International African Library 11
General editors: J. D. Y. Peel and David Parkin

STRANGERS AND TRADERS

International African Library

General Editors

J. D. Y. Peel *and* David Parkin

The *International African Library* is a major monograph series from the International African Institute and complements its quarterly periodical *Africa*, the premier journal in the field of African studies. Theoretically informed ethnographies, studies of social relations 'on the ground' which are sensitive to local cultural forms, have long been central to the Institute's publications programme. The *IAL* maintains this strength but extends it into new areas of contemporary concern, both practical and intellectual. It includes works focused on problems of development, especially on the linkages between the local and national levels of society; studies along the interface between the social and environmental sciences; and historical studies, especially those of a social, cultural or interdisciplinary character.

Titles in the series:

* *Published in the USA by the Smithsonian Institution Press*
† *Published in the USA by Indiana University Press*
‡ *Published in South Africa by Witwatersrand University Press*

Editorial Consultants

STRANGERS
AND
TRADERS

YORUBA MIGRANTS, MARKETS
AND THE STATE IN NORTHERN GHANA

J. S. EADES

EDINBURGH UNIVERSITY PRESS
for the INTERNATIONAL AFRICAN INSTITUTE, London

For Carla

Transferred to Digital Print 2009

Edinburgh University Press Ltd
22 George Square, Edinburgh

Typeset in Linotron Plantin by BP Integraphics Ltd, Bath, Avon,
and printed and bound in Great Britain by
CPI Antony Rowe, Chippenham and Eastbourne

A CIP record for this title is available from the British Library

ISBN 0 7486 0386 7

CONTENTS

Frontispiece: The successful trader: a retired *Alhaji* in Ogbomosho.

PREFACE

This book is a linear descendant of a Cambridge PhD thesis originally completed in 1975. This was in turn based on fieldwork carried out in 1969–70 in Ghana and 1971–3 in Nigeria, financed by a Hayter Studentship from the Department of Education and Science, and a Smuts Studentship from the University of Cambridge. I am grateful to these bodies, and also to Ahmadu Bello University, Zaria, Nigeria, and the University of Kent at Canterbury, for periods of study leave which enabled me both to write the original thesis and to recast it in its present form. The time which has elapsed since I first went into the field is all too long, but in a sense I found myself writing history rather than anthropology as soon as the Yoruba left Ghana part-way through my fieldwork, and I still feel that the experiences of the Yoruba in Ghana touch on issues such as migrant entrepreneurship and the relations between market traders and the state in the Third World which remain relevant today.

For help in Ghana, I would like to thank Malcolm McLeod, C.B. Gbeck, Tisiip Gandaa, Niara Sudarkasa, the Nigerian High Commission, officials of the Nigerian Community, the Yoruba Ilu Pejọ, and the various Yoruba town and religious organisations in Tamale, together with the staff of the Tamale markets, the Tamale branch of the National Archives of Ghana, the staff of the Tamale Grade II Court, and the Institute of African Studies, University of Ghana, Legon. In Nigeria, I would like to thank Rev. 'Dele Adeleru, Rev. and Mrs Whirley, Rev. and Mrs Sherrick, the Baptist and UMS Missions, the late Professor F.O. Okediji, Leslie Green, Vincent Milone and officials of the former Western State Ministry of Economic Planning and Reconstruction. Ganiyu Gbademasi, Lasisi Lawal, Razaki Braimah, Joseph Olugboye, Moses Iyanda, Felicia Sangotowo, Yekini Yusuf, Jimoh Balogun, Joshua Afolabi and 'Dayo Ayinla acted at various times as friends, informants and interpreters both in Ghana and Nigeria, and without their enthusiasm and help I would have got nowhere. For advice and help at various stages of writing, I am indebted to Keith Hart, Polly Hill, Ibrahim Tahir, Enid Schildkrout, my supervisor Jack Goody, and to the series editors John Peel and David Parkin for their continued assurance that this material was worth publishing, despite my endless ability to procrastinate and find other things to do with my life. Sections of some chapters were included in earlier versions in books published by Cambridge University Press, the International African Institute and the University of California Press, and I am grateful to these publishers for permission to reuse this material. I am also grateful to Cambridge University

Press for allowing me to reproduce two photographs originally published in *The Yoruba Today*. As in these previous publications, the names of the main protagonists in this account have been changed.

The two largest debts remain. The first is to my landlord in both Ghana and Nigeria, Alhaji Braimah Pakoyi, who was a constant source of friendship and encouragement in both Tamale and Igbetti, and who provided me with many of my most important insights into the nature of Yoruba migration and community structure. The second is to Carla, who abandoned the relative comfort of a life killing tame cockroaches in a Cambridge laboratory for the relative discomfort of a life killing wild cockroaches in the field. She played a vital role in helping collect much of the data on the women traders, and the study owes everything to the rapport which she was able to establish with our friends in Ghana and Nigeria. This is her book as much as it is mine.

Jerry Eades
Tokyo, 1993

LIST OF PLATES, MAPS, TABLES AND FIGURES

PLATES

MAPS

TABLES

FIGURES

LIST OF ABBREVIATIONS

AFRC	Armed Forces' Revolutionary Council
CFA	Communauté Financière d'Afrique: the CFA franc is tied to the French franc at a fixed rate, at the time of writing 50:1
CFAO	Compagnie Française d'Afrique Occidentale
CID	Criminal Investigation Department
CPP	Convention People's Party
ECOWAS	Economic Organisation of West African States
GNTC	Ghana National Trading Corporation
IMF	International Monetary Fund
NAL	National Alliance of Liberals
NC	New Cedi
NLC	National Liberation Council
NRC	National Redemption Council
NTS	Northern Territories
PDC	People's Defence Committee
PNDC	People's National Defence Committee
PP	Progress Party
UAC	United Africa Company
UMCA	United Missionary Church for Africa

A NOTE ON CURRENCY

Until the 1960s, the Gold Coast/Ghana used the British pounds, shillings and pence (£ s d) currency system, in which £1 equalled 20 shillings, and a shilling equalled 12 pence. The first attempt at decimalisation in the mid-1960s introduced the Cedi, equivalent to 8s 4d (i.e. 100 pence) of the old currency. This proved to be confusing to all, and, by the time of fieldwork, the New Cedi, equivalent to the old 10s, had replaced it. This was further divided into 100 pesewas. In 1969, thanks to devaluation, the New Cedi's official value was, rather conveniently, almost exactly one US dollar, though one could get up to 35 per cent more on the black market, depending on which Asian trader one dealt with. The word 'New' was gradually dropped. After so many subsequent years of hyperinflation, it is now sometimes difficult to recall that the Cedi has seen better days, but at the time of fieldwork it was still a substantial sum of money, more, in fact, than the daily minimum wage of 75 pesewas.

A NOTE ON ORTHOGRAPHY

Yoruba is written in a modified version of the Roman alphabet, using three special letters, ẹ, ọ and ṣ, to represent the three sounds e as in 'bet', o as in 'hop' and sh as in 'shop', instead of e, which sounds rather like the vowel sound in 'bait', and o as in 'hope'. These usages vary: in the towns where I worked, for instance, many people make no distinction between 's' and 'ṣ', pronouncing both as 's'. In addition, the language has a tonal structure which is conventionally represented by accents. As this book has little to say about the Yoruba language, in order to simplify matters for the general reader I have left out tonal marks and avoided many underdots in both personal names (most of which are fictitious) and place names, where I have used the familiar anglicised forms current in most of the literature on Nigeria.

1

INTRODUCTION

In April 1969 I arrived in Tamale in Northern Ghana to study the large numbers of Yoruba migrants, most of them traders, who had settled there during the colonial period and the early years of independence. These 'Lagosians', as they were commonly called by Ghanaians, many of them immediately recognisable from their dress and their facial marks, had established for themselves a dominant position in the country's distribution system. They were the largest group of immigrant traders in Ghana, with a population of around 150,000 in 1969.[1] In the major markets they provided a substantial proportion of the traders: 15 per cent in Accra in the 1950s, 23 per cent in Kumasi in the 1960s, and over a third in Tamale Central Market when I began my research.[2] The stalls of the wealthiest Yoruba traders were usually among the largest in any market, and in certain kinds of goods, particularly cloth, provisions, hardware, cycle parts and small manufactured goods collectively known as *worobo*, they had a virtual monopoly. In addition to these large markets, Yoruba traders could be found in most remote rural areas, and in many small villages they were the only resident full-time traders.

By the end of 1969, that community had ceased to exist. In response to the Ghanaian government's 'Aliens' Compliance Order', which stated simply that all foreigners without proper documents had two weeks to leave the country, virtually all the Yoruba in Ghana returned to their towns of origin in Nigeria.[3] In one of the more spectacular and tragic population movements in post-war West Africa, probably around 200,000 people left the country in the space of two weeks. Of these, the Yoruba were by far the largest group and many of the returnees to Nigeria lost virtually all their money and possessions in the process.

The ability of the Yoruba migrants to adapt to this situation, and the speed with which so many of them were able to reconstruct their lives is still a source of wonder to me: it said much for the strength and vitality of the Yoruba social institutions which had provided the foundation for the migration in the first place. My research, which had started off as a conventional study of ethnicity and trade in a migrant community, had suddenly become an exercise in historical reconstruction, and an investigation of the origins of the migration in these social institutions.

This, then, is an account of the Yoruba migration to northern Ghana, and in particular, to Tamale. The Northern and Upper Regions of Ghana, formerly the Northern Territories Protectorate of the Gold Coast, were by far the

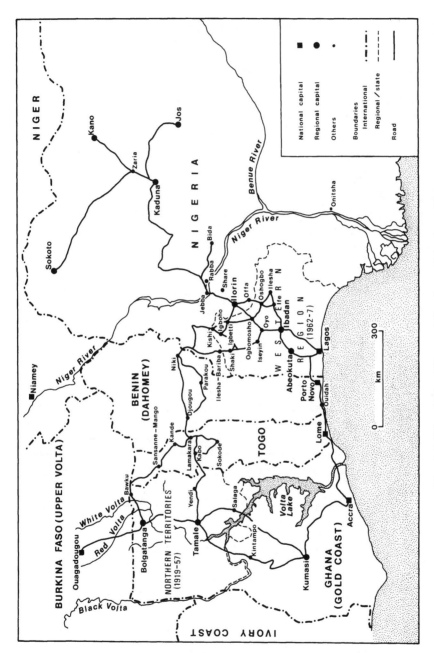

Map 1.1: West Africa: Western Nigeria and Northern Ghana.

poorest areas of the country, and yet many of the Yoruba had been able to establish successful trading enterprises there, in the process helping to open up the area to the market and the spread of the cash economy. Given the poverty and lack of development of the region, it is not surprising that the wealthiest traders in Tamale were by no means as rich as their counterparts in Kumasi and Accra, but allowing for the differences of scale in the larger cities of the south, many of the features of Yoruba trade, migration and community organisation appear to have been similar to those in other parts of Ghana. Some of the migrants in Tamale had worked earlier in southern Ghana, and others who had originally worked in Tamale had, by 1969, moved elsewhere in the north. These processes will be illustrated in later chapters, but the net result was a gradual diffusion of the Yoruba traders into many of the smaller and more remote towns and villages. The networks of Yoruba traders in the north were thus linked to those elsewhere in Ghana, which in turn formed part of an even larger network extending over much of West Africa.

Whether an account of these events is still worth publishing so long after they happened, I will have to leave to the reader to judge. I would justify it for three reasons.

The first reason is that the documentation of an extraordinarily successful migration by men and women who, with limited capital and a lot of hard work, played a major part in transforming the commercial economy of the Gold Coast in the first half of the twentieth century is of interest in itself, particularly in a period when the economies of so many African states are experiencing such difficulties. Their achievement was nowhere more remarkable than in the Northern Territories, the poorest and least developed area of the country. As elsewhere in West Africa, conditions in the markets of the Gold Coast, and particularly the Northern Territories, were such that access to goods and labour was crucial, and the social and economic structure of the northern Yoruba towns provided an ideal basis for the exploitation of these conditions. The result was rapid chain migration, a clustering of migrants from the same towns in Nigeria in the same towns in Ghana, and a tightly-knit community structure which helps explain why the Yoruba, of all the migrant ethnic groups in Ghana, were the most affected by the 1969 compliance order. In a recent survey of the development of business in Africa, Hopkins has written:

> If a comprehensive history of Africa is to be written 'from below', it must tell the story of small businessmen and artisans as well as of 'peasants' and wage-earners, and it must do so with a similar degree of empirical care and historical empathy.[4]

This book is in part an account 'from below' of the Yoruba entrepreneurs, both men and women, in northern Ghana.

The second reason is that the issues raised by the case of the Yoruba in Ghana are still important, and not only within Africa. In particular, it raises the question of the relationships between migrants, traders and the state in colonial and post-colonial West Africa, as well as further afield. The success of the Yoruba in the markets of Ghana and their departure illustrate well the constraints under which governments in West Africa formulate their economic policies and which they ignore at their peril. These constraints result, in part, from the political map bequeathed by the departing colonialists: with the exception of Nigeria, West African states are relatively small in terms of populations and internal markets, and have long, arbitrarily defined, land boundaries which divide ethnic groups and even families, and which are impossible to police effectively. Where borders are wide open and where trade is in the hands of hundreds of thousands of independent traders, economic policies based on prices, import duties and foreign exchange regulations which are widely at variance with those of neighbouring countries are unlikely to be fully effective. Few traders are wealthy enough to ignore income opportunities presented by the trading across the border, however often the politicians or the military call on them to obey the law. In any case, official pronouncements lack both credibility and legitimacy: laws are seen to change frequently, usually in an arbitrary fashion, and to be honoured in the breach rather than the observance, while individual administrators, soldiers and politicians are all too often themselves seen to be involved in corruption.[5] The exodus of the Yoruba is also a vivid reminder both of the increasingly closed borders and restrictive citizenship requirements of the states in the region, and of the increasing willingness of the state to intervene in the market place, usually to the detriment both of the traders and consumers alike. The success of the Yoruba in the Gold Coast in the early colonial period, based as it was on minimal resources, provides an ironic contrast with the situation in post-colonial Ghana in the early 1980s. The early traders had relied only on their feet and their heads for transport, but by the 1980s the system was falling apart because of a lack of petrol and vehicle parts. The Yoruba migration was able to develop in the way that it did because of the security provided by the colonial state, whereas a major danger for Ghanaian traders in the early 1980s was that of attacks by the military, whether in the name of the state or as the result of random indiscipline.

The final reason is theoretical. I would argue that the Yoruba migration to Ghana is of considerable theoretical and historical interest because it is so well documented both statistically and ethnographically. There are three main sources. The first is the 1960 Ghana Census which was one of the best and most comprehensive ever to have been undertaken in Africa. This, together with the less satisfactory 1948 Census provides an invaluable context in which this study can be located. Second, there is the mass of statistical information collected by the Nigerian government in 1969–70 when the Yoruba returned to Nigeria, which provides a detailed overview of both where the migrants came from in Nigeria, the towns where they settled in Ghana, and the kinds of work which they were doing there. Third, there is the ethnographic research on different Yoruba communities in Ghana, all carried out in the 1960s, by Oyedipe in Accra, Sudarkasa in Kumasi, and myself in Tamale.[6] This provides us with better overall documentation of this particular migration than any other in West Africa, and at both the macro- and micro-levels. The macro-level information suggests both a considerable concentration of the Yoruba in market trade, and of Yoruba from the same towns in Nigeria settling in the same towns in Ghana. What the micro-level ethnographic information is able to do is to provide a detailed account of the processes which produced this pattern at the level of the household and the individual. There is good reason to believe that Yoruba communities in other parts of West Africa have been formed in the same way, and the pattern is an extreme instance of chain migration which is common in other parts of the world as well. The social process of migration helps explain why the Yoruba were so extraordinarily successful in accumulating capital and penetrating both the urban and rural markets, and this should be of some interest in situations in other countries where there is a heavy incidence of chain migration involving a particular ethnic group or groups. However one of the reasons for the delay in publication of this material has been dissatisfaction with the theoretical terms in which successive versions of the argument have been cast with respect to the relationship between the macro- and micro-levels.

The theoretical basis of the original thesis was the urbanisation and entrepreneurship literature of the 1950s and 1960s. It tried to relate the success of the Yoruba traders to entrepreneurship and ethnic solidarity, but paid little systematic attention to the economic context in which they were operating, and particularly to the regional and world economies. I put aside the manuscript in order to write a general study of the Yoruba, and only took it up again when the latter had been published.[7] I was now equipped with a much better knowledge of the regional and historical context of the migration, so in a second version I drew heavily on the neo-Marxist development and dependency literature which had been published from the late 1960s onwards, and wrote a much more rigorous structural analysis, but it still seemed to fall short of what was required. Marxist structuralism was good at dealing with macro-level structures, but less satisfactory when it came to considering groups of people on the ground.

A good example which illustrates both the strengths and weaknesses of the approach is Amin's Introduction to his 1974 volume on *Modern Migrations in West Africa*.[8] Amin argued that the flows of manpower in the region could only be understood by looking at its integration into the international capitalist system, and the flows of capital which resulted from this. The general pattern was one in which most of the new investment took place along the coast, particularly in areas suitable for the cultivation of cash crops such as cocoa. As a result of this, not only did the economies of the forest areas develop more quickly than those of the savanna, but this development was speeded by the

flows of cheap labour which were attracted from further north. In the case of
Ghana, the development of the cocoa industry was made possible by the flow of
labour from the Northern Territories and Upper Volta.[9] There was a similar
pattern in Western Nigeria, where the cocoa belt running through what is now
Ogun, Ondo and southern Oyo and Oshun states absorbed labour from the
savanna areas of Yorubaland to the north, in northern Oyo and Kwara
States.[10] Most of the Yoruba migrants to Ghana came from towns in the
northern savanna areas of Yorubaland, and many of them accumulated their
trading capital working for cocoa farmers.

The problem with Amin's approach, however, was his single-minded
emphasis on the political economy to the exclusion of other factors. His
macro-level analysis went some way to accounting for the rate of migration –
what proportion of the population travels – as a function of the penetration of
the capitalist system, but he has less to say about the incidence of migration –
i.e. *who* – travels from a given population.[11] This is an important issue in the
case of the Yoruba, as their migration to Ghana was based on the movement of
clusters of kin, the general pattern being one in which younger migrants
helped their older relatives in trade. The effects of this extreme example of
chain migration can be seen in Chapter 2: the development of tightly-knit
communities of migrants in each town in Ghana from each of a small number of
towns in Nigeria. Ilorin migrants predominated in Accra, Ogbomosho
migrants in Kumasi, Offa migrants in Koforidua, and Oyan migrants in the
diamond areas. In Tamale the Yoruba community consisted of four relatively
equal groups from Ogbomosho, Igbetti, Igboho and Shaki.[12] Home town and
family ties were not only important in recruitment however: they were also
important in the organisation of trade, the transfer of information and capital,
and in the organisation of the life of the Yoruba community until the exodus in
1969.

To some extent this omission was rectified in the debate over the informal
sector of the economy and petty commodity production. Interest in, and
realisation of the importance of, petty trade and other kinds of small-scale
economic activity in the Third World owes much to the work of Keith Hart,
based on his research on Frafra migrants in Nima, one of the poorest areas
of Accra.[13] Hart found that conventional categories of 'employed' and
'unemployed' concealed a vast amount of economic activity in what he called
the 'informal' sector of the economy, and in his early papers he provided a
detailed classification of the kinds of activities he had in mind: primary and
secondary production, trade, rentier activities in housing and transport, and
transfers of resources, both legitimate in the form of begging, and illegitimate
in the form of theft. A lengthy debate then followed in the literature about the
nature of the informal sector and its links with the rest of the economy. The
conclusion generally was that the informal sector, far from being a dwindling
survival from the pre-capitalist period, was thriving precisely because of the

functions it performed within the capitalist system. It was in many cases organised around 'primordial' links of kinship and ethnicity, but its function was to provide goods and services more cheaply in many instances than they could be provided by bureaucratic capitalist firms, and thus to keep down the costs of living throughout the economy and to dampen down demands for higher wages both in the government and private sectors.[14]

What the informal sector literature suggested to me was a way of integrating a 'political economy' approach with an account of the social structure and of the strategies available to, and decisions taken by, individuals. This provided the framework for a brief general paper on migration I published in the mid-1980s, and I have recast the argument of this book in this form as well.[15] I argue that in order to fully describe and account for Yoruba migration to Ghana and the rest of West Africa, three levels of analysis are necessary. The first is that of the political economy, drawing on Amin and other neo-Marxist writers on development. The second is what Garbett and Kapferer have called the 'field of social relations' within which migration takes place, and I have already published a general account of Yoruba kinship, drawing on the work of Bascom, Schwab, Lloyd, Peel, Bender and Berry, and trying to relate changes in kinship organisation to regional economic change.[16] Third, I argue, we need to consider the level of individual decision-making within this 'opportunity structure' thus created. The important questions in the Yoruba case seem to be strategies which could be adopted by traders in difficulties, as well as alternative forms of investment open to those who were more successful. In a sense, these three levels of analysis are nested one inside the other, the outer 'shell' defining the broad parameters within which social groups are formed and individual strategies and decisions worked out. In fact, however, there is a dynamic interplay between all three levels. On the one hand it was the colonial political economy which provided the context within which the migration to Ghana took place and the Yoruba community was established. And it was the structure of kin groups which defined in large part who in the Yoruba towns was most likely to migrate. On the other hand, the result of individual decisions on migration could be the start of a new migrant chain and new growth points for the Yoruba migration in Ghana. And the cumulative effect of these migrations was to change the structure of both the kin groups and the regional political economy, in some instances challenging and undermining the economic policies of the state.

Given this focus on strategies and the interplay between levels of analysis, I have, even while writing this final version, become uncertain either that the strategies themselves or the relations between them can be specified sufficiently rigorously in standard English: the use of a block structured computing language, or something close to it, would allow the development of a more tightly defined and integrated set of models which could then be tested against the empirical evidence. However, there are constraints of readability and time and I have reluctantly decided that this is a line of argument which is best pursued in the future.[17] I suspect, in any case, that theory is often the most ephemeral aspect of a study like this, and that after only a few years it will be of interest, if at all, more because of the historical period and ethnography described, rather than the intellectual beauty of its theoretical underpinnings.

As for the layout of the rest of the book, the next two chapters describe the distribution of the Yoruba in Ghana as a whole, and the development of Yoruba migration to the north of the country. Chapters 4 and 5 describe patterns of Yoruba trade in Tamale and the surrounding areas in the 1960s, a period when the economy of Ghana was already going into recession.[18] For traders whose businesses were failing – and there were many, even before the exodus – there was a limited range of available options: changing trading lines in the hope that something else would sell better, moving to a more remote area where overheads would be less and profit margins higher, taking up another type of work, or returning home to Nigeria, usually to farm. Economic recessions are important in the history of the Yoruba in Ghana, for these are the periods both of innovation and movement into the more remote rural areas, making the Yoruba the most evenly distributed ethnic group in Ghana. For the trader whose business was yielding a profit, other decisions had to be made, this time about investments. As will be seen, the usual priorities were education for one's children, and construction of a house in one's home town in Nigeria, but after these had been satisfied there were other possibilities: property in Ghanaian or Nigerian cities, cattle, transport, rice farming, and (for Muslims) the pilgrimage to Mecca. Many of these choices were faced by women as well as men: an even larger percentage of women than men were involved in market trade, and though, for reasons to be discussed, most women were less successful than their husbands, some of them succeeded in amassing considerable wealth in their own right.

Chapter 6 deals with the organisation of the Yoruba community in Tamale. A recurring theme which emerges from the discussion of trade is the increasingly problematic nature of the relations between the Yoruba and the Ghanaians, and between the market traders and the Ghanaian state. As is well known, West Africa is an area in which political and cultural/ethnic boundaries seldom coincide, and ethnicity underlies (or is thought by western scholars to underlie) most aspects of everyday life. One of the features of the literature on ethnicity is that theories which claim to be general seem to arise out of very specific historical and political situations. The most famous example in West Africa is probably Abner Cohen's study of Hausa migrants in Western Nigeria, in which their ethnic identity was an important factor in their maintenance of control over the distribution and sale of cattle and kola nuts.[19] Not surprisingly, Cohen concluded that ethnic identities derive their strength from political and economic competition. Schildkrout's example of the Mossi in Kumasi Zongo is rather different.[20] The Mossi in Kumasi, unlike the Hausa in Ibadan, do not seem to have had a monopoly of a major sector of the market, nor do they appear to have been as segregated in residence and religion. Indeed, the Mossi were remarkable for the speed with which they assimilated into zongo life: the second generation spoke Hausa as their first language rather than More, they adopted Islam and zongo patterns of associational life, and they had comparatively high rates of intermarriage with other zongo groups. And yet, they still saw themselves as 'Mossi', and Mossi identity was of continuing importance in mosque and party politics.

What is clear in the Yoruba case is that, probably as a function of the pattern of their migration, they formed a tightly-knit community around the large groups of kin and fellow-townspeople to which the majority of the migrants belonged. They retained strong links with their home towns, links reinforced by ongoing flows of money and people, unlike the Mossi and Hausa who seem to have retained very few links at all.[21] While the intra-community links did not prevent individuals forming friendships and commercial relationships with Ghanaians and migrants from other ethnic groups, they did perform important functions for the Yoruba traders, both in settling disputes within the community cheaply and effectively, and keeping individuals out of trouble with the authorities. However, ironically, it was also the strength of these intra-community ties which produced the extraordinary response of the Yoruba to the Ghana government's compliance order in 1969: they left the country almost completely, while less well-organised groups such as the Hausa and Mossi tended to stay.[22]

The final chapter deals with the decline of the Ghanaian economy in the years following the exodus of the Yoruba, and the general lessons to be drawn from the history of the Yoruba migration and exodus for the economies of the region as a whole. During 1969–70, when I was in the field, life in Ghana still exhibited signs of the prosperity which had been the envy of the rest of Africa in former years. Goods were generally available in the markets, even if sales had suffered as a result of government retrenchment since the 1966 coup. The road network was still intact, petrol was available and transport functioned cheaply and efficiently. This was not to last long however: the economic difficulties encountered by the Busia regime led to a second military takeover in early 1972.[23] The Acheampong regime, after inital success in uniting the country politically, and in attracting foreign loans, became increasingly heavy-handed and inept as the decade wore on, and its leaders paid the penalty at the hands of the firing squads in 1979, during the brief period of rule by the Armed Forces Revolutionary Council under Flt Lt Rawlings.[24] But the inexorable economic decline of the country continued, through two further years of civilian rule under Limann and a second military regime led by Rawlings, who staged his second coup at the end of 1981. Two years of revolutionary zeal and unorthodox economic measures, including attempts to shift the distribution of essential goods and foodstuffs into the state sector, also failed to revive the

shattered economy, and it was only with the adoption of the measures
prescribed by the IMF late in 1983, which included removing many of the
constraints on market trade, that life in the country began to assume an air of
normality once more. The economic stability since has been maintained at the
price of a crippling foreign debt burden and hyperinflation which caused the
value of the Cedi to sink like a stone.[25] Since 1983, the revival of the Ghanaian
economy has been in part due to the regime coming to terms with crucial
features of economic life in West Africa: that given the prevailing economic
conditions, much of the distribution and retailing network is likely to remain
in the hands of small scale operators; that it is impossible to control their
activities administratively given both the scale of the task and the personal
interests of officials at all levels entrusted with this task; and that consequently
it is very difficult for a country to pursue an economic policy of its own which is
seriously out of line with those of its neighbours. In order to ensure that an
efficient, cheap distribution system develops, the real role of the state should
perhaps be to provide a framework within which the small-scale entrepreneur
can operate with a degree of security, rather than try to carry out these
functions itself. For better or worse, there is a high probability that the most
efficient distribution network can be provided most quickly by chain migration from outside. The tragedy is that so many governments, like that of
Ghana, regard migrants as a problem and a threat rather than as a valuable
economic resource, and so the probability that episodes such as the departure
of the Yoruba from Ghana will be repeated elsewhere is, unfortunately, very
high.

2

THE POLITICAL ECONOMY OF A MIGRATION

This chapter and the one that follows deal with the distribution of Yoruba migrants in Ghana, the reasons why they went there, and the reasons why some of them began to trade in the north, despite the fact that it was the poorest part of the country. This chapter deals with macro-level structural factors: the transformation of the Ghanaian and Nigerian economies in the twentieth century and the patterns of migration which resulted from this. Chapter 3 discusses the micro-level factors, the relationship of the pattern of migration to the social organisation of the Yoruba town, and the ways in which the early migrants were able to adapt these institutions to enable the establishment of viable enterprises in such an apparently unpromising economic environment.

THE YORUBA IN NIGERIA

The Yoruba-speaking peoples occupy much of the south western quarter of present-day Nigeria, forming the bulk of the population in Lagos, Ogun, Oshun, Oyo and Ondo States, a large proportion of the population in Kwara State, and spilling over the border into neighbouring Benin and Togo. Yoruba is one of the major languages of Africa, and is spoken by over twenty million people in Nigeria where it is second only to Hausa in importance.[1]

The Yoruba homeland is divided into three geographical zones: a strip of creekland along the coast, an inland forest belt, much of it suitable for cocoa cultivation, and, further inland still, a belt of more open orchard bush and Guinea savanna grasslands. In the twentieth century it was the forest areas which developed most rapidly, thanks to the rise of the cocoa industry, and this in turn depended on flows of labour and foodstuffs from the savanna areas to the north.[2]

Until the early nineteenth century, the pattern of development was very different. The Yoruba were divided between a number of independent kingdoms, sharing closely related dialects and cultures and common traditions of origin from Ile-Ife, but often at war with each other.[3] The largest of these states was Oyo which flourished in the savanna, and which exploited its middleman position in the trade between the ports along the Atlantic coast and the West African interior.[4] Complex exchanges of slaves, European manufactured goods and horses, the basis of the Oyo war machine, enabled the state to expand its influence to the coast, and major trade routes criss-crossed the map. While Oyo controlled the Dahomey kingdom to the south-west, it exported many of its slaves from the port of Ouidah. Once Dahomey had reasserted its

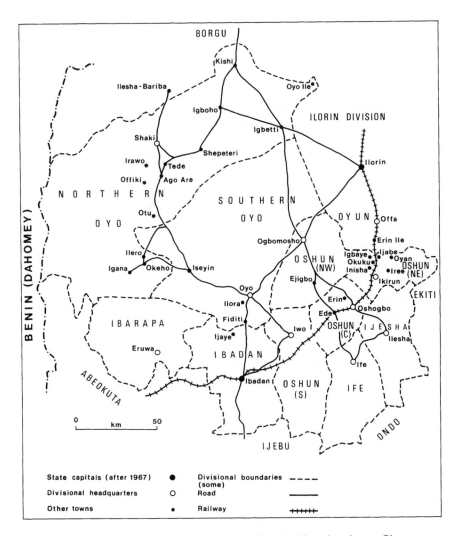

Map 2.1: Western Nigeria: principal areas involved in migration to Ghana.

autonomy in the late eighteenth century, the trade was shifted to the east, with the main route running down through Egbado to Lagos. In the north the trade routes running up from the coast joined the major routes of the interior.[5] The most important route of all in the early nineteenth century, from Salaga in northern Ghana to Kano in northern Nigeria, passed not far to the north of Oyo Ile, the former capital of Oyo to the north of Igbetti, which was abandoned in the 1830s. Islam reached Oyo in the sixteenth century, and there must have been early, if undocumented, trade links between the Yoruba states and their Akan counterparts, both via the interior and coastal routes.

If trade had stimulated the expansion of Oyo, a change in the patterns of trade probably contributed to its spectacular collapse in the first three decades of the nineteenth century. The European market for slaves declined, a shortage of horses undermined Oyo's military capability, and political dissension led to the kingdom's fragmentation. For the rest of the century much of the Yoruba homeland was engulfed in a series of wars between successor states trying to fill the power vacuum left by the collapse of Oyo: Ilorin, Ibadan, Ijaye and Abeokuta.[6] Numerous settlements were destroyed, and refugees regrouped at sites which could be easily defended, on hill tops and along the fringes of the forest. The net result was a massive shift of population from the northern savanna to the edge of the forest in the south and east, where many of the largest Yoruba towns – Oyo, Ibadan, Ogbomosho, Iwo, Ede, Ejigbo and Oshogbo – are still located.[7] The Oke Ogun, the Upper Ogun River basin running from Shaki to Igboho, Igbetti and Oyo Ile, once the heartland of the kingdom, became a sparsely populated periphery, away from the main roads, the railway, the major administrative centres and the cocoa belt. With its abundance of land and low population density it was an area of considerable agricultural potential, but during the colonial period the main axis of development lay elsewhere.[8]

The nineteenth-century wars and the imposition of colonial rule produced a number of effects of direct relevance to this study. First, as we have seen, it led to the emergence of a new urban hierarchy and the marginalisation of once strategically important areas. Second, the early colonial period coincided with the rise of the cocoa industry, which helped shift the locus of economic development to the south and east. Third, it led to the establishment of a new road and rail network, and the towns which were on it tended to grow faster than the towns which were not. As we shall see, there are links between railway construction and early migration to Ghana. Fourth, it led to a new administrative structure, with the new administrative centres gaining ground at the expense of the old, and with zero-sum competition for resources between administrative units, and between towns within each unit, becoming the basis of politics in the region. This has remained the case ever since, and is a factor of enormous importance. The nineteenth century led to an increase in the size of the larger towns, making Western Nigeria the most urbanised area in Africa during the colonial period, and most Yoruba see themselves as townspeople, even if they spend most of their lives farming in smaller hamlets and villages outside.[9] The distinction between 'children of the soil' – real town members – and 'strangers' from other towns is rigidly maintained, and has important implications for access to land, particularly where it is scarce.[10] Towns not only provide a form of identity but, through access to farmland, an ultimate source of security as well. Yoruba migrants tend to retain strong links with home, however long they stay away. 'Upstairs' houses (*ile pẹtẹsi*) built by migrants resident elsewhere in West Africa are a common feature of the Yoruba urban landscape, a visible sign of their owners' success and commitment to the town, even if many of them do stand empty. Town unions (*parapọ*) and improvement associations flourish, with branches throughout West Africa, wherever migrants from the town live in sufficient numbers to make them viable, and they function as channels through which remittances from abroad can be invested in development projects at home.[11]

Finally, the imposition of colonial rule and the end of the wars meant a change in the nature of trade. With improved security and communications, the large trading caravans which had dominated long-distance trade in the nineteenth century became obsolete, and the markets were opened up to individual traders, working on their own or with the help of relatives. Within Western Nigeria itself trade boomed, and groups of Yoruba migrants as well as outsiders like the Lebanese and Hausa, were quick to exploit the new opportunities created by the expansion of the cash economy, the cocoa industry and the rising imports of European manufactures.[12] Within Yorubaland itself, many of the most successful traders came from areas where capital could be accumulated quickly: the Ijesha *oṣomaalo*, who sold manufactured goods in the savanna areas to the north, and the Ijebu who came to dominate many sectors of the labour market in Ibadan, are good examples.[13] Would-be traders from other more outlying areas had to look elsewhere: in northern Nigeria, and the rest of West Africa, including the Gold Coast, which in 1957 became Ghana.

THE YORUBA IN GHANA

The Yoruba migration to Ghana is one of the best documented migrations in Africa, partly – and ironically – because of the data generated by the 1969 exodus. The Western State Ministry of Economic Development and Reconstruction in Nigeria registered over 88,000 returnees from Ghana between December 1969 and April 1971, and this complements the excellent material contained in the 1960 Ghana census, and the less detailed information from the census of 1948. In addition there are the ethnographic accounts of Yoruba in various parts of the country by Stapleton, Oyedipe, Sudarkasa and myself. Taken together, it is possible not only to trace the growth of the Yoruba population in each area of the country, but also to identify the main towns from which the migrants in each area came, and their economic role in Ghana.[14]

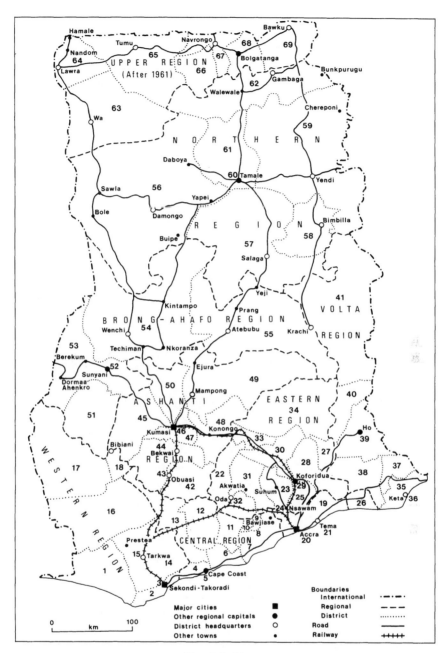

Map 2.2: Ghana.

Note: The map is based on regional and district boundaries in the early years of independence, before the filling of the Volta Lake. The numbers correspond to those in the list of local authorities in Table 2.2.

Table 2.1: Coefficients of concentration of Yoruba migrants in Ghana, 1948, by enumeration area.

Area	Concentration	
Accra	1.97	(2.77)
Ahanta-Nzima	1.90	(2.23)
Akwapim-New Juaben	1.84	(2.10)
Birim	0.99	(1.35)
Cape Coast	0.90	(0.90)
Ho	1.16	(0.84)
Keta	0.42	(0.35)
Sefwi	1.67	(1.20)
Volta River	0.98	(0.72)
Wassaw-Aowin	4.73	(3.38)
Bekwai	0.38	(0.75)
Kumasi	1.18	(1.13)
Mampong	0.90	(0.66)
Wenchi-Sunyani	0.65	(0.47)
Dagomba	0.68	(0.50)
Gonja	0.66	(0.47)
Krachi	0.05	(1.49)
Mamprusi	0.25	(0.19)
Wa	0.22	(0.18)

Source: Population Census of the Gold Coast, 1948, Table 23, pp. 367–9. The figures in brackets assume that 'Northern Nigerians' and 'Nigerians' were also Yoruba. The coefficient of concentration for each division is calculated by dividing the percentage of the Yoruba population by the percentage of the total population in that division.

The Yoruba population of the Gold Coast at the start of the colonial period was probably quite small, but it may have grown to around 10,000 by 1930. It increased to 35–40,000 by 1948, stood at over 100,000 in 1960, and may have grown to 150,000 by 1969.[15] The 1948 census gives information on the different levels of concentration in different parts of the country (Table 2.1).

The highest concentrations were in the larger towns in the south and the mining areas. The concentrations in the economically less developed Volta and Northern Regions were lower. The 1960 census, with smaller enumeration areas and better ethnic classification presents a more detailed picture (Table 2.2). It shows clearly the relatively heavy concentrations in the urban areas, as well as the continued under-representation in parts of the east and north. Comparing the two censuses is difficult because of the changes in enumeration areas and regional boundaries, but a rough comparison (Table 2.3) suggests a slight rise in the concentrations in Brong-Ahafo and the north as the level of development increased.[16]

In 1931 there were only 840 Yoruba recorded in the whole of the north, 305 of whom were in Tamale, with the others concentrated in the eastern towns of

Table 2.2: Total population and Yoruba population of Ghana, 1960, by enumeration area.

Enumeration area	Total population	Yoruba population	Concentration
All Regions	6,726,820	100,560	1.00
Western and Central Regions	1,377,550	22,900	1.11
1. Nzima-Evalue-Ajomoro-Gwira	93,080	380	0.27
2. Ahanta-Shama	76,690	1,550	1.35
3. Sekondi-Takoradi	123,310	3,650	1.98
4. Komenda-Edina-Eguafo-Abrem-Asebu	72,120	760	1.70
5. Cape Coast	56,910	1,320	1.55
6. Mfantisman	124,850	640	0.34
7. Gomoa-Awutu-Effutu	171,110	2,480	0.97
8. Swedru	20,550	690	2.25
9. Agona (Southern Ghana)	51,090	1,610	2.11
10. Nyakrom-Nkum	23,870	340	0.95
11. Breman-Ajumako-Enyan	101,440	870	0.57
12. Asin	55,720	680	0.81
13. Denkyira-Twifu-Hemang	73,740	960	0.87
14. Wassaw-Fiase-Mpohaw	91,830	1,590	1.16
15. Tarkwa-Aboso	49,270	2,280	3.10
16. Amenfi-Aowin	76,100	470	0.41
17. Sefwi-Wiawso	67,480	1,090	1.08
18. Sefwi-Anhwiaso-Bekwai-Bibiani	48,390	1,540	2.13
Accra Capital District	491,820	9,260	1.26
19. Ga-Dangbe-Shai	76,290	260	0.23
20. Accra	388,400	8,530	1.47
21. Tema	27,130	470	1.16
Eastern Region	1,094,200	25,680	1.57
22. Western Akim	103,830	4,750	3.06
23. South Akim Abuakwa	113,360	1,250	0.74
24. Nsawam	29,790	780	1.75
25. Akwapim	78,750	410	0.38
26. Ada	50,120	40	0.05
27. Akwamu-Anum-Boso	32,680	170	0.35
28. Manya-Yilo-Osokodu	163,710	1,200	0.49
29. New Juaben	53,820	1,660	2.06
30. East Akim Abuakwa	118,090	1,130	0.64
31. West Akim Abuakwa	161,350	10,060	4.17
32. Oda-Swedru	52,540	3,410	4.34
33. South Kwahu	71,310	740	0.69
34. North Kwahu	64,850	80	0.08
Volta Region	777,280	6,400	0.55
35. Anlo South	69,870	220	0.21

Table 2.2: (continued)

Enumeration area	Total population	Yoruba population	Concen- tration
36. Keta	29,710	400	0.90
37. Anlo North	141,430	790	0.37
38. Tongu	86,060	350	0.27
39. Ho	116,990	720	0.41
40. Kpandu	118,990	570	0.32
41. Buem-Krachi	214,230	3,350	1.04
Ashanti	1,109,120	19,720	1.19
42. Adansi-Bankwa	68,050	790	0.78
43. Abuasi	26,580	810	2.04
44. Amansie	149,370	1,270	0.57
45. Kumasi West	153,760	1,960	0.85
46. Kumasi	218,170	9,530	2.92
47. Kumasi South	108,890	610	0.37
48. Kumasi East	120,450	1,770	0.98
49. Sekyere	136,420	1,580	0.77
50. Kumasi North	127,440	1,400	0.73
Brong-Ahafo Region	587,920	6,150	0.70
51. Brong-Ahafo South	81,590	700	0.57
52. Sunyani	15,810	250	1.05
53. Brong-Ahafo Central	230,370	2,710	0.79
54. Brong-Ahafo North	194,300	1,630	0.56
55. Brong-Ahafo East	65,850	860	0.87
Northern and Upper Regions	1,288,920	10,450	0.54
56. Western Gonja	62,440	590	0.63
57. Eastern Gonja	55,790	1,070	1.28
58. Nanumba	45,950	870	1.27
59. Eastern Dagomba	122,470	900	0.49
60. Tamale	58,180	1,400	1.61
61. Western Dagomba	82,290	150	0.12
62. South Mamprusi	104,460	940	0.60
63. Wala	130,980	710	0.36
64. Lawra	114,190	820	0.48
65. Tumu	43,540	140	0.21
66. Builsa	50,920	200	0.26
67. Kassena-Nankanni	93,400	340	0.24
68. Frafra	150,030	600	0.27
69. Kusasi	174,290	1,720	0.66

Source: *Population Census of Ghana, 1960*, Report E, Table S1, pp. c.3–c.9. The numbers of the enumeration areas correspond to those shown on Map 2.2 (Ghana). The index of concentration is given by the percentage of the Yoruba population divided by the percentage of the total population in each district.

Table 2.3: Comparison of coefficients of concentration of Yoruba migrants in Ghana in 1948 and 1960 by 1948 enumeration area.

Area	1948		1960		Change
Accra	1.97	(2.77)	1.26	−0.71	(−1.51)
Ahanta	1.90	(2.23)	1.27	−0.63	(−0.96)
Akwapim	1.84	(2.10)	2.10	+0.26	(+0.00)
Birim	0.99	(1.35)	2.09	+1.10	(+0.74)
Cape Coast	0.90	(0.90)	0.92	+0.02	(+0.02)
Ho					
Keta	0.42	(0.35)	0.31	−0.11	(−0.04)
Sefwi	1.67	(1.20)	1.52	−0.15	(+0.32)
Volta River	0.98	(0.72)	0.47	−0.51	(−0.25)
Wassaw	4.73	(3.38)	1.34	−3.39	(−2.04)
Bekwai	0.38	(0.75)	1.27	+0.91	(+0.52)
Kumasi	1.18	(1.13)	1.32	+0.14	(+0.19)
Mampong	0.90	(0.66)	0.79	−0.11	(+0.13)
Wenchi	0.65	(0.47)	0.70	+0.05	(+0.23)
Dagomba	0.68	(0.50)	0.61	−0.07	(+0.11)
Gonja	0.66	(0.47)	0.93	+0.27	(+0.46)
Krachi					
Mamprusi	0.25	(0.19)	0.44	+0.19	(+0.25)
Wa	0.22	(0.18)	0.39	+0.17	(+0.21)

Sources: Population Censuses of Ghana, 1948, 1960. The figures in brackets assume that 'Northern Nigerians' and 'Nigerians' were also Yoruba. Comparisons between the figures for Ho and Krachi are not possible because of changes in the boundaries of enumeration areas.

Yendi, Bawku and Krachi (see Table 2.8 below). The number rose to 4,000 in 1948 and 10,000 in 1960, and became more evenly distributed. A gradual diffusion of migrants seems to have taken place from the wealthier to the less developed areas, and from larger to smaller settlements, a process which will be illustrated in later chapters. By the 1948 census, the general pattern of Yoruba settlement in Ghana had been established, and it changed little in the following twenty years. They were by far the most evenly distributed ethnic group in the country.[17]

The sex ratio of the Yoruba in Ghana in 1960 stood at 116 males to 100 females, an unusually even balance for an immigrant population. The Yoruba women, most of them self-employed traders, had been able to join the migration at an early stage. Their age distribution was also significant. With the exception of the Igbo (a group of even more recent arrivals) the Yoruba had the lowest proportion of men over 65 of any ethnic group in Ghana, reflecting not only their comparatively recent arrival, but also the tendency of the older migrants to retire to Nigeria. Nearly all the Yoruba migrants gave their religion as either Islam (two-thirds) or Christianity (one-third), reflecting the relative strength of the two religions in their home regions.

But perhaps the most significant fact to emerge from the census data is the

Table 2.4: Numbers and percentages of returned migrants registered by the Western State Government of Nigeria, 1969–71.

Division	Number	Percentage
Oyo North	13,857	15.7
Oyo South	3,869	4.4
Oshun North West	25,552	29.0
Oshun North East	25,016	28.4
Oshun Central	8,610	9.8
Oshun South	421	0.5
Ibadan	2,275	2.6
Ijesha	1,022	1.2
Egbado	290	0.3
Egba	834	0.9
Ekiti	2,268	2.6
Ijebu	541	0.6
Other/Unclassified	3,549	4.0
Total	88,104	100.0

Source: Ministry figures, Western Nigerian Ministry of Economic Development and Reconstruction, Ibadan.

extent of the Yoruba involvement in trade. The Yoruba were primarily 'commercial migrants':[18] 48 per cent of the men were in trade, a higher proportion than in any other ethnic group, while a further 20 per cent worked on their own account in various types of crafts and services.[19] The pattern among the women was even more striking, with over 90 per cent of those employed involved in trade.[20] The pattern was not totally uniform, however, as the 1969 data makes clear.[21] There were differences both between Yoruba migrants from different towns, and migrants in different areas of Ghana. Overall, 66 per cent of the returnees registered by the Nigerian government in 1970–71 were traders. Nine per cent were farmers, and 18 per cent were craft workers. Over 80 per cent of returnees from towns like Ogbomosho, Igboho, Igbetti and Shaki were registered as traders, but other towns, like Oyo, Iseyin and Fiditi, registered large proportions of craft workers. This is partly a function of regional differences within Ghana. Towns well represented in the north of Ghana tended to have large proportions of traders. The lowest proportions of Yoruba traders were to be found in towns like Techiman in Brong-Ahafo (only 50 per cent thanks to a large number of Yoruba farmers) and in the coastal cities of Tema (49 per cent), Takoradi (58 per cent) and Accra (61 per cent), with their more diverse labour markets. By contrast over 85 per cent of the adult returnees from northern towns like Bawku and Tamale were registered as traders.

The 1969 data also makes clear the overwhelming importance of the savanna areas of north-west Yorubaland in the migration to Ghana. At the time, the Western State of Nigeria was divided into twenty-five administrative divisions, and the vast majority of returnees from Ghana originated from just four of them – Oyo North, Oshun North East, Oshun North West and Oshun Central – together with two divisions in the neighbouring Kwara State, Ilorin and Oyun (Table 2.4). The 1969 figures also reveal the importance within these divisions of specific towns, the figures for which are given in Table 2.5. The extraordinarily high levels of migration from some towns are shown dramatically when the numbers of returnees is contrasted with the 1952–3 census figures for the area: in two of the towns, the number of returnees exceeded the total resident population only fifteen years earlier (Table 2.6).

A final feature of the Yoruba distribution in Ghana which emerges from the 1969 data is the degree of clustering of migrants from the same home town in the same town in Ghana, and regional differences in the distribution of Yoruba from different towns suggest the main directions through which the migration developed.

Oshun North-East

Over half the migrants from this division came from the towns of Inisha and Oyan: there were also significant contingents from Igbaye, Iree, Ijabe and

Table 2.5: Numbers and percentages of returned migrants registered by the Western State Government of Nigeria, 1969–71, by town.

Rank	Town	Division	Number	Percentage
1	Ogbomosho	Oshun NW	20,556	23.3
2	Inisha	Oshun NE	14,550	16.5
3	Oyan	Oshun NE	8,800	10.0
4	Shaki	Oyo North	6,997	7.9
5	Ejigbo	Oshun NW	4,288	4.9
6	Oshogbo	Oshun Central	3,636	4.1
7	Ede	Oshun Central	3,420	3.9
8	Igbaye	Oshun NE	3,050	3.5
9	Ibadan	Ibadan	1,948	2.2
10	Igboho	Oyo North	1,783	2.0
11	Okeho	Oyo North	965	1.1
12	Kishi	Oyo North	887	1.0
13	Shepeteri	Oyo North	744	0.8
14	Abeokuta	Egba	716	0.8
15	Ilero	Oyo North	597	0.7
16	Igbetti	Oyo North	535	0.6
17	Ago Are	Oyo North	530	0.8
18	Tede	Oyo North	435	0.5
	Other towns		13,760	15.6

Source: Registration forms, Western Nigerian Ministry of Economic Development and Reconstruction, Ibadan.

Table 2.6: Comparison of the number of returned migrants registered by the Western State Government of Nigeria in 1969–70 on their return from Ghana with the 1952 Nigerian Census figures.

Town	Returnees	1952 Census	Percentage Ratio
Ogbomosho	20,556	139,535	14.7
Inisha	14,550	9,830	148.4
Oyan	8,800	6,610	133.1
Shaki	6,997	22,983	30.4
Ejigbo	4,288	15,851	27.0
Oshogbo	3,636	122,728	2.9
Ede	3,420	44,808	7.6
Igbaye	3,050	–	–
Ibadan	1,948	459,196	0.4
Igboho	1,783	8,476	21.0
Okeho	965	15,807	6.1
Kishi	887	7,827	11.3
Shepeteri	744	–	–
Abeokuta	716	84,451	0.8
Ilero	597	11,168	5.3
Igbetti	535	10,955	4.8

Sources: Mabogunje (1968: 329–30); Registration forms, Ministry of Economic Development and Reconstruction, Ibadan.

Okuku (cf. Barber, 1991: 217–19). Most of these migrants were in southern Ghana. The Inisha were widely scattered, and the only areas of significant concentration were Kumasi, Dormaa Ahenkro and Sunyani. The Igbaye were similarly scattered. The Oyan migrants were the largest Yoruba group in the diamond towns of Akim Oda and Akwatia, and they were also well-represented in Kumasi.

Oshun North-West

The great majority of migrants from this division were from Ogbomosho, with smaller contingents from Ede and Ejigbo. The Ogbomosho were the largest single group of Yoruba migrants in Ghana. Their main centre was Kumasi, but they were among the most numerous migrants in a number of other towns, including Accra, Tamale, Sekondi-Takoradi, Techiman, Suhum, Berekum, Bibiani, Prestea and Wa. The Ejigbo migrants were found mainly in Accra and the Volta Region, while the Ede migrants were strongest in the Central Region, particularly in Bawjiase.

Oshun Central

The two major towns involved here were Oshogbo and Erin. Both groups were well-scattered in the Eastern, Central and Ashanti Regions, while the Erin migrants were in the Western Region as well. There were large Oshogbo groups in Tema, Koforidua, Akwatia and Cape Coast.

Oyo North

This was the most important area of origin as far as the Yoruba in Northern Ghana were concerned. The Shaki migrants were by far the most numerous, with large groups in Tamale, Bawku, Bolgatanga, Salaga, Yendi, Wa, Nandom, and Chereponi. The Igboho migrants were the next most widely distributed, with large groups in Tamale, Bawku, Bolgatanga, Walewale and Navrongo. The Kishi migrants were found mainly in the towns in the Upper Region, while the Igbetti were concentrated in Tamale. Okcho and Ilero were exceptions: both had major concentrations of migrants in Kumasi and Accra. The Okeho were also the largest Yoruba group in Hamale, in the extreme north-west on the Upper Volta border.

Oyo South

Southern Oyo, unlike Northern Oyo, lies on the edge of the cocoa belt, and produced far fewer migrants to Ghana, though there were sizeable groups from Oyo, Iseyin, Ilora and Fiditi. The migrants from all four of these towns included a relatively low percentage of traders and a high percentage of craft workers. Apart from a large group of Iseyin migrants in Yendi, they had settled mainly in towns in the south.

Other divisions

Only three other divisions of the Western State were at all well represented in Ghana: Ibadan, Egba (Abeokuta) and Ekiti. The Ibadan and Egba migrants were concentrated almost entirely in Kumasi and Accra, while the Ekiti migrants, mainly from Ogotun and Oke Mesi, were in the mining areas of the Eastern Region. The number of migrants from these areas in Ghana, was small relative to the size of their populations in Nigeria, and small in comparison with the large migrations from the towns further north. Smaller still was the number of migrants from Ijebu: though many of the migrants in Ghana acknowledged that the Ijebu were among the most skilful traders in Yorubaland, they had migrated mainly to Ibadan and Lagos.[22] Sudarkasa mentions a group of Ijebu dealers in vehicle parts in the Magazine area of Kumasi.[23] Migrants from the other southern and eastern Yoruba areas such as Lagos and Ondo were very few and far between. One of the ironies of the migration to Ghana is that the 'Lagosian traders' included very few indigenous Lagosians at all, though a number of migrants from the northern Yoruba towns had used Lagos as their point of departure.

Kwara State

Migrants from Kwara state came mainly from Ilorin and Offa but figures are only available for the migrants from Offa and Erin Ile. These towns are very near Inisha and Oyan, and the Offa migrants were also widely distributed in southern Ghana. Indeed, with the exception of the Ogbomosho, they were the largest single group of Yoruba in Ghana. They were the largest group in Koforidua where many had been involved in the cocoa industry, and they were also strong in Nsawam, Kumasi, Konongo, Odumasi, Prestea, Sunyani, Techiman, Berekum, Accra, Akim Oda, Tema and Sekondi-Takoradi. The Ilorin migrants, for which no figures are available, were probably among the earliest Yoruba migrants in Ghana, and were strongest in Accra, where they were the largest Yoruba group.

MIGRATION AND ECONOMIC DEVELOPMENT

A number of geographical and historical factors appear to underlie this pattern of the distribution of the Yoruba migrants. Hundsalz suggests that the migrants from the drier savanna areas of Oyo North tended to go to the drier savanna areas of Ghana, while the migrants from towns like Oshogbo or Ibadan, on the edge of or within the cocoa belt, tended to go to the south.[24] This is partly true, but geographical determinism hardly explains, for instance, the Ilorin concentration in Accra. A more complex explanation in terms of the transformation of both the Nigerian and Ghanaian economies in the late nineteenth and early twentieth centuries is required, and it is to the Gold Coast economy that we now turn.

Like Nigeria, the Gold Coast had well-defined core and peripheral areas, and increasingly in the twentieth century it was the coastal and forest areas in the south which provided the economic core, while the savanna areas, which became the Northern Territories under colonial rule, became increasingly peripheral. This was not always the case: in the nineteenth century this area had been of strategic importance in the economy of the Ashanti state. Its marginalisation resulted from the collapse of the Ashanti economy after the British invasion of 1874, and the increasing redirection of trade towards the coast.

In this section, I discuss the changing structure of trade between Ashanti and the north, the development of the economy of the southern Gold Coast in the early colonial period, and the non-development of the north which created a north-south divide in the country which has persisted until the present day. Each of these processes had implications for flows of manpower both within the Gold Coast and from outside, including an increasing flow of migrants from Nigeria and together they provided the framework for the emergence of the patterns of distribution noted above.

Geographically, the north of Ghana consists of a large expanse of savanna, the more densely populated plains of the present Upper West and East Regions being divided from the more sparsely populated Northern Region by the Gambaga scarp. Gonja, in the south, is very sparsely populated in places, while the Bolgatanga area of the Upper East Region is one of the most densely populated in Africa.[25] There has long been a trade in staple foodstuffs between north and south Ghana, and in the 1970s the area around Tamale, the largest town, saw the commercial development of rice production.[26] But initially the 'Ashanti hinterland', as it was tellingly described, was seen primarily as a source of cheap labour for the south: slaves in the nineteenth century, and migrant labour in the twentieth.[27]

In the nineteenth century, much of this labour had been 'produced' by raiding the small, less politically centralised areas to the north, among the Dagarti, Sisala, Frafra and Kusasi. The major trade routes, on the other hand, ran through the centralised Gonja and Dagomba states which were, from 1740 until 1874, under Ashanti control. Much of the trade was in the hands of outsiders, such as the Dyula and Hausa, and towns like Buipe, Salaga, Kintampo and Atebubu developed as trans-shipment points along the savanna–forest divide. From the early nineteenth century, Salaga became the most important of these, as the Ashanti state excluded Muslim merchants from the area further south and retained a monopoly over long-distance trade itself.[28] Major trade routes ran from Salaga, through the Dagomba capital at Yendi, and from there across the present-day Togo and Benin, either through Gurma country in the north or through Borgu in the south. The northern routes crossed the Niger at Yauri. The southern road joined up with the routes running north through Yorubaland, crossed the Niger at Rabba, and passed on through the Nupe kingdom to Hausaland.[29] The main export from Ashanti to Hausaland was kola,[30] but the traders in the caravans which travelled the route also dealt in slaves, livestock, and ivory, as well as in craft goods such as leather, beads and textiles. The long-distance trade routes were dominated by Dyula and Hausa, but some Yoruba involvement was also likely. Long-distance trade was a Muslim specialty, and Islam had begun to spread in Oyo from the sixteenth century. After the collapse of Oyo, Ilorin, the southern outpost of the Sokoto Caliphate, became a major commercial centre.[31] Yoruba cloth circulated widely, and after the destruction of Oyo Ile, its weavers shifted production to other towns, notably Ilorin and Iseyin.[32] According to Sudarkasa, there may have been Ilorin traders settled in Salaga in the mid-nineteenth century.[33]

The established pattern of trade collapsed in 1874. The British invaded Ashanti and captured Kumasi. Gonja and Dagomba rebelled, and Ashanti officials were killed. In retaliation the Ashanti diverted the kola trade to Kintampo, and Salaga market suffered. Prior to 1874 it was estimated that Salaga's population had been 40,000, in addition to a huge transit population of traders, 10,000 of whom arrived or left daily.[34] Many of the permanent residents were landlords, servicing the needs of these traders. By 1876 the population was reduced to between 12,000 and 15,000, and 80 per cent of the houses were falling into ruins. However, as more travellers passed through, reports of Yoruba traders in Salaga began to multiply.[35] Trade revived a little in 1877, when the British opened up an eastern route to Accra, bypassing Ashanti, only to collapse finally in the 1890s, thanks to a civil war and the town's destruction.[36] By this time, many of the traders had moved south, founding migrant communities and starting to trade with Nigeria along the coast. There was a distinguishable Yoruba community in Accra in the first decade of the twentieth century, which included both traders from Salaga and Yoruba soldiers who had settled in the Gold Coast after being taken there during the Ashanti wars.[37] Yoruba traders from Salaga also moved north. Skinner mentions a group moving to Ouagadougou in the late nineteenth century because the trade in kola and cloth with Dyula traders from Timbuktu had been disrupted.[38] New groups of Yoruba started to arrive, like the Shaki traders who appeared in Yendi about the turn of the century.[39] By 1908 the District Commissioner in Navrongo was able to note that most of the local trade was now in the hands of the Hausa, Mossi and Yoruba.[40]

The political background to all this was provided by competition between the British, the Germans and the French. It became clear that trade in the interior of West Africa could not be exploited without direct political control, and the British government was finally persuaded to move into the interior by a combination of the demands of the trade lobby and the fear that the French and Germans would beat them to it. In 1884 the Germans declared a protectorate in Togo. To safeguard their interests in the hinterland of the Gold Coast the British negotiated an agreement which created a neutral zone consisting of much of eastern Gonja, Dagomba and south eastern Mamprusi, in 1888. The zone lasted for twelve years, during which the British and Germans both tried to establish their spheres of influence in and around it, anticipating its eventual division between them. Meanwhile the British bargained with the French over the question of boundaries in the north and north-west.[41] With the rivalry between the powers resolved, the Protectorate of the Northern Territories of the Gold Coast came into being at the start of 1902. The Order-in-Council set up a military administration with the powers of the Governor in Accra exercised in the north by a Chief Commissioner, together with a number of District Commissioners, and a detachment of British troops to enforce the Pax Britannica. The only subsequent major change in the boundaries of the region came with the occupation of the western part of northern Togoland in 1914 and its formal assimilation in 1923.[42] The British headquarters had already been shifted from Kintampo to Gambaga in 1898, and were moved again to the new and more central location of Tamale in 1907.[43]

ECONOMIC DEVELOPMENT AND MIGRATION IN SOUTHERN GHANA

If the colonial takeover of the north of Ghana prepared the way for several decades of neglect and stagnation, the situation to the south was very different.

The period from 1891–1911 saw the transformation of the economy here into one of the most dynamic in Africa,[44] attracting migrants from far and wide who cashed in on the new opportunities. Among the first of these were the troops taken there from Nigeria by the British. Although the majority of the British troops in the campaigns of 1874 and 1900 were Hausa in origin, substantial numbers of Yoruba were recruited into the army until about 1905,[45] and some of them settled in Kumasi and Accra after the Yaa Asantewaa War.[46] Yoruba migrants also became involved in the Gold Coast transport, mining and cocoa industries.

The first twenty years of colonial rule saw the construction of both the railway and road networks in the Gold Coast, and their main outlines have changed little since. Railway construction involved importation of labour from Nigeria, where the line from Lagos to the north was already being built. It may be significant that the Yoruba population of southern Ghana included large groups from most of the major towns along the line in Nigeria, including Abeokuta, Ibadan, Ede, Oshogbo, Offa, Oyan and Ilorin. Yoruba labour was also employed in road construction,[47] as well as in the mines.

By 1911, mining employed 19,000 men, but wages were low and working conditions poor, so the government tried recruiting in Nigeria. Yoruba workers seem to have been used for cutting firewood in the gold industry, though generally mine labour seems to have been unpopular. The majority of Yoruba mine workers eventually turned to trade.[48] Yoruba migrants also became involved in the diamond industry, in the Akwatia and Akim Oda areas, which in 1960 had the highest concentrations of Yoruba migrants in Ghana. The town from which most of them came, Oyan, had one of the highest levels of outmigration in Nigeria. A majority of the diamond diggers were Yoruba from the 1930s until 1963, when the Ghana government tried to exclude them from the industry.[49]

But the number of people involved in mining was only a tenth of the number involved in cocoa production – 185,000 by 1911. The industry's expansion was due almost entirely to African initiative, and it created a massive demand for migrant labour. The migration from the Northern Territories and Upper Volta is well documented: less well-known is the involvement of Yoruba traders, brokers and transporters who did much of the buying and bulking in the rural areas.[50] They acted as money lenders, advancing loans against the next season's crop, and they included many of the Offa migrants who were the largest Yoruba group in Koforidua.

But the diamond and cocoa industries were, in the context of the country as a whole, local specialisms. Throughout the entire country the Yoruba were fast becoming established in the retail trade in manufactured goods, and some of the wealthier ones doubled as wholesalers. This was true in both the towns and the rural areas. Many of the traders had initially been involved in the coastal trade, exporting kola to Nigeria and importing Yoruba cloth. The Nigerian

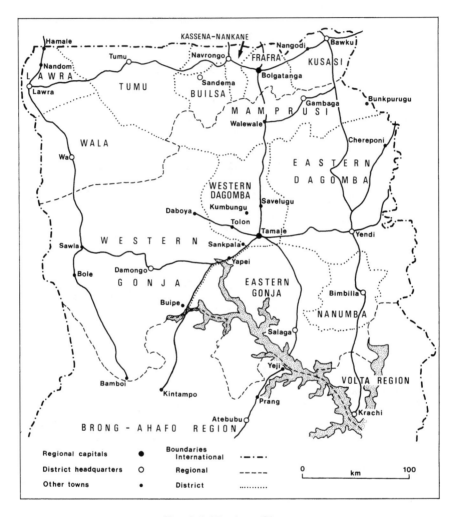

Map 2.3: Northern Ghana.

cloth trade was particularly profitable in the period after the First World War when supplies of European cloth were scarce, but demand for it in the south dwindled as more varied European textiles reappeared.[51] The kola trade also went into decline as the Nigerian government restricted imports and production within Nigeria itself increased.[52] Increasingly the Yoruba turned to the sale of manufactures bought from the large European firms and the Lebanese merchants in Accra and Kumasi, selling them both in the major urban markets and in the smaller towns and villages. The trade in Nigerian cloth survived longer in the north, where tastes were more conservative, and it remained an important item of trade until the 1950s. It is to the economic development, or lack of it, in the north that we turn next.

'DEVELOPMENT' IN THE NORTHERN TERRITORIES

The process of economic change in the north was much slower than in the south, so slow at times as to be almost imperceptible.[53] Individual administrators stationed there might wax lyrical about the region's economic potential, but, with the possible exception of Guggisberg in the 1920s, governors in Accra were much more sceptical. Governor Hodgeson's views in 1898 were typical:

> The country as far as is known is destitute of mineral wealth, it is destitute of valuable timbers, and does not produce either rubber or kola nuts or indeed any product of trade value . . . For the present I therefore cannot too strongly urge the employment of all the available resources of the Government upon the development of the country to the south of Kintampo leaving the Northern Territories to be dealt with in future years . . . I would not at present spend upon the Northern Territories . . . a single penny more than is absolutely necessary for their suitable administration and the encouragement of the transit trade.[54]

These views persisted: even as late as 1938, the Annual Report for the Northern Territories could state that the people of the region were regarded as: 'an amiable people; useful as soldiers, police and labourers in the mines and cocoa farms; in short fit only to be hewers of wood and drawers of water for their brothers in the Colony and Ashanti'.[55]

In the early colonial period, therefore, the interests of the south of the country, the Colony and Ashanti, were paramount, and all the north could supply was unimpeded access to their markets, and a supply of cheap labour. In order to encourage the transit trade and the flow of livestock from the north, the tax on caravans was abolished, despite the fact that this was the Northern Territories' only significant form of revenue. The administrators of the NTs bitterly resented it:

> At present we are merely a stepping stone towards the down country markets, and, as a Protectorate, do not benefit at all by the caravan traffic. If anything we are losers by it . . . That these alien coloured traders

overrun the protectorate without doing good to the inhabitants is naturally a sore point with political officers. It is no exaggeration to say that the caravan people do only harm to our natives. They sell and buy no wares en route, and, as regards foodstuffs, what necessities they do not bring with them they practically filch from the inhabitants.[56]

In contrast, government efforts to promote trade in the north itself were limited. Markets were established and improved in the main towns and a start was made in introducing silver coinage. Government stores were set up in Gambaga, Wa, Yeji and Kintampo before 1900 and European merchants arrived in Tamale and Gambaga in 1908.[57] Cloth sold well, but other goods were considered too expensive and could not compete with those brought in by African traders from the north east or up through Togo. The costs of labour and transport were lower in Togo and there was a fear of the northern markets being flooded with German goods.[58] Customs duties were instituted, regular searches of the main markets for French and German goods brought in illegally were carried out, and fines imposed on those who were caught. Long-distance trade was only permitted as long as it did not conflict with the interests of the government and European firms. The cattle trade was allowed to continue and even expand, but the trade in manufactured goods brought in from neighbouring countries which competed with those from the Colony was now either subjected to duty or categorised as 'smuggling'. The quantity of goods in the markets coming up from Ashanti rather than through Togo increased, but after 1911 the sales of the European stores in Tamale and Salaga declined.[59] They were eventually closed.

A major problem in the early years was the cost of transport. Until the use of motor vehicles developed, goods had to be brought up by headload. A start was made on the road network, built largely by corvee labour provided by the local chiefs, but even after the motor car had started to prove itself in the south, the government delayed the construction of the road from Kumasi to Tamale, hoping to open up the Volta River as an alternative. The road was not finished until the 1920s, and was not tarred until the 1950s.[60] In the 1920s Guggisberg considered building a railway from Kumasi to Tamale, but owing to the onset of the depression, nothing came of the plan.

Despite the aim of the administration to encourage the flow of trading caravans to the south, the administrative controls, the improved security situation and the gradual improvement in transport actually rendered them obsolete. Small groups or individual traders could now operate on their own, and this allowed increasing numbers of Yoruba to join the previously dominant Hausa and Dyula in the local markets. Some of the old landlords who had serviced the caravan trade turned to farming.[61] However, even for the new arrivals, the prospects for business hardly looked promising, given the lack of a colonial development policy, the shortage of coinage in circulation, and the difficulties of transport. But as the Yoruba traders found, demand for the goods which they were selling did exist if one was prepared to travel widely enough, and this initially meant travelling on foot, and, where possible, using junior relatives to increase both the geographical coverage and the quantity of goods which could be carried.

Demand was a function of the amount of cash in circulation, and, though this increased only slowly, it did nevertheless increase. First, there were the earnings of labour migrants to the south, even though much of them went into the pockets of traders in the south. Not everyone in the north was enthusiastic about outmigration: the chiefs complained that it cut down the amount of labour at their disposal, and at times such as the influenza epidemic of 1918, it was genuinely in short supply.[62] Northern migrants tended to head for the cocoa fields rather than the mines, where pay and conditions were so poor that the government resorted to forced labour in the 1920s, with disastrous results.[63] During the First World War there was massive recruitment into the army from the north, where 90 per cent of the Gold Coast troops originated.[64] In the 1920s migration increased once more with the completion of the road to the south, and although it declined during the depression, it picked up once more with the imposition of taxation in the late 1930s, and with renewed army recruitment during the Second World War.

In addition to labour migration, a further stimulus to trade came from the growth of the colonial administration in the main towns, and in the number of people it employed. Tamale itself was also expanding rapidly. The 1920s and 1930s saw the construction of the aerodrome, the waterworks, the power station and a new agricultural station. There were now soldiers, police, clerical workers and government labourers stationed there in large numbers. After 1918 the Mossi Zongo had been laid out, taking its name from the demobilised Mossi troops who settled there. The layout of the Hausa Zongo soon followed, and by 1927 all the plots had been allocated.[65] Commercial activity was also increasing rapidly, as a report for 1929–30 described:

> Tamale continues to increase in population. Buildings are going up everywhere, and it is becoming a difficult matter for the town authorities to cope with the number of applications for building plots. A great many of these people are traders in a small way . . . The market is becoming so large as to be almost congested on 'big market' days [i.e. on the day of Tamale market, held every six days] . . . Extra accommodation in the way of stalls has been erected.[66]

The Annual Report of the following year noted that the market had quadrupled in size in the previous three or four years, and that Tamale had now become a major livestock and kola market.[67] With the development of transport Syrians had started to operate stores and transport businesses in Tamale and in 1930 four expatriate firms opened stores there as well. These trends were accentuated by a dramatic improvement in communications with the south. Even if the railway failed to materialise the road from Kumasi to Tamale

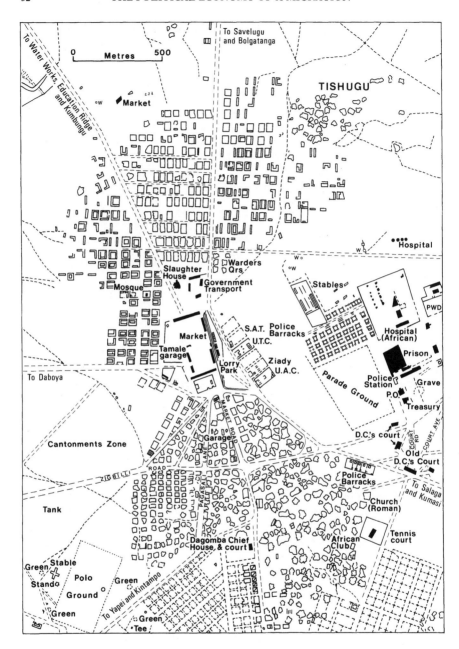

Map 2.4: Central Tamale in 1932.

was finished in the early 1920s and the Yeji ferry was now able to take motor vehicles. The decade which followed saw the rapid development of motor transport throughout the north. Each year in the 1920s produced a large increase in the numbers of vehicles making their way over the ferries to and from the south, and by 1925 the Tamale–Kumasi road could be used throughout the year. By 1924 traffic was able to reach Wa, Lawra and Bole for the first time.[68] The journey from Kumasi to Tamale now only took two days. Syrian and African transport owners began to operate in Tamale, and lorries also started to appear in the rural markets around Tamale – Tolon, Savelugu and Nyankpala. Further afield there were reports of a lorry service to Wa and the development of trade in Bawku with the construction of a drift over the river into Upper Volta at Mogonori. As a final sign that the motor age had arrived, the Governor and a party of royal visitors made a grand tour of the Protectorate entirely by road. By 1929 there were 2,500 miles of road in the north, and the bridges were being consolidated with concrete culverts. In the same year the number of lorries and trailers making the Yeji crossing rose to 15,685, a 43 per cent increase over the previous year.[69]

The population of the town in the 1931 census was 12,941, having trebled since 1921. A breakdown of these figures gives a good idea of the occupational structure of the town. Of these 1,286 people were listed as 'traders', 866 as 'market traders' and a further 385 as 'hawkers'.[70] The difference between these categories was not explained, but it appears that nearly 2,500 of a population of 13,000 were engaged in some form of trade, compared with the 3,028 listed as 'farmers'. The figure included both men and women, and no doubt many of the traders operated on an extremely small scale, but it does indicate the importance of Tamale as a trading centre, and many of those enumerated there probably sold goods in the outlying villages as well. The census also gave an impression of the distribution of Yoruba migrants in the Northern Territories as a whole.

Tables 2.7 and 2.8 give the figures which I could locate in the Tamale Archives on the distribution of the Yoruba in the north in 1931. Most were concentrated in Tamale, Krachi, Yendi and Bawku, with only a few in the other areas. It was only later that they started to spread to the west in larger numbers, but even here they had been noticed by the administration. The District Commissioner for Lawra-Tumu District complained:

> Local trade is almost entirely in the hands of non-natives – Lagosians etc. – who are the most worthless class of traders, as they take out of the District the money which they obtain for their wares instead of purchasing local commodities, and return again with fresh commerce, thereby draining the District of its available monetary resources.[71]

It was not only here that the presence of the Yoruba had been noticed by the authorities. It seems that by this time they had become a conspicuous and easily identified group. Syme noted in Kusasi in 1931 that sixty-four of the

Table 2.7: Distribution of the Yoruba in the Northern Territories of the Gold Coast, 1931, by district.

District	Number	Percentage
Kusasi	162	19.3
Zurungu	?	?
Navrongo	14	1.7
Lawra-Tumu	10	1.2
Wa	?	?
Western Gonja	0	0.0
Western Dagomba	85	10.1
Tamale	305	36.3
Eastern Dagomba	70	8.3
Eastern Gonja	93	11.1
Krachi	101	12.0
Total	840	100.0

Source: District Census Reports, 1931, Ghana National Archives, Tamale. Percentages are of available figures. I could locate no figures for Wa or Zurungu Districts. Although the figures for Western Gonja gave a breakdown by ethnic group, there was no mention of Yoruba in it.

stalls owned by the government in Bawku market, as well as thirty-four other stalls, had been occupied by Yoruba.[72] Most markets in the area contained a few Yoruba from whom the 'usual trinkets, scents and cloth from the coast could be bought.' By 1937, it was reported from Eastern Dagomba that most of the trade outside that in foodstuffs was in the hands of the Lagosians who made their headquarters in Tamale, Yendi and Bimbilla, and who could be seen cycling with enormous loads on their carriers to all the large markets in the District, often travelling forty or fifty miles a day.[73] They were also involved in other types of trade, as the Annual Report of 1939 showed:

Table 2.8: Yoruba population of the Northern Territories of the Gold Coast, 1931, by age and sex.

District	Males				Females				Total
	0–15	15–45	45+	Total	0–15	15–45	45+	Total	
Eastern Gonja	23	32	5	60	8	20	5	33	93
Western Dagomba	16	32	3	51	9	19	6	34	85
Kusasi	11	92	8	111	8	39	4	52	162
Navrongo	1	8	0	9	2	3	0	5	14
Totals	51	164	16	231	27	81	15	123	354
Percentages	14.4	46.3	4.5	65.3	7.6	22.8	4.2	34.7	100.0

Source: District Census Reports, 1931, Ghana National Archives, Tamale. The Western Dagomba figure excludes Tamale.

The Lagosians are the most enterprising traders. They are now seen in the smallest markets selling their junk and Japan goods, and 'Japan' has now become a word in most dialects of the country to describe an article not of the highest quality. In Dagomba District, numerous cases of smuggling were brought to light during the year. The offenders were all Lagosians, and the goods smuggled included cigarettes, matches and leaf tobacco. It is suspected that smuggling is very much on the increase.[74]

The number of Yoruba in the north during the period was therefore growing and they were to a large extent taking over the developing market in manufactured goods in the rural areas. This was a position of dominance that was to last until the exodus thirty years later. There were signs that they had come to stay. First it was mentioned that they were among those applying for house plots in various towns in the north, and a note from Kusasi District on the lodging houses in Bawku mentions the presence of Yoruba landlords.[75] Second, the 1931 census figures gives a breakdown of the Yoruba population by age and sex in some districts, and over a third of those recorded were female. The earliest descriptions of trade in Northern Ghana that I received from informants spoke of a variety of goods being taken there from Nigeria, including beads and bracelets from Bida, antimony (*tiro*) natron (*kaun*) and various types of Yoruba cloth from a number of different Yoruba towns. It was in the period after 1918, however, that Yoruba cloth became the most important item being sold by the Yoruba traders in the north, and this remained the case throughout the inter-war period.

Yoruba woven cloth (*aṣọ ofi*) is still a highly prized and relatively expensive item of dress throughout Yorubaland, and large quantities of it are still produced, particularly in towns like Iseyin and Ilorin. But many other towns have their own weavers and styles, including Ogbomosho, Oyo, Igboho, Shaki and Okeho. The Yoruba traders taking the cloth to Ghana drew on a variety of sources. There were two main types of woven cloth taken to Ghana. The first was the familiar type woven on a horizontal loom in narrow strips five or six inches wide. This is normally woven by the men, and the strips can then be cut up into shorter lengths and sewn into cloths of various sizes. Numerous variations both in the colours of the cloth and forms of ornamentation used on it are possible, and it is still the cloth which is worn by many on important occasions. In the towns where it is produced whole compounds were traditionally involved in its production and the craft was passed down in the descent group.[76] Its popularity in the post war period seems to have been due to two factors. First supplies of European cloth, according to informants, were in short supply. Second, it proved popular among groups like the demobilised soldiers who had money to spend and who spent it on more elaborate forms of traditional dress.

The second type of woven cloth is produced by women on a broader vertical loom and is known as *aṣọ kejipa*. It is a thicker type of cloth and consists of strips about 15 or 16 inches wide and five feet or so long. A woman's wrapper consists of two of these pieces sewn together, while three are enough for a man's cover cloth. The loom on which it is woven is much simpler than that for the narrow strip cloth, and in many northern Yoruba houses looms of this type are found with half-completed cloths on them on which the women work in their spare time. Most of this cloth used to be either plain white or plain indigo in colour, but these days a variety of threads and patterns are found. A single strip of cloth of this type is often used by a woman to secure her baby on her back.

A third type of cloth often taken to Ghana by the Yoruba traders was *aṣọ adirẹ*, plain white cotton sheeting dyed with indigo, either by tying it or by using wax or cassava resist techniques.[77] Many Yoruba women in the markets in Ghana used to wear this type of cloth themselves, and the indigo colour, together with the method of tying their headscarves, made them instantly recognisable. Good quality *adirẹ* cloth with hand-painted designs is very expensive, but cheaper *adirẹ* made with stencilled or tied designs became very popular in northern Ghana, as it was one of the cheapest forms of coloured cloth available there. Initially most of the *adirẹ* sold in Ghana came from Abeokuta in Nigeria, but later it was produced in Ghana itself. Some of the *adirẹ* designs were later copied by European manufacturing firms.[78]

In the 1930s, a man's cover cloth made of *kejipa* cost around 3/- in Nigeria. This could be sold for 5/- in French territory or for 7/- in Ghana. After 1945 the price rose to 7/- in Nigeria and 15/- or more in Ghana. The largest number of cover cloths that could be carried in a single headload was usually forty. A single piece of *kejipa* weighs between 2–300 gm depending on the weave, and thus forty men's cloths represents a weight of around 24–30 kg. In the 1930s, such a load meant an expenditure of £5 or £6. This represented the minimum investment for the would-be trader, in addition to travelling and food expenses on the way to Ghana. Narrow loom *aṣọ ofi* was more expensive.

While many of the Ogbomosho traders had enough capital before 1939 to travel on the coastal route by steamers and railway, foot transport on the inland route remained the norm for the northern Oyo traders until the end of the Second World War, and, for some, even later than this. There was little cross-country motor traffic, and even when it was available (for instance between Tamale and Yendi) the cost was too high for the poorer traders. In Tamale the newly arrived traders stayed at the houses of the few that had already settled there. Tamale was not only an important market in its own right, but also served as a base for traders going round the northern towns and surrounding villages where the bulk of the cloth was sold. Many of the early migrants reported making regular trips on foot not only to the markets in the immediate vicinity of Tamale, but as far afield as Wa, Bole, Bawku and Yendi. Travelling conditions were difficult during the rains, when trade frequently involved wading through flooded streams, but it could be worthwhile. According to one informant, his sales were best when the villages were the most

isolated because of the rains, and when other traders made no effort to get
through. The traders could not always be sure of the welcome that they would
get in a new village:

> At that time, immediately the Dagomba saw us, then they started to run
> away from us because they knew nothing about us and our tribal marks
> were also strange to them. If they wanted to buy something from us, they
> used to point to it with their sticks. If their children came near us, they
> told them to keep away because they did not know who we were and where
> we were from and they were afraid of us.

However, this fear could be overcome through the presentation of gifts of
natron or cloth to the chief and the children in a new village. Most traders built
up a regular clientele in this way, and a new trader could be taken round by a
friend or relative in order to get to know the area, and to learn enough Hausa or
Dagbane in order to be able to communicate with the local people.

Most of the early migrants from northern Oyo followed routes to northern
Ghana which corresponded closely both to the old trade routes and the modern
laterite roads. After buying cloth, usually in Igboho, Ilorin or Okeho, they
would pass through Kishi, Ilesha Bariba, and then over the border to Niki,
Djougou, Lamakara, Kabo, Yendi and Tamale.[79] There were Yoruba settled
in many of these towns who provided the traders with shelter on the way. The
most usual time to travel for the new trader was the start of the dry season, after
the harvest, when he was able to buy the cloth with the proceeds from the
farming season, but the established traders would travel at any time of the year,
including the rains. The weather was cooler, though rivers in flood had to be
crossed with the help of local swimmers using calabashes as floats.

As early as the 1930s the traders could take a lorry from Yendi to Tamale,
and by the 1950s there were lorries travelling on the roads in the French
colonies as well. Alternatives to the main route might take the trader through
Parakou in the south or up to Kande in the north. The exact route taken by the
small groups of traders would depend on the latest news about the activities of
the border guards, who from time to time proved troublesome to the traders.
Apart from their demands for customs duties, there are reports of the French
border guards attempting to recruit some of the traders into the army during
the Second World War. The response of the traders was to develop skills in
dealing with the guards which ranged from bribery to avoidance, skills which
were retained after Ghanaian independence.

The development of transport within Ghana brought diversification in the
commodities dealt in by the Yoruba. This was partly a result of the increased
use of the coastal route for the transport of the cloth, as it had been for kola.
The commonest variation was to transport the cloth from Ilorin to Lagos by
rail, to Accra by sea, and to Kumasi by rail, bringing it on up to Tamale by
road, or using porters if the road was closed during the rains. There seems to

have been cooperation between the richer Yoruba traders who regularly travelled on the coastal route and those who could not afford to:

> Sometimes we used to buy the cloth in Bida. The Gambari [i.e. Hausa] used to take our loads to Jebba and the railway. The people at Jebba would write down the number of the cloth and weigh it, and it would be put on the ship at Lagos. In Accra the ship money was paid, together with the duty. It was the rich people like Alhaji Karimu [from Ogbomosho, later the Yoruba chief in Tamale] who used to bring it up from Accra for us. Meanwhile we would walk to Tamale, which took 25 days, and we collected the cloth there.

A rich trader like Alhaji Karimu was, even before 1939, bringing over consignments of over a thousand pounds worth of cloth at a time, both for his own use and for that of other traders, including his own junior relatives. According to Sudarkasa, the Ogbomosho traders in southern Ghana employed clerks in both Lagos and Accra to handle the transport of the cloth between the two countries.[80]

The changing patterns of transport brought the Yoruba in Tamale more into contact with the south and they started to sell other goods brought up from Lebanese or expatriate wholesalers in Kumasi and Accra. The goods they started to sell were much the same standard lines that they remained selling until 1969. They acted as bulk-breakers for the larger firms, selling in small quantities, both to the local people in Tamale, including the government workers, and to people in the rural areas to which the larger firms had little interest in extending their activities. Here, packets of cigarettes, boxes of matches, bars of washing soap, and even jars of pomade, could be broken down into smaller units for sale. Yards of cloth were divided into thin strips for use as loin cloths (bante) by some of the northern groups such as the Frafra and Konkomba. Enamelware and pots were another popular selling line. The use of a single member of the group buying cloth in Nigeria for a number of traders in Ghana allowed the permanent settlement of Yoruba traders in Tamale on an increasing scale.

The other transport innovation was the more widespread use of the bicycle, though my own data suggest that most of the Yoruba traders remained on foot until after 1945. In pre-war years, bicycles were difficult to obtain in Tamale. A report from 1936 noted that:

> The pushbike is steadily growing in popularity and it seems a pity that English firms neglect this market ... as soon as there is any news of an old or new cycle for sale, purchasers come crowding in. The District Commissioner recently ordered six cycles for six of his road overseers from Kumasi. As soon as they arrived there were three or four people wanting each cycle.[81]

Another observed that 'even a senior chief has been observed cycling along the road with his panting entourage preceding at a smart trot'.[82]

The cycle also began to play a role in the trade between Ghana and Nigeria. Goods could be brought to Ghana by cycle on the inland route in six days, a quarter of the time that it took on foot. During the war, this method of transport was especially useful with the disruption of trade links along the coast, and until the exodus in 1969 the use of cycles along the bush paths near the borders remained important for the traders involved in smuggling.

By the start of the Second World War, therefore, numbers of Yoruba had already become established in the Northern Territories, selling a variety of goods, though their success was still largely based on the sale of Yoruba cloth brought from Nigeria. Most of the Igboho and Igbetti traders still used porters to transport this. It was the traders from Ogbomosho who were the first to bring cloth in large quantities along the coastal route. The cloth was sold not only in Tamale itself but all over the north of the country, and this involved travelling considerable distances on foot, or, later, by bicycle. The trade in Nigerian cloth was gradually supplemented with the trade in other goods, mainly European cloth and small manufactured items brought up from the towns in the south. Their capital was gathered from a variety of sources – farming, migrant labour, craft work and trade in Nigeria. But once a trader was successful in Ghana he would be followed there by friends and relatives, either working for him or trading with their own capital. With the establishment of the coastal route, buying and transport came to be left more and more in the hands of a single member of the group, leaving the other members free to spend more time selling goods in Tamale and further afield. Despite the low level of economic development in the north, there was an increasing amount of money in circulation. This came from labour migration, from government workers (including soldiers during the two wars), and from those selling foodstuffs and livestock for the markets of the southern towns, following the construction of the main roads and ferries. The demand for manufactured goods was diffuse and scattered, and while the Lebanese and the European firms confined their activities to the large towns, the Yoruba were able to exploit this demand through their willingness to headload goods over long distances through the rural areas.

CONCLUSION

So far, we have dealt with the macro-level context of Yoruba migration to Ghana in the early twentieth century: the transformation of the economies of western Nigeria and the Gold Coast, the creation of new growth poles and opportunities for capital accumulation, and the breakdown of the pre-colonial trading system based on long-distance caravans. The growth of the cocoa industry and the market economy in Western Nigeria coupled with the survival of a thriving weaving industry meant that the Yoruba were in an excellent position to exploit new entrepreneurial opportunities throughout the region. Some, like the Ijesha, 'discovered' Ibadan, Lagos and the rest of Nigeria.[83]

Others made their way to the Gold Coast as troops, labourers or traders and laid the basis for the steady expansion of Yoruba migration throughout the colonial period. Why the Yoruba rather than other ethnic groups were able to capitalise on these opportunities is a complex question. Various factors were undoubtedly significant: the proximity of western Nigeria to the Gold Coast, the sheer size of the Yoruba population (greater than that of Ghana) and the vitality of the Western Nigerian economy which made capital accumulation possible. There was also the information available on the opportunities in the Gold Coast which came from troops, labourers, railway workers and pioneer traders who had been there, as well as from workers moving in the opposite direction. Even in the north of the country there were opportunities available, thanks to the growth of the administration, labour migration and the army.

The evidence suggests that there were a number of distinct streams of early migrants to different parts of Ghana, though as a result of secondary migration within Ghana and continued migration from Nigeria the boundaries between these flows became increasingly blurred. The earliest migrants to Salaga were probably from Ilorin, which lay within the Sokoto Caliphate in the nineteenth century and which became an important trade centre. After the sack of Kumasi by the British in 1874, Ashanti control of trade to the north was shattered, and northern traders, including Yoruba from Ilorin, made their way to Accra and other towns in the south, founding colonies of migrants there.[84]

A second wave of Yoruba migration resulted from the intervention of the British in the political economy of the south. The troops used by the British in the Ashanti wars included Yoruba, and some members of the 1900 contingent settled in Kumasi afterwards. They appear to have come from the towns of the Ibadan empire, and may have included not only troops from Ibadan but also from Oshogbo and Ogbomosho. All three towns were well-represented in Kumasi, which had the largest Yoruba community of any town in Ghana, perhaps as many as 20,000 by 1969.[85] Ogbomosho migrants later moved north, settling in the major towns along the way such as Ejura, Prang, Atebubu, Kintampo, Techiman, Tamale and Wa. Transport and mine labourers were also recruited, mainly from Ogbomosho and the towns to the east, including Offa, Inisha and Oyan. These towns produced the largest groups of migrants in Southern Ghana. The early labour migrants eventually moved into trade in which they were joined by their relatives from the 1920s onwards. In addition, many of the Offa migrants moved into the cocoa industry, while the Oyan took up diamond digging.

The other major stream of migration was from the towns of Northern Oyo to the Northern and Upper Regions of Ghana, and particularly from Shaki, Igboho, Kishi and Igbetti. Shaki migrants arrived in Yendi about the turn of the century[86] but the main period of migration was from the 1920s onwards. The attraction of these areas for migrants from these towns was threefold. First, they lie relatively near northern Ghana: the routes followed by the early traders, travelling on foot, cut straight across northern Togo and Benin. Second, this is the least developed area of Nigerian Yorubaland. The economic transformation resulting from colonial rule took place later than in other parts of Yorubaland, and so did large-scale migration to Ghana, by which time the more promising economic opportunities in Southern Ghana had been exploited already. The northern Oyo migrants tended to look for opportunities in the poorer Northern Territories, and they were joined there by other groups of migrants, mainly from Ogbomosho, who had had little success in the Colony and Ashanti.

These areas of primary migration tended to overlap and merge as secondary migration took place within the Gold Coast. Three general features of the migration stand out. First, the overwhelming majority of the migrants came from towns in the northwestern parts of Yorubaland, and particularly from the towns outside the cocoa belt. The higher level of economic development in and around the larger Yoruba towns like Abeokuta, Ibadan, Oshogbo and Ife has tended to curtail outmigration, and the main movement has been in search of cocoa land. Similarly many of the trading opportunities within western Nigeria were monopolised by migrants from more wealthy areas. Yoruba traders from the poorer towns had to look further afield.

Second, the migrants were heavily clustered by town of origin. These groups of migrants from different towns remained distinct until 1969, most notably in their marriage patterns and associational structure. The clustering was a function of the migration process itself, and is crucial to an understanding of the success of the Yoruba migrants in trade, their social organisation in Ghana, and their relations with their hosts, culminating in the 1969 exodus.

Third, the Yoruba were able to take over particular niches in the labour market extremely quickly once they had arrived in Ghana, and the reasons for this are related to the social structure of trade and its links with the organisation of the towns from which they originated. This enabled the traders to exploit the demand which did exist and to secure a regular supply of labour in the market. It is with these social processes that the next chapter is concerned.

YORUBA TOWNSMEN IN THE NORTHERN GOLD COAST

If the last chapter described in broad outline the Yoruba migration to the Gold Coast as a whole, the present one provides some of the finer-grain description of the migration process to the northern Gold Coast from the four main towns represented in Tamale: Ogbomosho, Igbetti, Igboho and Shaki. The argument is that this process was a function of three sets of factors: the political and economic legacy of the nineteenth century wars in northern Yorubaland, the social structure of the Yoruba town, and the economic requirements of the trades in the Gold Coast in which the Yoruba migrants were engaged. These factors are, of course, intimately linked. The social structure of the four towns in the early twentieth century was very much a product of the nineteenth-century wars, and has been further modified by the success of their migrants scattered all over West Africa. Secondly, the changing requirements of trade tended to reinforce processes of modification in Yoruba kinship and residential organisation which were already underway. The complexities of the relationship between the three sets of factors will become apparent as the histories of two groups of traders, from Igbetti and Ogbomosho, unfold.

THE LEGACY OF THE NINETEENTH CENTURY

As was seen in the previous chapters, the main demographic effects of the collapse of Oyo and the nineteenth century wars were the destruction of many of the settlements in the Oke Ogun, including Oyo Ile itself, and a shift of population to the south and east. The population density increases appreciably to the east of the road between Ogbomosho and Ilorin. Most of the migrants to the southern Gold Coast originated to the east of this line, while most migrants to the Northern Territories came from the area to the north and west. Ogbomosho, situated on the boundary between the two zones, was appropriately well represented in both halves of the country.[1]

To the north and west, the towns which survived the wars were those which could be defended easily against attack, either like Igboho because they were heavily fortified, or like Igbetti because of their location. When Clarke visited Igbetti in the 1850s the town was actually situated on top of a massive inselberg,[2] and it was only during the colonial period that the townspeople were persuaded to move to the present site in the valley below. Shaki and Igboho were much more important centres in the Oyo empire prior to its collapse, as the massive fortifications around Igboho demonstrate.[3] The towns survived, but only as shadows of their former selves. Igboho, which had had a population of 40,000 at its height in the nineteenth century, had fewer than 10,000 people in 1953. The problems for both Shaki and Igboho in the new order of things was their location.[4] They lay well to the west of the main road and rail links between the south and north of Nigeria, and the economic opportunities available to their people were consequently severely curtailed. Weaving survived there, but failed to become the major factor in the economy that it was in Iseyin and Ilorin, with their better access to raw materials and markets. Farm land was abundant, but again their remoteness prevented them from fully exploiting the markets to the south for their produce. The other options available were labour migration and long distance trade, the one, in many cases, providing the capital for the other. Igboho migrants clustered in the Mamu area of the cocoa belt, and financed their trade with their cocoa earnings. But there was one advantage from their location, and that was their proximity to the Nigerian border. With the increased security provided by colonial rule, the Shaki and Igboho traders were quick to move outside Nigeria to trade. Igboho traders became established throughout the Northern Territories of the Gold Coast, the Ivory Coast and Niger, and the dispersal of the Shaki traders was even more spectacular, with sizeable groups to be found in every country from Guinea to Niger.[5]

Development in these towns however remained painfully slow, partly as a function of the low esteem in which the colonial government held them. Igboho, together with Igbetti and Kishi, makes up the Irepo District, the most northerly part of Oyo State. As late as 1948, the Oyo Province Annual Report observed: 'This is the remotest, wildest and most impoverished area in this Division, and has on occasion given the appearance of being scarcely under administrative control at all'.[6] Even by the late 1960s, progress had been limited. Shaki was now the administrative headquarters for Oyo North and was becoming a centre of rice and tobacco production, while a good tarred road now looped through Shaki, Kishi and Igboho, connecting them to Iseyin and Ibadan. Igboho had acquired a secondary school, part of a distribution of facilities between the Irepo towns which left Igbetti with the hospital and Kishi with the council headquarters. Yet there was still much to be done. The roads from Igbetti to Kishi and Igboho remained untarred, and all three Irepo towns lacked the basic facilities of electricity, piped water and sanitation. Most people had to make do with kerosene lamps, compound wells and the bush. The water situation in Igboho during the dry season of 1970–71 was particularly desperate, with the women and children having to trek several miles to the nearest streams, all the wells in the town having run dry. Paradoxically, the main signs of progress in all three towns appeared to be the large number of well-built two-storey houses, but many of these were standing empty, having been built with remittances from migrants still resident abroad.

The position of Igbetti was slightly different. It had originated as a refugee settlement rather than as an administrative centre. The huge black rock which overlooks the town, Oke Iyamapo, provided security against attack, and enabled it to attack others. A report from 1901 described it as 'the home of robbers and idlers, who ... find it a safe harbour from which to plunder travellers and neighbouring towns.'[7] The difference between the location of Igbetti, compared with Igboho and Shaki, lay in its position on the main roads from Ilorin and Ogbomosho, and the colonisation of the areas surrounding it by migrants farmers from Ilorin in the 1910s onwards. This allowed Igbetti to become a major marketing centre for staple foodstuffs, as well as for their production. In the 1960s the town was still surrounded by small villages of Ilorin and Ogbomosho migrants, as well as camps of Fulani pastoralists, and the night market held every four days was one of the largest in Western Nigeria, attracting produce traders from Lagos and Ibadan.[8]

The opportunity structure in the early part of the century was thus slightly different from that in Igboho and Shaki. Igbetti was closer to the road and rail networks and further from the border with Dahomey. At the same time, both farming and dealing in farm produce provided a marginally greater degree of local opportunity than existed to the west. Igbetti migrants went to the Gold Coast, but most of them were concentrated in Tamale, with small offshoot communities in Damongo and Yendi. Perhaps significantly, the Igbetti migration started through contacts with Shaki, as we shall see. There was the usual outmigration to the cocoa areas, the most frequent Igbetti destination being Ajilete. It is not surprising that while the Igbetti migration to Tamale was as large, if not larger than that from Igboho, the Igbetti migration to the Gold Coast as a whole was much smaller. By the late 1960s, Igbetti's problems were similar to those of Igboho: no electricity, piped water or sanitation, though the supply in the local wells did seem to be holding up better than that in Igboho during the dry season. Despite its marginally more buoyant market economy, however, Igbetti lacked the scale of migrant remittance that flowed into Shaki and Igboho, their value increased by the fact that many of them were in CFA currency, and this was reflected in the comparative number of two-storey buildings in the town. By 1969, Igbetti had just five.

Ogbomosho's position differed yet again. Even if the vagaries of Nigerian census taking make a precise estimate of its size in the 1960s very difficult, with around 80,000 inhabitants it was much larger than Shaki (20,000) Igbetti or Igboho (around 10,000 each).[9] Ogbomosho was on the edge of the densely settled zone where the population had been swelled by the influx from the north west. Unlike the other three towns it had became a major protagonist in the nineteenth-century wars, a northern outpost of Ibadan in its struggles with Ilorin, 33 miles to the north. When the road was not closed because of the hostilities, Ogbomosho was a major centre on the north–south trade route. As the history of Chief Akintola's family showed, some of the Ogbomosho traders shifted from the trade in slaves in the nineteenth century to the trades in kola, foodstuffs and European manufactures in the twentieth.[10] Ogbomosho traders were much quicker to exploit the foodstuffs trade round Ilorin than were the Ilorin people themselves, and in the early years of colonial rule they were also quick to join the army, before the Yoruba ceased to be thought of as a 'martial race'.[11] They were among the migrants recruited for the railway and mining industries in the Gold Coast, and in all these cases the capital accumulated was ultimately invested largely in trade. But perhaps the most important result of colonialism for the town was to open up the cities of Northern Nigeria for Ogbomosho enterprise.[12]

Entrepreneurship was all the more attractive because of Ogbomosho's comparative political and economic marginality. It lies well outside the cocoa belt, and, despite its location on the main road to the north, it is well away from the railway line, which passes through Oshogbo further east. Plans to build a line through Ogbomosho in the 1920s never materialised, and Oshogbo has remained the more important commercial centre ever since. Provincial administration also bypassed Ogbomosho. It was based at Oyo, 33 miles to the south, and the 'new Oyo empire' as Atanda dubbed the colonial administrative order, left little room for local autonomy.[13] The British view of Ogbomosho was similar to their view of Irepo District. The 1948 Oyo Province Annual Report noted that it was the largest town in the province apart from Ibadan, but that it shared with Iwo the distinction of being the most backward.[14] However, the outlook for progress was not entirely bleak. The 1949 Annual Report noted that the townspeople were 'united through the mechanism of various societies, the aims of which are the progress of their towns and people'.[15]

The most active people in town politics and associational life were the new generation of graduates from the secondary schools and the Baptist Seminary, and some of them became active in regional and national politics.[16] The most prominent was Chief S.L. Akintola, who was Premier of the Western Region from 1958 to 1966. It was during this period that the town acquired a new waterworks, a catering resthouse and a shoe factory. More turbulent times lay ahead: Akintola was killed in the military coup of January 1966, and the town's ruler was killed in a tax riot in 1968. The succession was still being bitterly contested two years later.[17]

Despite the obvious differences in size and location, all four towns had much in common with other Yoruba towns which have been the subject of recent studies. Like Ilesha and Ife, they had political upheavals, thanks to the interpenetration of national and regional party politics with local chieftaincy disputes. The arrival of Christianity had had an impact on all four through the access to literacy and education which it provided. All the towns had their parapọ, their progressive unions which channelled remittances from migrants abroad into development projects at home, and which lobbied government officials for the allocation of resources.[18] Migrant remittances might produce impressive results in terms of the number of churches, mosques, and public facilities which they financed, but when it came to getting resources and facilities from the state the towns were hampered by the scarcity of representatives in top places, in comparison with other areas of Yorubaland. Ogbomosho during the Akintola period is the exception which proves the rule. Most other developments were the result of local capital and initiative. This was noticeable in all four towns in 1970 as the landscape was transformed by a building boom financed by capital repatriated from Ghana. But the lack of cocoa in the area, the relatively low level of education and the general indifference of government, both before and after independence, made entrepreneurship and long-distance trade an attractive proposition in all of them.

Starting capital could be acquired from a variety of sources, and these expanded along with the cash economy in the first three decades of the century. The first was labour migration, whether to the cocoa fields or the urban centres of the coast. The second was farming, though this depended on the farmer's ability to sell the crops for cash at the end of the season. As the foodstuffs trade in the rural areas of northern Yorubaland grew, this became easier, and the proceeds of a single harvest might be enough to buy an initial load of goods. Many younger men were farming for their fathers, but they were usually allowed to cultivate their own plots in the afternoon and evening, and it was the proceeds of these over which they had control. The third way of raising capital was through the money earned from other skills, acquired from relatives or apprenticeships. These ranged from traditional skills such as weaving and drumming to more recently introduced ones such as tailoring and cycle repair. Fourth, capital could be acquired by working as a porter for an established trader. Until the Second World War, most of the traders still travelled on foot, and so the amount of goods carried was directly proportional to the number of porters used. The trip to the Gold Coast took 25–30 days, and the porters were provided with food on the way, and a lump sum at the end of the trip. They were paid according to the number of cloths that they could carry, but the average seems to have been around £1.00. Other jobs were undoubtedly more lucrative, but an added advantage was useful first-hand experience of trading conditions in the Gold Coast. But for most entrants to trade the source of capital was a senior relative for whom they worked for a time before starting on their own, and this brings us to the links between migrant recruitment and the Yoruba kinship system.

KINSHIP, RESIDENCE AND MIGRATION

The main outlines of northern Yoruba kinship organisation are well documented, and fairly uniform for the main towns involved in the migration.[19] Yoruba towns are usually divided into quarters (*adugbo*) which are further divided into compounds (*ile*). These are named residential units, and provide the citizens of the town with their primary focus of loyalty and identity. They vary enormously in size and layout. In earlier years, many compounds consisted of a single large building, containing a series of rooms arranged around a large central courtyard. By the 1960s most of these buildings had been demolished or modified. Many of them had been replaced by a series of smaller buildings, built by the wealthier members of the compound for themselves and their immediate families. In the more crowded parts of the town, new building on the original site is sometimes impossible, and many present-day compounds consist of buildings in different parts of the town. Over time, the offshoots take on an identity of their own, and a new name.

In the northern towns, residence has a strong patrilocal bias, and the residential core of many compounds consists of a group of patrilineally-related males, together with their wives and children. In the nineteenth century, it would also have included slaves and pawns. There is no tidy one-to-one relationship between descent group and compound, however. Many compounds consist of more than one descent group, while many of the larger descent groups are now divided between a number of separate compounds, thanks to fission. Descent groups who used to live together in a single compound have sometimes gone their separate ways.

The pattern is complicated still further by the cognatic elements in Yoruba kinship ideology. Women retain membership of their own compounds after marriage, even though they live with their husbands, and they continue to take part in family events and meetings. Occasionally, a woman after widowhood or divorce moves back to her natal compound permanently, and as a result her children may grow up there and continue to live there as adults. Eventually they may gravitate to their father's compound to live, especially if they want to build houses of their own, but otherwise their stay may be permanent, allowing them to inherit land, property and even chieftaincy titles belonging to their mother's group.[20]

Yoruba kinship also places considerable emphasis on the relative seniority of compound members, and this is defined in terms of birth order for those born in the compound, and by date of marriage for women marrying in.[21] There are two kin terms, egbon and aburo, meaning 'senior' and 'junior' (classificatory) sibling, the use of which constantly reinforce members' consciousness of their relative positions in the pecking order. Traditionally, supreme authority was in the hands of the bale, the most senior member of the core agnatic group, who allocated living space and farm land, settled disputes between group members, and acted as mediator between compound members and the political authorities in the town.[22] Junior kin, together with slaves and pawns, provided the older members with a pool of labour on which they could draw in production or trade.

None of these principles are inflexible however, and it has always been possible for individuals with drive and initiative to carve out their own leadership position in Yoruba society using their skills, knowledge or wealth.[23] With the increasing amount of wealth in circulation outside their control, the authority of the elders has been gradually eroded in the twentieth century. Initially this was a result of the growth of the cash economy and the market for wage labour. Younger men were becoming less dependent on their elders for their livelihood or the means to get married. In addition to farming at home, they had the alternatives of migrant labour and, if they could accumulate the capital, migrant trade.[24] Wives also increased their economic independence, and began trading on their own account rather than transporting, processing and selling goods for their husbands.[25]

These features have important implications for the Yoruba traders in the Gold Coast. First, in the early days of migration, the elders had a considerable pool of labour within the compound on which they could draw. Second, as the transport infrastructure developed, and the need for head porterage declined, the structure of the family groups of traders was also modified, a change which coincided with the decline of the trade in Yoruba cloth, and the growth of the trade in European manufactures. Third, the development of independent trade among women also took place earlier, and in the regional economy in the 1960s and 1970s it was the Ogbomosho, Ilorin and Ibadan women who dominated the trade in foodstuffs, not the women from the Oke Ogun. In Tamale with few exceptions, the wealthiest Yoruba women traders were from Ogbomosho, rather than from Igbetti, Igboho or Shaki.

The implications of these features of Yoruba social organisation for the development of trade in the Gold Coast can be seen in the following pair of case studies.

Ile Olowo, Igbetti

The earliest Igbetti migrant in the Gold Coast was Alhaji Sadiku, who in the 1960s was the *bale* of Ile Olowo.[26] He first travelled to the Gold Coast with traders from Shaki in 1917. Before this, he had been farming and trading with his elder brother, buying foodstuffs in Borgu to the north. The Shaki traders used to stay in their house on their buying trips to Ilorin and Bida because Sadiku was one of the first Muslims in the town.[27] Using money from his brother in addition to his own, Sadiku bought cloth, beads and bracelets from Bida, together with antimony and natron, and began to trade in Yendi and Gambaga, before settling in Tamale. He eventually returned home to marry, and after an unsuccessful attempt to learn Arabic, he returned to the Gold Coast in 1924, taking a group of junior relatives as porters and assistants: Sanusi, the son of his senior brother; Sule and his two brothers, the sons of a senior sister; and David, the son of a half-sister (Figure 3.1).

This time he took Yoruba cloth, and after several journeys back and forth, he settled at home once more in 1933, leaving the others in the Gold Coast. In addition to Yoruba cloth, they were also selling manufactures from the south. Sadiku's eldest son, Lasisi, travelled to the Gold Coast with porters and more cloth to join them in 1936. According to his own account, he gradually became

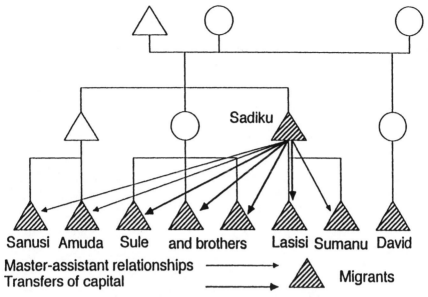

Figure 3.1: The start of migration to Ghana from Ile Olowo, Igbetti.

dissatisfied with the way in which they were trading, and wrote to his father telling him to come back and sort out the group's affairs. Sadiku eventually did so in 1943, accompanied by his second son, Sumanu. He paid off the group's debts, divided the remaining capital among them, and left them to trade independently of each other. He himself settled in Damongo with Amuda, Sanusi's junior brother. They stayed there until 1948, when Sadiku's senior brother died. Sadiku was now the oldest member of Ile Olowo, and returned to Igbetti as its *bale*. The group had already begun to disintegrate. Sule died in the Gold Coast in 1945, and Sumanu returned to Igbetti with the news of his death, where he stayed to learn Arabic. David returned home to marry. Sule's two brothers ran out of money and returned home with help from Lasisi. After Sadiku's departure, Amuda joined Lasisi in Tamale. He became a driver with the Public Works Department, and eventually moved to Tema to work on the site of the new town. Lasisi alone remained trading in Tamale, and was the key figure in the group's post-war expansion.

This sketchy account illustrates some of the main features of Yoruba trade in the Northern Territories during the period up to 1945. The group's initial involvement in trade there came about through contacts with Muslims in Shaki, and at first involved a lengthy stay in the Gold Coast, selling a variety of goods, presumably bought there once the initial stock had been sold. The growth of the trade in Yoruba cloth after 1918 meant that during this second period in the Gold Coast, Sadiku frequently returned to Nigeria to buy new

Plate 3.1: The Seriki and Pakoyi: two of the earliest Igbetti migrants to Ghana, at a Muslim festival in 1970.

supplies.[28] The rest of the group stayed in the Gold Coast, where they sold manufactures from the south in addition to the cloth. Though Sadiku's second wife joined him in Damongo after 1943, his first wife remained in Igbetti throughout. The organisation of the group's activities was extremely loose, though in theory the capital and goods belonged to Sadiku until the group's formal dissolution in 1943. The members of the group organised the purchase and transport of Nigerian cloth jointly, but in day-to-day buying and selling they had considerable autonomy, taking what they needed from the profits to cover their own living expenses. The degree of direction which Sadiku could exercise was probably limited to infrequent stock-taking to see how business was going. The older a member of the group became, the more latitude he had in running his own part of the business. In other trading groups, senior members who still regarded themselves as working for their leader had in fact recruited their own groups of assistants. These groups of traders were not formal 'family firms' with centralised direction and policy, but looser aggregates of individuals, each with their own interests in addition to their group obligations. If business appeared to be going well, they would be left largely on their own. This was desirable in conditions where the scattered demand for goods could be best served by allowing individual traders to make long solo trips to the small towns and villages and the rural markets, able to make decisions without reference to their senior relatives. Economies of scale were important, however, in the purchase of cloth in Nigeria, and this was usually in the hands of the most senior member of the group.

Ile Isalẹ, Ogbomosho

The Ile Isalẹ migration to the Gold Coast developed around two related groups of traders who settled in Kumasi and Tamale.[29] Braimah arrived in Kumasi in the 1920s, and began to trade with Shittu, a sister's son. Both used capital earned from farming. In 1931 they were joined by Rahimi, Braimah's senior half-brother's son, and his own son Ganiyu who had been farming in Nigeria. The group sold Yoruba cloth brought to Kumasi along the coast by rail and steamer, and Braimah was in charge of buying it. The pattern which developed was similar to that in Ile Olowo: a loose-knit group of traders buying jointly but selling individually, this time in the southern Gold Coast. During the 1930s, when the market in the south was slack, Rahimi started to travel to Navrongo and Tamale to buy foodstuffs. By this time, Joseph Ola had settled in Tamale selling beads, assisted by his eldest son. The war disrupted the flow of cloth from Nigeria, and in 1940 the traders in the south decided to move to Tamale. They now included Braimah's second son, Mohammed, and Lawani, a half-brother of Shittu (Figure 3.2).

In terms of their composition and trading operations, the two groups shared many similarities. The main differences were that the Ile Isalẹ migration started initially in the south, and that the transport of Nigerian cloth took place

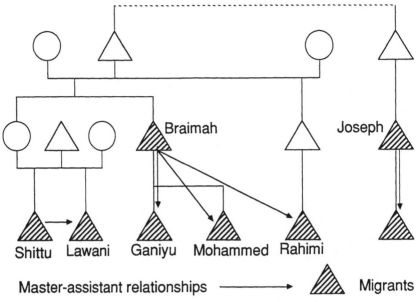

Figure 3.2: The start of migration to Ghana from Ile Isalẹ, Ogbomosho.

along the coastal route, using rail and steamer links, rather than across the inland route using head porters. Not surprisingly, these links were disrupted by the war and the ban on cloth exports from Nigeria, and the group decided to move to the north, where the trade in foodstuffs was actually stimulated by the war, and where it was easier to evade restrictions on trade with Nigeria.[30] In both cases trade seems to have suffered during the war, but it was to take off again with the rapid expansion of the Gold Coast economy in the 1950s, and this led to an equally rapid expansion of both groups of traders in the post-war period.

THE POST-WAR ECONOMY

The post-war history of the country up to 1969 can be divided into five periods: the political agitation which produced the Convention People's Party (CPP) between 1945 and 1950; the period of 'dyarchy' with Nkrumah in power during the last years of British rule, from 1950 to 1957; the first years of Ghanaian independence from 1957 to 1960; the years of the Republic with Nkrumah as President from 1960 to 1966; and finally the period after the military coup of 1966.[31] Each of these periods had its own economic characteristics, and these were reflected in the patterns of Yoruba migration and the growth of the Yoruba migrant community.

The end of the war saw the economy in a depressed state. There had been an almost universal decline in real incomes during the hostilities, and the disruption of world trade had made many types of goods unobtainable. The incomes of the cocoa producers had been held down by the marketing boards, and the failure of living standards to rise in line with expectations lay behind the riots of 1948. High prices, which many blamed on collusion between large firms and the government, were officially identified as a major grievance.[32] However, the upturn soon came. World cocoa prices rose and remained high throughout the 1950s, and rural incomes increased, despite the marketing boards creaming off a large slice of the profits to finance the CPP's elaborate development plans.[33] There was a massive expansion of government spending on infrastructure, health, education, industry and the bureaucracy. The construction of the dam across the Volta River at Akasombo and the new town at Tema were both started. There was a surge in food imports, which doubled between 1954 and 1960, as per capita incomes rose steadily.[34] As the towns boomed, and as educational provision and state employment expanded, the popularity of imported manufactured goods grew, and a start was made in the establishment of industries to produce them locally. The booming economy meant a shortage of labour in the south, and the numbers of migrants crossing on ferries rose from 131,000 in 1945 to 392,000 in 1952.[35] Comparatively few of them came from the Tamale area, where food production for the market and cattle dealing were both proving lucrative alternatives to migration.[36] And as incomes and supplies of imported goods increased, so did the numbers of Yoruba traders selling them.

Although the popularity of Yoruba cloth continued for a time in the north, manufactured goods increasingly became the basis of Yoruba trade, just as they had in the south in the 1920s. Most of these were imported by the large expatriate firms, against which so much hostility had been expressed in 1948. Partly as a result of this, and partly in response to competition from Lebanese, Indian and African traders, the large firms reduced their role in retailing, and relied on local traders for bulkbreaking and distribution. In some cases they set up their African storekeepers as independent agents. In others, they distributed goods through their wholesale outlets in the larger towns to regular 'passbook' customers, who passed them on to retailers and consumers throughout the country.[37]

Between 1961 and 1966, the direction of economic policy changed drastically as Nkrumah and his advisors attempted to bring about a structural transformation of the economy based on increased state intervention and control, the establishment of state farms, and rapid industrialisation.[38] State expenditure rose rapidly, and resources were systematically diverted from the private to the public sector through taxation and the marketing boards, a wage freeze, and the imposition of exchange and import controls. All this took place against the background of a falling world price of cocoa. Despite the massive effort and expenditure the attempt was a failure, resulting in 'modernisation without growth'. For the public it meant rapid inflation, a drastic decline in living standards, and increasing shortages of essential commodities.[39]

The trades in smuggled goods and foreign currency flourished, and the Yoruba were in a good position to exploit these conditions to the full. The government nevertheless kept up its level of expenditure and launched another ambitious development plan in 1964, intended to run for seven years and financed largely through supplier credits. This meant that a high level of employment was maintained, despite the difficult economic climate.[40]

The situation changed with the coup of 1966. The response of the National Liberation Council, the new military regime, to the economic situation was to prune public expenditure and devalue the currency by 30 per cent. The development plan was largely abandoned, after considerable expenditure but before many of the supposed benefits had begun to appear.[41] After the coup, although the supplies of many goods in the markets increased, thanks to the relaxation of import restrictions by the NLC, demand in many areas slumped owing to the increased unemployment which resulted from government cuts in the development programme.[42]

Two further trends were noticeable after independence. The first was the involvement of the government in the commercial sector of the economy. The second was the gradual growth of feeling against the immigrant population of the country, both the Indians and Lebanese on the one hand, and the nationals of other West African countries on the other.

Nkrumah's attitude towards the structure of the distributive system in the country was as critical as had been that of the Watson Commission in 1948 which had laid some of the blame for the economic situation after the war on the 'market mammies' through whose hands most goods passed on their way to the consumer.[43] Nkrumah's attitude was similarly negative. Traders were seen as unproductive: they simply bought and resold essential commodities at overly high prices.[44] The government moved into the commercial sector with the formation of the Ghana National Trading Corporation (GNTC) in 1962, after the purchase of the Ghanaian assets of AG Leventis.[45] Other moves also had a direct and serious effect on commerce in Ghana. The balance of payments crisis and government policies meant a reduction in the level of imports of consumer goods, but, in addition, the closure of the border with Togo for some years meant the loss of the regional *entrepôt* trade for many Ghana-based traders, as well as a massive increase in smuggling along the Togolese border.[46]

After the coup the NLC generally took a more favourable view of private enterprise, and the voices of Ghanaian businessmen had a greater weight than they had done in the days of the CPP. However, one of the demands that they were making was that measures should be taken against foreign enterprises in the country, to make room for Ghanaian entrepreneurs.[47]

There had already been several instances of hostility towards aliens in Ghana in the period after 1945, though the reasons for it differed from instance to instance. In the 1950s the reasons were usually political, and the measures were aimed at political opponents of the CPP. The best-known example of this was the deportation in 1957 of leading politicians from the Kumasi Zongo who were sent back to Nigeria and Upper Volta.[48] This was made possible by the Ghana Nationality and Citizenship Act of 1957, by which birth in Ghana did not automatically confer citizenship. To be a citizen one had to be born of 'Ghanaian' parents as well. Thus, in some instances, children of migrants born in Ghana were legally stateless. The act was the first in a series defining and redefining the position of Ghana's aliens and the criteria for citizenship.[49]

After the consolidation of the CPP government, the pressure on aliens in the country was reduced for a time, thanks to Nkrumah's pan-Africanist political stance. While the 1963 Aliens' Act made residence permits a necessity for foreign nationals, until 1969 this was never regularly enforced.[50] However, there were still moves against aliens in particular sectors of the economy, notably in the diamond industry. In 1960 there were 236 licensed diamond diggers, of whom 145 were aliens, mainly Yoruba from the single town of Oyan.[51] In 1962 the alien diggers were deprived of their licences, but many were able to stay in business with the help of Ghanaian partners. The result was a massive increase in diamond smuggling, intensified by the import and currency restrictions. A second attempt to control the situation in 1968 made it necessary for aliens living in the diamond areas to obtain permits.[52]

Pressure for additional moves against aliens after the coup seems to have come from the local businessmen. Much of their criticism was aimed at the Lebanese. They had been attacked both by the expatriates and the local traders for many years, and the government had been restricting their immigration, even prior to independence.[53] The Ghanaian Nationality Bill of 1957 was partly aimed at them, and strong feelings were expressed in the press about their business practices. After the coup this feeling intensified. A committee was set up in December 1967 to review immigration quotas and the question of Ghanaianisation of certain sectors of the economy. The result was the 1968 Ghanaian Enterprises Decree which proposed restricting certain areas of business activity to Ghanaian citizens. The areas included the ownership of taxis, small-scale manufacturing enterprises, retail establishments with an annual turnover of less than NC500,000, and wholesale establishments with an annual turnover of less than NC1,000,000. It was not at all certain at the time whether this was directed just at the Lebanese and Indians, or at the nationals of other West African countries as well.[54]

In July 1969, the embassies of the other West African countries were given nine months to register their nationals and provide them with the necessary documents to obtain residence permits.[55] Progress was slow, and after the 1969 general election, which returned Ghana to civilian rule, the new Busia administration took action. The climax of the moves against Ghana's aliens came with the 'compliance order' of 1969. Along with this came enforcement

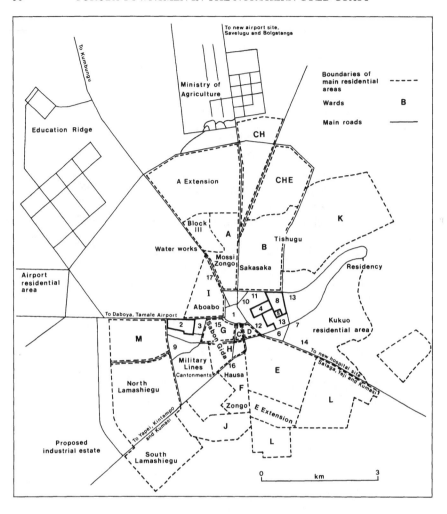

Map 3.1: Tamale in 1969.

Notes:

1. central market	7. high court	13. government offices
2. new market	8. hospital	14. Catholic cathedral
3. main lorry park	9. West Hospital	15. First Baptist church
4. police station	10. Rivoli Cinema	16. UMCA church
5. prison	11. post office	17. Second Baptist church
6. local court	12. stores and banks	

of some of the provisions of the 1968 Decree, including a prohibition on participation in market trade by non-Ghanaians from 2 December, 1969. It was this last provision, announced a couple of days before the expiry of the deadline of the compliance order, which prompted the decision by many of the Yoruba to pack up and leave the country.

THE GROWTH OF TAMALE

Despite the economic crisis in the country as a whole, Tamale continued to grow in the 1960s. Between 1948 and 1960 the population of the town had trebled, reaching 43,000. In 1970, just after the exodus of the Yoruba, it stood at over 80,000. Its heterogeneity is shown by Table 3.1 showing the ethnic composition in 1960. The annual growth rate between 1960 and 1970 had been

Table 3.1: Ethnic composition of the population of Tamale, 1960.

Ethnic Group	Number	Percentage
Dagomba	35,820	61.6
Ewe	2,590	4.5
Ashanti	2,070	3.6
Fanti	1,360	2.3
Othan Akan	1,450	2.5
Mossi	1,670	2.9
Grunshi	1,670	2.9
Ga-Adangbe	1,620	2.8
Frafra	1,470	2.5
Yoruba	1,400	2.5
Hausa	950	1.6
Gonja	780	1.3
Other Guan-speaking	430	0.7
Gurma	630	1.1
Builsa	570	1.0
Mamprusi	520	0.9
Dagarti	450	0.8
Busanga	400	0.7
Wala	360	0.6
Fulani	320	0.6
Kusasi	290	0.5
Kotokoli	240	0.4
Zabarima	180	0.3
Wangara	110	0.2
Ibo	20	0.0
Others	560	1.0
Unclassified	250	0.4
Total	58,180	100.0

Source: Population Census of Ghana, 1960, Report 'E', Table S1, pp. c3–c9.

7.1 per cent, rather faster than the urban growth rate of 4.7 per cent for the country as a whole.[56] This was in spite of the creation of the Upper Region in 1960 and the transformation of Bolgatanga into a new regional capital, making it the fastest-growing town in Ghana.[57] By 1969, Tamale had, in addition to the regional administrative offices, four secondary schools, two training colleges, two agricultural stations, a hospital and two army camps located in and around the town. A number of modern commercial buildings, housing the large firms and the banks, had appeared along the main streets in the late 1950s,[58] while in 1969 a new international airport and a new hospital were both under construction. There were also the symbols of urban status so common throughout English-speaking West Africa: an élite (formerly expatriate) club, a polo ground, two Lebanese-owned cinemas, and a Kingsway store. However, some projects had run into difficulties with the government cuts in expenditure after the 1966 coup. Plans for an industrial estate had resulted in a single *pito* factory which opened early in 1970. The international airport had been proposed first in the 1962 development plan, but work on it had stopped after the coup. Pressure was put on the NLC and work started again in 1968,[59] but it was generally felt that the future of the project was uncertain. The general employment situation in the town had thus worsened since 1966 and trade had suffered as a result.

Outside the town, the major addition to the infrastructure of the north was the new road to Kumasi via Kintampo. This had been constructed to the west of the old Salaga road, and had the great advantage that it crossed the Volta River with bridges at Yapei and Buipe rather than with ferries. The ferry crossing at Yeji now took much longer than it had done previously owing to the growth of the Volta Lake: by 1969 there were only three crossings a day in either direction. The new road, on the other hand, though still untarred, allowed traffic to flow to the south around the clock, and the Yoruba traders made full use of overnight buses to and from Kumasi. The construction of the road had attracted large numbers of labourers and provided openings for traders in the villages which lay near it. The other main road out of Tamale, running through Bolgatanga in the north, had also received some attention and the ferries on this had been replaced by bridges. It had been tarred as far as Navrongo and Nangodi, beyond Bolgatanga.

The effects of these developments on trade in Tamale, and especially on the Yoruba, were mixed. The import restrictions of the early 1960s and the policy of channelling goods through the GNTC produced acute shortages. The Yoruba who had passbooks or personal contacts in the large firms with the managers and storekeepers, or who were involved in smuggling, were able to capitalise on the situation and increase their profits. The north of Ghana provided ideal conditions for the smugglers: a long, unprotected border, a force of customs officials not averse to informal sources of income, and supplies of goods readily available over the border in Togo and Upper Volta. This helps to explain the presence of large numbers of Yoruba traders, most of them from Shaki, who had settled in border towns like Bunkpurugu and Hamale, small towns not otherwise known for their economic dynamism. The Yoruba traders, however, who were unable to capitalise on the shortages, found themselves under increasing pressure, and this intensified after the 1966 coup. Before this, demand in the markets had held up, despite falls in workers' real incomes, thanks to the number of projects that were under way in the north. After the coup, the rate of inflation dropped,[60] but demand slumped as many of the workers were laid off. Supplies of goods in the market, on the other hand, increased and the Yoruba found themselves in increasing competition with local Ghanaian traders who now had easier access to goods than they had done before 1966.

It is against this background of developments in the Ghanaian economy that the post-war expansion of Yoruba migration to the north has to be seen. The next section deals with the impact of these trends on the two groups of traders discussed in the previous chapter.

Ile Olowo

For the Yoruba traders in the north of Ghana in the immediate post-war period, the shortages of European goods, including cloth, meant another rise in the demand for Yoruba cloth. Lasisi, now unencumbered by less efficient relatives, was able to capitalise on this. He had started to trade on his own with the division of the capital between the various members of the Ile Olowo group in 1944. His assets at that time consisted of £16 worth of European cloth, £7 10s. in cash which he had managed to save, and a cycle which he was able to hire out. He remained in Tamale, selling mainly European cloth when it was available, until 1948, when he managed to collect enough money together to return to Nigeria to buy a consignment of Yoruba cloth. Large profits were possible. On his first trip he took with him £300, on the second he was able to take £330, and on the third he was able to increase this to £500 by selling four cows he had in Nigeria. For some years after this, he returned to Nigeria every four months to buy cloth, and Yoruba cloth remained his main selling line until the mid-1950s. By this time, he was well established in Tamale. He had married two wives and was building himself a house in the town. As his business expanded he began to take or attract a whole series of junior relatives to Tamale to help him. The relationships of the family members involved in the post-war phase of the migration are shown in Figure 3.3.

In 1951 he took with him his half-brother, Tijani. In 1956 he loaned Tijani £60 with which to start trading on his own, but Tijani had no success in Tamale. He moved to Damongo where his father had lived previously, and had more success there as a cycle repairer, farmer and exporter of dried meat to the south. In 1958 he was joined by Ganiyu, his junior brother, who worked for two years as an apprentice cycle repairer, after which he returned home to learn

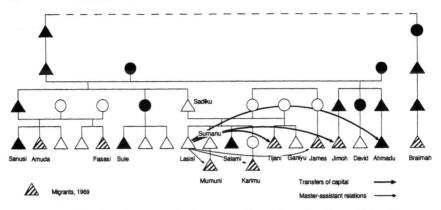

Figure 3.3: Relationships of migrants to Ghana from Ile Olowo, Igbetti.

Arabic from Sumanu, his half-brother, now established as a Koranic teacher in Igbetti. Tijani was now joined by Fasasi, a half-sibling of Amuda. Fasasi had been a cycle repairer in Igbetti and continued with the work in Ghana. By 1969, Tijani had acquired houses of his own in Igbetti and Damongo, and had married three wives, one of them a local Gonja girl. Also with him in Damongo for a time was Ahmadu, a more distant agnate whom Lasisi had invited to come to Ghana in 1960. He was given capital of £100 on his arrival, and joined Tijani in Damongo where he stayed until his death in a road accident in 1967.

In 1952 Lasisi took his junior full brother, Salami, to the Gold Coast. He gave him the remains of the European cloth which he had in stock and concentrated on the sale of Nigerian cloth. Salami proved to be an excellent trader, and, when in 1960 Lasisi built himself a larger stall in the market, he gave Salami the old one together with £160 capital. Salami's success continued until his sudden death in 1968, by which time he had married three wives and had built a house of his own in Tamale, on a site near to that of his brother.

Jimoh was less of a success. He joined Lasisi in the Gold Coast in the early 1950s as well, after leaving Ilorin where he had trained as a motor mechanic. Lasisi decided to set him up as a trader and gave him money to buy cloth in the south. Jimoh spent all the money on himself, then, in order to buy the goods in the south, he broke into Lasisi's room and took some more. Unfortunately he was seen, and, on his return from Kumasi, he was greeted by a group of irate relatives at the lorry park. After this confrontation he vanished and lost all contact with the others, though it was rumoured that he had taken a job as a tractor driver in the Volta Region.

Lasisi continued to attract relatives to Ghana in the 1960s. Braimah arrived in 1966 and became a washerman with equipment which Lasisi provided. He returned to Nigeria to marry in 1969 and then started to trade with the capital he had collected as a washerman. Lasisi also brought over James, a mother's sister's son, to drive the car which he bought in the early 1960s, and to manage the rice farm which he planted for the first time in 1968. The last two people that Lasisi took to Ghana were Mumuni, the eldest son of his brother Sumanu, and Karimu, a young boy, the son of his junior sister. At the time of the exodus these two were helping him in his stall, together with his own two senior sons. The third and fourth sons were both in secondary school and unlikely to help him in trade. Throughout Lasisi had maintained his close links with his home town. His eldest son and daughter had both been educated there, while in 1959 he had helped Sadiku to rebuild their house. In 1967 he came perhaps to the climax of his career, when he was able to send both his father and his junior half-brother to Mecca.

Ile Isalẹ

Ile Isalẹ was also affected by the expansion of the economy after 1945. Initially Rahimi and then Mohammed took over the buying and the transport of the cloth from Nigeria. In addition to Yoruba cloth the group also took foodstuffs to Accra and bought European goods for sale in Tamale. It was in this post-war period that they started to separate. In 1948 Rahimi was given £200 and some goods to start trading on his own. From then on he dealt in *worobo*, changing to the sale of fishnets in the 1950s and to shoes around 1960.

This period saw a rapid influx of junior relatives and the house which the established traders rented in the Mossi Zongo was soon bursting at the seams with the boys recruited from Nigeria to help them. Most of these came to help Rahimi and Mohammed, the two most successful traders. Also relatively successful in the early 1950s was Peter Ola, who had taken over when his father had died, just before the war. Rahimi was being helped by Raji, his half-brother, and four other agnates. Shittu was helped by Gbademasi, his second son, and later by Salami, the third. Lawani had a brother's son and the son of a friend working for him. Mohammed had two father's brother's sons and a mother's brother's son to help, while Peter was helped by his two junior full brothers, a half-brother and the son of a friend. The one who was not a success was Ganiyu, the eldest son of Braimah. He was given trading capital but lost it all. He moved to join Ogbomosho friends in Atebubu, and from there he went to Damongo. Despite repeated help from his brother he finally give up trade altogether and became a tailor in 1957. He learned from an Ede man, paying him £3 for the tuition instead of the going rate of £7 because he was a friend. Six months later, Braimah, his father, returned to Nigeria to become the head of his compound in Ogbomosho.

After the heady days of market expansion in the early 1950s the going gradually became harder. In addition to Ganiyu, with his chronic financial difficulties, Shittu and Peter were both having their problems as well. Mohammed did better, but had made unsuccessful attempts to diversify his activities. His trade had been going well: he had been taking £500 to Accra two or three times a month, and his assistants were helping him to increase his turnover by cycling out to the rural markets each day. After his father went home Mohammed sent money to help him build an 'upstairs' house in Ogbomosho, and he also invested in a taxi and a diesel truck for a time. Neither of the vehicles paid off. As many of the wealthier Yoruba in Tamale found, the main problem lay in the supervision of the drivers. Mohammed sold the vehicles and started to build a house in Tamale instead.

Peter and Shittu had more serious difficulties. The most obvious symptom was the way in which their helpers drifted off into other occupations. Yesufu, Shittu's son, had already fallen out with his father over education, and gone to work for an expatriate. Gbademasi, the second son, went to Ibadan to learn tailoring. After Salami finished primary school in 1959, Shittu packed up and followed Braimah to Ogbomosho where he returned to farming. Salami was sent off to join relatives in Jos where he attended technical school. Later he helped to sell motor parts in the market there. Peter soldiered on with trade, but his brothers dropped out. One of them became a driver in 1960, and the second followed him two years later. They were taught to drive by a Yoruba from Offa who worked for the State Transport Corporation. The third brother became a labourer with the Public Works Department. Finally, Peter himself gave up trade in 1966 and became a daily contribution collector.[61]

The final stage in the development of the group came with the separation of the remaining younger members during the 1960s. The economic climate by this time was still more difficult. While the senior traders continued to make money, with the exceptions noted above, the junior ones found it increasingly difficult to get started. Rahimi and Mohammed were both able to build houses of their own in Tamale and both of them by now had three wives. But Raji, Rahimi's half brother, spent the capital he had been given in 1961 and had to beg Rahimi for more. Rahimi was at first angry and refused to help him again, so Raji learned how to repair watches from an Ogbomosho friend. After a while the brothers resolved their differences and Raji started to trade again. He had his own stall, but also helped Rahimi buy goods in the south when necessary. Peter's remaining helper, the son of one of his friends, had similar problems. Peter arranged his marriage in 1966 and gave him £15 trading capital. Given the effects of inflation over the years, this was much too little, and by 1969 the boy had given up trade and gone off to join a brother in Nkoranza.

The other helpers of Rahimi and Mohammed had gradually dropped out of trade as well. Three of the boys helping Rahimi left for Kumasi and later joined other relatives in Zaria (Nigeria). Two of them left in the early 1960s and the third left in 1968 after Rahimi had arranged his marriage and given him £60. He too had little luck in trade on his own. The fourth brother's son fared better. Rahimi gave him the same amount of £60: by the time of the exodus he had a stall in the market nearly as large as Rahimi's. Mohammed's mother's brother's son had disliked trade and Mohammed's attempts to convert him to Islam (his own father was a Christian). After completing Middle School, he took a secretarial course and became a clerk at one of the local schools. Raufu, Mohammed's father's brother's son, was given capital and Mohammed arranged his marriage in 1967. His brother, Kelani, was unmarried and still working for Mohammed in 1969.

Figure 3.4 shows the relationships involved in the later phase of the migration. A final chapter in the saga was the reappearance of Shittu. Rahimi and Mohammed had suggested that he should return to Ghana, and he did so in 1968, bringing Salami with him. He started trade again with the aid of a loan from the other two, using a spare stall belonging to Mohammed. Salami, who married in the same year, did most of the buying and selling for him.

In comparing these two histories, many similarities become apparent. The general pattern is one in which the original migrant recruits junior relatives, mainly agnates, who in turn become independent traders and recruit their own helpers. A migrant who is successful recruits first senior siblings' sons, and then his own junior siblings, and finally his own sons when they are old enough to participate. Finally, continued success attracts more distant agnatic and cognatic relatives, and in some cases the sons of friends.

The result of this process was similar in both cases. It led to a proliferation of independent small-scale trading enterprises established by descent group members, all in the same area of the market, and selling similar lines of cloth, *worobo* or shoes. In the case of Ile Olowo, where a higher number of those who participated in the migration had died or dropped out of trade over the years, there were four members left in trade in 1969, two each in Tamale and Damongo. In addition, it should be noted that all the wives of the members of both groups in Ghana were also involved in trade. In both cases, the main period of expansion had come after 1945. The trading lines in both groups had been diversified and turnover had been increased by the recruitment of junior members who could take the goods to the rural areas. In both cases there was a

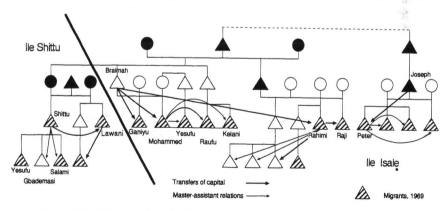

Figure 3.4: Relationships of migrants to Ghana from Ile Isalẹ, Ogbomosho.

gradual move away from the trade in Nigerian cloth to that in European manufactured goods. In the case of Ile Olowo, Lasisi sold Nigerian cloth until independence with a fair degree of success. This was true of a number of the wealthier Yoruba traders in Tamale, but by the 1950s the trade in Nigerian cloth had become a relatively capital-intensive affair, with a few wealthy traders organising the purchase and transport of the cloth. Most of the junior members, when they become independent, tended to turn to other selling lines.

In both cases, the post-war period saw the emergence of one or two successful members of each group who became the nuclei for further recruitment. However, not all of the members had equal aptitude for trade. A number of them remained in the market, trading on a small scale until the exodus, but others left Tamale for other towns, or gave up trade altogether. This was particularly common in the increasingly adverse economic climate after independence. The general pattern was that a trader worked for a senior relative for some time, in return for which the senior relative would arrange his marriage and provide him with trading capital. In the late 1960s, the capital was often too limited to start a viable enterprise. In Ile Isalẹ, for instance, the most successful traders were those who had started with £200 or more during the post-war boom. The traders that separated after 1966 in this group received £50 or £60 at the most. In some cases it was rumoured that younger traders who were successful had managed because of the additional capital they had been able to embezzle from their masters over the years. More honest ones found it more difficult to become established.[62] In both cases the most successful traders were responsible for the establishment of a number of other enterprises over the years, and the eventual aim of nearly all the migrants was to retire to Nigeria, after having built a house there, to assume the responsibilities of age in their own descent group.

A final point to note is the geographical mobility of the group over the years. The early histories of the two groups are different: the Ile Olowo traders went initially to Tamale, though later there was a secondary migration to Damongo. The initial migration from Ile Isalẹ had been to Kumasi, and the move to Tamale was itself a secondary migration. In both cases, however, a similar process was at work: unsuccessful traders from the larger towns tended to gravitate to the smaller ones, in more and more remote parts of the county. Once a network of relatives was established in different parts of West Africa, it provided a framework within which the other members of the group could move. The movement of Salami, Shittu's son, from Ghana to Ogbomosho, then to Jos and back to Ghana, was typical of the way in which the Ogbomosho traders could make use of their particularly extensive networks.

In both cases the results of the migration process were essentially conservative. There was little by way of innovation, beyond the adoption of new selling lines when the market in the old ones declined. The only major capital

Plate 3.2: Chain migration continues: a group of migrants from the second and third generations, Ogbomosho 1971.

investments by the members of either group were in housing, both in Ghana and Nigeria, apart from Lasisi's rice farm and Mohammed's flirtation with transport ownership. Even in trade, the result was a series of one-person enterprises: there was little additional cooperation in the sense of pooling capital or taking advantages of economies of scale.[63] On the other hand, the limited size of the enterprises and the number of people involved were probably crucial factors in the success of the Yoruba diaspora as a whole. The sheer number of decision-makers gave the system a flexibility which enabled it to respond very rapidly to changes in the market and the discovery of new opportunities. And the small size of the enterprises meant that the risks of market trade were widely shared. In times of recession traders operating at a marginal level were squeezed out of the markets of the larger towns or out of the market completely. The wealthier traders would have to cut back and limit their expenditure, but would still survive.

These detailed case studies prompt another question: how typical were they of the Yoruba migration to northern Ghana as a whole? To answer this, we need to extend the discussion to consider, in rather less detail, other groups of migrants from Ogbomosho and Igbetti.

THE OGBOMOSHO MIGRATION

The core of the Ogbomosho community in Tamale consisted of four large groups of kin, accounting for over a third of the Ogbomosho migrants. One of these, the Ile Isalẹ group, has been discussed already. The other three came from three other compounds in Ogbomosho: Ile Isalẹ Alagbẹdẹ, Ile Iyanda and Ile Oke.

The first member of Ile Isalẹ Alagbẹdẹ to go to Tamale was Alhaji Karimu. He came across on the inland trade route through Yendi, rather than from Kumasi. He was the first Ogbomosho trader in Tamale and one of the first Yoruba to own houses there. He used to accommodate many of the early traders on their first arrival in the town in the 1920s and 1930s. He was thus a key figure, not only in the Ogbomosho migration, but in the growth of the Yoruba community as a whole. He dealt mainly in Yoruba cloth and in the 1930s he headed a group of eight related traders, each with their own capital. Karimu did most of the buying and was already making use of the rail and steamer links along the coast in the 1920s.

The relatives that made up the group initially included a sister's son, Ahmadu, the sons of a father's junior brother, Muftawu and Lasisi, and Raji, the son of a senior brother (Figure 3.5). By 1939, Karimu had started to bring his own sons to the Gold Coast, and later the junior brothers of Raji were recruited as well. This group produced some of the richest Yoruba traders in

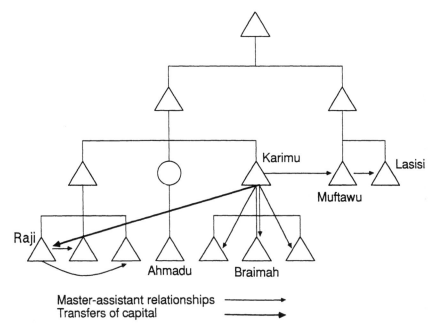

Master-assistant relationships ———————▶
Transfers of capital   ———————▶

Figure 3.5: Relationships of migrants to Ghana from Ile Isalẹ Alagbẹdẹ, Ogbomosho.

Tamale: one indication of their success is the fact that by 1969 eight of them had been to Mecca. Towards 1969, however, there was more diversification. Most of Karimu's grandchildren had been educated to Middle School and beyond, and were not involved in trade. Only one of Lasisi's four sons and none of Ahmadu's were trading in 1969. Three of Lasisi's sons had become drivers and Ahmadu's sons included a painter with the Public Works Department and a store manager with the Union Trading Co. in Accra. Karimu himself had retired to Nigeria in 1962 and only made occasional trips to Tamale after that. Apart from Lasisi, who still continued to sell Nigerian cloth on a small scale, and Braimah, Karimu's second son, who was rumoured to be a smuggler, the group's members left in trade all sold European cloth.

The third of the large groups, and the last to become established in Tamale, was from Ile Iyanda. This migration started with the arrival in Tamale of a pair of agnates from the south around 1945. They sold Yoruba cloth. The relationship between them is not certain, though their fathers were possibly full siblings. Bamidele, the senior partner, left for home soon after, leaving Mustafa Iyanda in charge. Iyanda became one of the most successful of the Yoruba traders in Tamale, and, by his death in 1968 he had acquired six houses in Tamale and two in Ogbomosho, both of them large 'upstairs' buildings. Until the middle 1950s he was trading in Tamale market together with his junior brother and other junior relatives including the sons of Bamidele. The relationships between them are shown in Figure 3.6. By this time he had started to sell European cloth and the other members of the group started to separate and run their own stalls. Lawani, Bamidele's senior son, and Jimoh, Iyanda's junior brother, started to trade on their own in 1958. Each was given £500 to start,

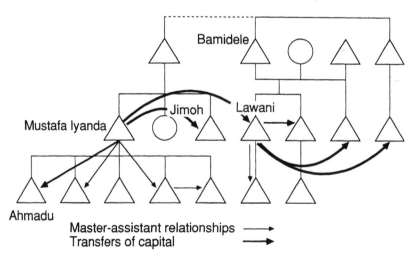

Master-assistant relationships ⟶
Transfers of capital ⟹

Figure 3.6: Relationships of migrants to Ghana from Ile Iyanda, Ogbomosho.

and Ahmadu, Iyanda's own oldest son, was given a similar amount in 1961. Lawani had three relatives working for him, over the years, to whom he gave capital: his father's brother's son, his own junior brother, and a half brother by the same mother. In 1969, he was helped by his eldest son, and the two of them were selling drugs and provisions. Iyanda's own stall was taken over by one of his younger sons on his death. Although most of his adult sons were by this time working independently, they still held joint stock-taking sessions and they had a joint bank account into which they paid the money they received from the tenants in their father's houses. In 1969, three of the brothers had stalls in the market. A fourth used to take cloth round to the rural areas and other towns in the north, and a fifth had a barrow from which he sold *worobo* in the streets of Tamale. The younger brothers were all at school, but helped out in the evenings and the holidays. Iyanda's second son was an exception. He had gone to secondary school and by 1969 he was a civil servant with the Ministry of Agriculture in Walewale. He also had a Ghanaian wife, but still remained in close touch with the other brothers. The final member of the group was a cognatic relative of Iyanda's who had come to Ghana with his own trading capital, but who lived with the others and sold *worobo* in front of one of their market stalls.

The fourth of the Ogbomosho groups is in some ways the most interesting, and the career of one of its senior members, Isaac Ogundiran, will be examined in more detail in the next chapter. It was the only one of the four large Ogbomosho groups to be predominantly Christian, and it was also the one which showed the greatest degree of economic innovation.

The first member of Ile Oke in the Gold Coast was Joseph Ade, who made his way there in 1912. He spent ten years in Accra and three in Kumasi before going on to Tamale in 1925. In 1931 he took his junior brother, Luke, to join him, and in 1937 they were joined by Isaac Ogundiran, a son of Joseph's father's half brother. Members of other segments of the compound also migrated to Tamale, but it is with this segment that I will be primarily concerned. Like the other major Ogbomosho groups, the Ile Oke traders sold Yoruba cloth until after 1945. Joseph, Luke and Isaac were successively responsible for buying and transporting the cloth from Nigeria. In the 1950s they were joined by other agnates, including the three sons of Joseph Ade, and by John, Isaac's younger brother. Luke became a licensed dealer for the Compagnie Française d'Afrique Occidentale (CFAO) in the early 1950s, transferring to the United Africa Company (UAC) in 1955. In 1962 he started his own store, bought grinding mills, and started to sell spare parts for the mills along with provisions. Grinding machines became his main source of income, and he ploughed the profits back into more machines and, later, houses which he bought in various parts of Tamale. By 1969, he had seven mills and six houses, and he ran the mills with the help of Ade's second son. After the coup, he borrowed money from the bank using the houses as collateral, and started a

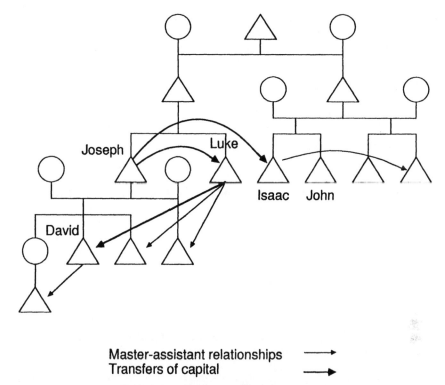

Master-assistant relationships ⟶
Transfers of capital ⟶

Figure 3.7: Relationships of migrants to Ghana from Ile Oke, Ogbomosho.

substantial rice farm on the road to Bolgatanga.[64] The list of his major assets
also included an ancient car and the 'upstairs' house in Ogbomosho which he
had built together with Ade in 1950, when the latter retired to Nigeria for
good. Luke also acquired five wives. In 1958 he set up David, Ade's eldest son,
in a UAC store in Bawku. In 1966 David sold up and bought three grinding mills
of his own which he operated until 1969.

Isaac's fortunes had been more mixed. He married in 1950 and started
working on his own in 1953, with a substantial amount of cash and with
passbooks for CFAO and UAC. He and his brother John were selling provisions in
Tamale and they also made trips to Togo and Upper Volta until 1958. After a
serious road accident Isaac decided to become a registered UAC dealer, and he
began to sell cycles and provisions in Tamale. His relations with his junior
brother were poor for reasons which will become clear later. Isaac arranged
John's marriage in 1964 but never gave him the capital to trade on his own. In
1969 John was working for a Lebanese merchant in a store opposite his
brother's shop. The relationships of the members of the group involved in the
migration are shown in Figure 3.7.

Despite the obvious differences between these four Ogbomosho groups, some common features do emerge. The general conclusions reached above seem to be valid: the processes of the recruitment of migrants, the proliferation of trading enterprises, the movement from the sale of Nigerian cloth to the sale of manufactured goods, and the diversification of occupations among the younger generation are common to all four groups. Two other features appear to be shared. The first is the importance of the father's brother/brother's son relationship which has played a part in four of the five migrations discussed so far. (The exception is Ile Iyanda, where the relationship of the original migrants is more obscure.) The second is the way in which the larger trading groups segment into subgroups, each relatively independent and centred around a single successful trader. In the case of Ile Isalẹ Alagbẹdẹ, there were the two groups centred on Karimu and Lasisi. In the case of Ile Isalẹ, there were the groups centred on Shittu, Rahimi, Mohammed and Peter. These groups segment further over time, with the death or retirement of their leaders and with the junior members marrying and asserting their own independence.

THE IGBETTI MIGRATION

The development of migration in other Igbetti descent groups was similar. In 1969 Lasisi of Ile Olowo was one of a group of ten or so prosperous Igbetti traders in Tamale, and nearly all of them had their clusters of junior relatives. The main Igbetti compounds involved were as follows.

Ile Ajanina

The earliest trader from this compound was Sarumi who went to the Gold Coast with Alhaji Sadiku of Ile Olowo before 1914. He was later followed by Yesufu, a junior full brother, and Gbademasi, a junior half brother. Sarumi retired to Igbetti before 1939, and Yesufu died in the 1950s. This left Gbademasi in charge of the junior relatives that had joined them in the Gold Coast. These included the sons of two other brothers, and the son of a classificatory sister. His father came from Ile Babalola. These three had all been given capital of their own, and the son of the sister, the eldest of the three, started to take his own brother's sons with him. In 1969 Gbademasi was being helped by two of his own sons.

Ile Raji

Alhaji Raji was a member of one of the Igbetti compounds which had originally consisted of more than one descent group, Ile Ago Are. Ile Olowo and Ile Ago Are are adjacent to each other, and Raji first went to the Gold Coast with Alhaji Sadiku from Ile Olowo. In the 1920s, Raji was the first Igbetti migrant to the Gold Coast to be really successful. He took a large number of friends, relatives and other compound members as porters and assistants. He also built the first house in Igbetti to have a corrugated iron roof, and it has been called Ile Raji or

Ile Panu (because of the 'pan' roof) ever since.[65] By 1969 he had retired to Igbetti and his trade had been taken over by his sons and other junior relatives in Tamale. The most senior of those left in the Gold Coast, a son of Raji's senior brother, had moved to Daboya because of his financial difficulties after the coup. There he joined members of two of the other lineages of Ile Ago Are. The first Igbetti man in Daboya was Jimoh Akanni who had gone there on his own in 1945. By 1969 he had become a grinding mill owner and had acquired a local wife. His success had attracted other Igbetti men in addition to his own relatives. These included members of a third descent group in Ile Ago Are. The most senior member of the compound in the Gold Coast was Yesufu Ladebo. He had taken his own brother's son to the Gold Coast, and his eldest son, Kasumu, had become a cycle repairer in Daboya around the time of the coup. Yesufu himself made frequent visits to Daboya to buy foodstuffs, his main selling line after the coup.

Ile Asumọde

If Ile Ago Are was an example of a single compound with several descent groups within it, Ile Asumọde was an example of a single descent group which had segmented into three different compounds in different parts of the town. There were independent migrations to the Gold Coast from each of these. The smallest of the three segments, Ile Ajayi, on the original site of the compound, produced only two migrants, a pair of brothers. They went to the Gold Coast after 1945, one on his own and one at the suggestion of a friend from Ile Seriki. The two other segments produced more migrants. One of them, Ile Orioko, produced two of the wealthiest Igbetti traders in Tamale, both of whom had been to Mecca by 1969. Alhaji Lawani had originally gone as a porter for the traders from Ile Ajanina, and then he borrowed money and went on his own account. Alhaji Moyibi went to the Gold Coast independently about the same time, in the late 1930s. In 1969 Lawani was still being helped in the market by his eldest son, Yesufu, whose two marriages he had arranged. He had also taken Busari, the son of his senior brother, but by 1969 Busari was himself independent and had in turn taken his own junior brothers. Moyibi was the only child of an only child, and so he had had to turn to his cognatic relatives for help. He took first Rahimi from Ile Ọlọgbọn, Moyibi's mother's compound. In 1958 Rahimi left him to study Arabic, and Moyibi replaced him with his mother's brother's son, Amusa, from Ile Adekunle who worked for him until the exodus.

The third segment also produced a number of migrants. The first of these was Gabriel, one of a large sibling group, who was accompanied by his junior brother, Amos, to Togo and, later, to Tamale, in the late 1920s. Two other junior brothers and the sons of senior brothers later joined them there. After 1945 Gabriel retired to Igbetti, leaving his eldest son in Damongo where Amos had now settled. The son stayed there while Amos himself moved back to

Tamale, where he built a house after independence. A final recruit was the son
of a senior sister. He worked for Amos for a time, but there was no capital
available for him and in 1969 he was working as a washerman in Tamale.

Ile Seriki

This is by far the largest compound in Igbetti, and contains members of six
different descent groups. It produced a number of migrations to the Gold
Coast. The first involved Amos Oni who went to the Gold Coast for the first
time with a father's brother, Samuel, who had been another of Raji's porters in
the 1920s. Samuel retired home in 1948 on the death of Amos's father, leaving
Amos in charge in the Gold Coast. He took with him his own half brothers and
the children of his full brother who had died. He was also responsible for the
recruitment of various friends. Together they formed a tightly-knit *egbe* within
the UMCA church in Tamale, the church to which nearly all the Igbetti Christians belonged.[66] The first of the friends, Zaccheus, who came from another
descent group in Ile Seriki, was in fact a junior brother of David who had been
taken to the Gold Coast several years before by Sadiku in Ile Olowo. Zaccheus
also took with him his half-brothers, and later he took David's son to whom he
gave trading capital in 1967. Another, independent, migration from Ile Seriki
was that of Suleman Oloya, who went with his family to trade at Yapei on the
Kintampo road in the 1950s.

Ile Oriade

This house consisted of a single lineage, but it also produced a number of
independent migrants. The first migrant was another of Raji's recruits. Later
on this man's senior half brother went to the Gold Coast with Samuel from Ile
Seriki, who was a close friend of his: later still his full brother went with Amos
Oni. This latter brother, Isiah Oke, took with him in 1950 the son of a
classifactory sister who had married a man in the adjacent compound, Ile
Koko. The sister's son was joined by one senior and one junior brother and the
three of them worked together in Tamale until 1969. Their father's junior half
brother had already been to the Gold Coast, as had a number of other migrants
from Ile Koko who had gone independently.

It will have become clear from the above examples that the Igbetti migrants
to the Gold Coast were linked to each other by a complex web of agnatic,
cognatic and affinal ties, as well as through ties of friendship and neighbourhood stemming from the home town. Nearly all the migrations discussed
so far from Igbetti are linked in one way or another to the original migration of
Alhaji Sadiku from Ile Olowo (Figure 3.8). Over time these links were further
reinforced by intermarriage between the members of the various compounds
both in the Gold Coast and Igbetti. Amos Oni's sister, for instance, was
married to Raji's brother, while 1969 saw the wedding in Tamale of one of
Raji's sons to a daughter of Zaccheus's half-brother. Numerous other

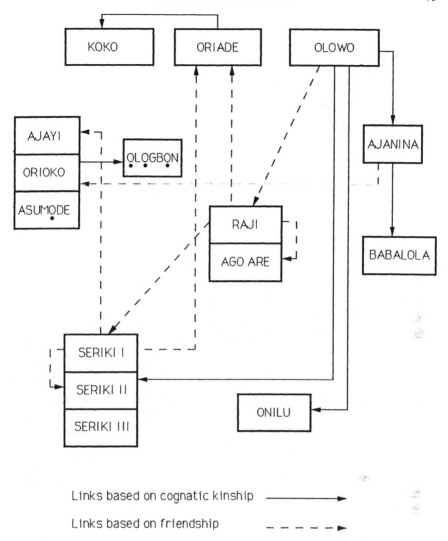

Links based on cognatic kinship ⟶

Links based on friendship − − − − ➤

Figure 3.8: The spread of migration between compounds in Igbetti.

examples can be given, and it is not surprising that the Igbetti community which developed in Tamale was extremely close-knit.

There is a broad similarity in patterns of chain migration in Ogbomosho and Igbetti. The successful migrant looked to his home town for assistance: this usually meant the recruitment of agnatic relatives, though cognates were recruited as well. Two other features of Igbetti migration are worth noting. The first is that more than one independent migration could take place within the same descent group. The second is the importance of friendship networks in recruitment, especially in the 1920s and 1930s when most of the cloth was still being taken by porters, and also in the 1950s when the market in the Gold Coast was expanding most rapidly. One of the most important features of Yoruba society this century has been the proliferation of associations (*egbe*) which have sprung up in every town.[67] *Egbe* can mean anything from a small, informal group of friends to a more formal association with a specific function, but the most important *egbe* in many towns are those which are affiliated either to the churches or the mosque. They provide the individual with most of his or her closest friends, and have an important function in the rites of passage – marriages, funerals and naming ceremonies – involving individual members. Small cliques of friends, many of whom were members of the same *egbe*, were an important factor in the recruitment of new migrants, in addition to kinship links. Igbetti is a small and compact town: many of the early migrants came from adjacent compounds – Ile Raji, Ile Olowo, Ile Oriade and Ile Koko lie side by side. In the early stages, Islam appears to have been a factor. Sadiku (Ile Olowo) and Sarumi (Ile Ajanina) were among the earliest Muslims in Igbetti and went with Muslims from Shaki. The father of Jimoh Akanni was a Koranic teacher who lived in Ile Ago Are, and he converted most of the younger men in it to Islam. After the second war, Christianity also became an important factor, particularly in the case of Amos Oni and his friends, who became members of the same *egbe* in their church in Tamale.

My data on friendship networks among migrants from the other towns is less complete, but they were certainly significant in the case of the migration from Igboho. Many of the Igboho migrants had been recruited by a group of three close friends who were working together transporting cloth from Nigeria on bicycles in the 1930s. All three took junior relatives with them, and all came from the same area of the town and belonged to the same Baptist church. One of the resulting groups, from Ile Balogun, later moved to Bolgatanga while the others stayed in Tamale.

Thus, through the processes of recruitment, the formation of friendship networks and intermarriage, an unusually dense network of kinship and friendship ties developed between migrants from the same town. As will be seen ties between Yoruba migrants from different towns were less frequent, and intermarriage between migrants from different towns very rare, though this pattern was changing among the second generation migrants.

MIGRATION AND SOCIAL STRUCTURE

It remains to link these patterns of migration to the patterns of Yoruba social organisation outlined earlier. Table 3.2 gives details of the links through which migrants were recruited, and it appears that the great majority were recruited by close relatives, especially their parents, full siblings, and fathers' full siblings. Matrilateral links were common though less frequent. But a developmental sequence has to be borne in mind. It was only if a migrant was

Table 3.2: Relationships of people responsible for the migration of Yoruba men to Northern Ghana.

Relationship	Ogbomosho	%	Igboho	%	Igbetti	%	Total	%
Parent	12	24.5	6	10.2	5	11.4	23	15.1
Sibling	12	24.5	15	25.4	9	20.5	36	23.7
Father's brother	12	24.5	13	22.0	13	29.5	38	25.0
Mother's brother	5	10.2	7	11.9	6	13.6	18	11.8
Other agnate	3	6.1	6	10.2	3	6.8	12	7.9
Other cognate	2	4.1	5	8.5	1	2.3	8	5.3
Affinal	0	0.0	1	1.7	1	2.3	2	1.3
Non-relative	3	6.1	6	10.2	6	13.6	15	9.9
Total	49	100.0	59	100.0	44	100.0	152	100.0

Source: Male interviews, 1970–1. Figures exclude migrants born in Ghana or who went on their own initiative.

successful that a migration chain would be started. In many cases this would consist only of the migrant himself, along with his wives and children, but in others a number of close relatives, and eventually more distant relatives, would be recruited as well. Finally, the major periods of expansion in the Gold Coast economy, the 1920s and the 1950s, produced a flood of migrants including the friends of those who had already gone, anxious to try their own luck in the Gold Coast. These processes reflect a number of the basic features of Yoruba social organisation. First, the principle of seniority provided the basis for authority and decision-making within the groups of migrant traders working in the Gold Coast. Second, cognatic ties were important in migrant recruitment, alongside agnatic ties. The close ties of women with their own descent groups are reflected in the number of sisters' sons recruited by the migrants to the Gold Coast, and it was quite normal for women with brothers who were successful migrants to urge them to take one of their own children with them as well. In some cases, where there were no close agnatic relatives of the right age available, sister's sons were the obvious source of assistance for the trader. Many women went to the Gold Coast initially to stay with mothers' sisters and help them with trade, moving to live with their own husbands after marriage. Indeed, it might be argued that migration, in which problems of land tenure, inheritance and traditional office are not involved, might lead to a strengthening of cognatic ties, as they provide additional flexibility for the migrant trader looking for assistance.

The strength of a woman's ties with her natal compound reflect the strength of the ties between full siblings in Yoruba society. There is a saying '*okun ọmọ iya yi*' – the rope which binds the children of the same mother is strong. This extends to both males and females within the sibling group. In recruitment, full siblings and fathers' full siblings played a much more important part than half-siblings and fathers' half-siblings. The contrast between groups of full and half-siblings is also important in segmentation within the Yoruba descent group and also in inheritance patterns. Full siblings are expected to cooperate, and informants seemed to feel that full siblings could be expected to form far more durable trading partnerships than half-siblings.

The question arises, therefore, under what conditions could half-siblings be recruited? The answer lies in the way in which a father with more than one wife attempts to ensure that the children of each wife are treated in an equivalent fashion. Sadiku of Ile Olowo retired leaving his eldest son in the Gold Coast. Instead of recruiting his own junior brother first, Lasisi turned instead to the elder son of his father's second wife. He argued that had Sadiku remained in the Gold Coast he would have recruited a son from this marriage to help him: as Lasisi had taken over his economic obligations in the Gold Coast, he had to do the same. However, the more long-lasting trade partnership was the one he had with his full brother when he was finally joined by him. The unity of the full sibling group is expressed in other ways too. It is full siblings who tend to foster one another's children, and who take over the responsibility for the children of members of the descent group who die while their children are still young.

A further feature of Yoruba social structure reflected in the migration pattern is the close relationship between a man and his eldest son. While in many West African societies this relationship is often one of tension and avoidance, in this case it is very close. In towns like Igbetti it was common for an eldest son to live with his father, even if his full siblings had built their own house elsewhere. In the early stages of the migration to the Gold Coast, it was the younger members of the sibling group who tended to migrate. The eldest son tended to stay at home to farm. In the Gold Coast, the most durable trading partnerships were often those between fathers and eldest sons. Normally traders tended to start their own businesses on marriage, but there were examples of eldest sons continuing to work with their fathers long afterwards, even when they had two wives and when other more junior relatives had separated long since. As one informant put it, 'Why should he bother to separate? When the old man dies it will all be for him.'

But most of the trading partnerships eventually dissolved as the younger partners married and were given their own capital, and the tendency was for this to happen more quickly in the post-war than in the pre-war period. The pre-war pattern was for a group of several traders to work together under the nominal leadership of the senior members. The relations between them were usually amicable and each member of the group, especially the older members, tended to have a good deal of autonomy. The post-war pattern was one of individual enterprises, a single trader working with the help of younger unmarried assistants. The assistants were usually given the capital to start trading on their own as soon as their master arranged their marriages, and at times the relationship could be both exploitative and antagonistic. Masters suspected their assistants of cheating them, while it was in fact in the interests of the younger man to make as much as he could out of the arrangement in order to become established more quickly once he gained his independence. It is possible to see why full siblings, along with fathers and their eldest sons, established the most durable partnerships. These were the situations in which there was the greatest identity of interest between master and assistant.

The process of the individuation of trading enterprises parallels that of the fragmentation of the compound and descent group in the home town. In the northern Yoruba towns, the availability of alternative sources of wealth has undermined the authority of the *bale* and the other elders. They are still accorded a great deal of respect, but their actual power, especially over the labour of their junior relatives, is greatly diminished.[68] The migration to the Gold Coast and elsewhere, by creating new sources of wealth outside the control of the elders, only accelerated the process. These changes are visible in the very fabric and layout of the compounds. Many of the older and larger compounds have been replaced by a number of smaller structures which reflect fairly precisely the wealth of those who built them. The poor build in mud. The richer builders plaster the mud with concrete to make it more durable, while those who are richer still build with concrete blocks or stone. The ultimate in the 1970s for the very wealthy, was an '*ile petesi*', built of concrete blocks with louvred glass windows replacing the corrugated iron or wooden window shutters. Increasingly these large prestigious buildings were being erected, not on the site of the owner's natal compound, but on new sites by the main roads leading out of the town. In the more developed towns, some of the rooms could be rented out.[69] In towns like Igbetti and Igboho, many of the houses stood almost empty as their owners continue to live elsewhere. But the normal pattern, once more, was for full siblings to cooperate in building a house: groups of siblings by different mothers tended to build separate houses.

Among the migrants in the Gold Coast, however, the fragmentation of the trading group was also a reflection of the changing conditions in the market. By the 1950s the trade in Yoruba cloth was in decline, even in the north. Most of the Yoruba traders now sold manufactured goods, and there was no need for the more elaborate organisation found in the earlier Yoruba cloth trade, with a specialist buyer travelling back and forth to Nigeria. The wider kinship group remained important for labour recruitment, child fostering, and education, and groups of related migrants often continued to live in the same compound in the Gold Coast, but in the markets, the traders increasingly worked on their own.

WOMEN AND MIGRATION

It will have been noticed that I have said very little so far about the role of women in the migration process. This is because I have been dealing in this chapter with the main streams of migration which led to the build-up of large clusters of kin, and there is no doubt that these were mainly dependent on relationships between the men from the same households and kinship groups in Nigeria. The influence of women, and the continuing relationships between brothers and sisters were obviously a factor in the recruitment by many traders of their sisters' sons, one of the factors which led to the migration spreading from compound to compound. But despite the fact that women travelled with their husbands from an early stage in the migration, they seldom initiated migration themselves.

Two factors which accounted for this were the difference in marriage age between men and women, and the differential access of men and women to capital. Women marry younger than men, and so moved straight from adolescence, in which their movements were controlled by their parents, to an adulthood in which their movements were largely determined by their husbands. Some of them did go to live with and to work for other relatives in childhood or adolescence, but after that their marriages would be arranged for them and their movements would then once more be determined by those of their husbands. Older independent women, either widows or divorcees, had more freedom of movement, but seldom had the capital to recruit large numbers of helpers. If they did have relatives working for them, they were usually girls, whose marriages in due course would be arranged, and who would move in turn to join their husbands. So, women's mobility was more constrained than that of men, and migration by women rarely gave rise to the migrant chains and clustering that resulted from the migration of their male counterparts. As we will see in a later section, differential marriage age, the expenses of childrearing and more limited access to capital were factors which reduced the scale of women's market trade as well. Thus, there arises the paradox that, though a large percentage of the migrants and a majority of the Yoruba traders were women, it was the movements of the men which determined both where, and the speed at which, clusters of Yoruba traders appeared in the local markets in Ghana.

CONCLUSION

In the post-war period, the Yoruba community in the northern Gold Coast continued to expand along the lines already established before 1939. Many of the new migrants joined relatives or friends already established there. The period of most rapid expansion was in the early 1950s, the period of most rapid economic development in the Gold Coast. After 1960, the growth rate slackened off, though perhaps less so in the north, where towns like Tamale and Bolgatanga continued to grow faster than average. Although individual traders were squeezed out of the market before the 1966 coup, it was after it that the chronic stagnation of the Ghanaian economy began to affect most Yoruba traders.

At the same time, there was a trend towards occupational differentiation in the Yoruba community. Many of those who had failed in trade had moved into other occupations rather than returning home. In addition, there was a growing second generation of migrants born in Ghana who had been drawn into formal education during the 1950s and who had, as a result, moved into clerical occupations or teaching. A growing number of Yoruba in Tamale were from Kumasi or other towns in the south, having come to the north either for education or employment, and many of the children of migrants in Tamale now worked in the south. This was paralleled by a shift in the type of migration from Nigeria. Increasingly during this period, younger migrants were joining relatives in Ghana not to trade, but for middle-school or secondary education which was easier to obtain and cheaper than in Nigeria. The slow-down in the Ghanaian economy meant a slow-down in commercial migration, and many of those worst affected by it were already contemplating moving back to Nigeria when the Ghanaian government made their decision for them.

All this meant changes in the shape of the migrants' networks of social relations which now encompassed migrants in other parts of Ghana and Nigeria as well as Tamale and the home towns. In their search for employment and education, people in all parts of the network made the most of the opportunities which it presented, often through the geographical extension of patterns of child fostering. The fragmentation of the compounds at home may have meant the increasing restriction of the fostering to an immediate circle of kin – parents and siblings – but close kin were now likely to be living in Lagos, Ibadan or northern Nigeria, as well as in their home town or in Ghana.

It was within this network of kin and friends and the constraints imposed by the Ghanaian and Nigerian political economies that individual migrant decisions were made, and individual decisions could, over time, lead to the formation of new clusters of migrants. We have seen how much of the Igbetti migration to Tamale can be traced back to one initial contact: had Alhaji Sadiku decided to stay in Yendi, migration patterns from the town might have been very different. Similarly much of the Ogbomosho migration can be traced back to the arrival of a handful of traders from Yendi and Kumasi. By 1969, the search for opportunities had taken Yoruba traders to all the major markets and most of the larger villages in the north: in the Tamale area, towns like Yapei, Sawla, Buipe and Daboya now had their resident traders, many of whom had worked previously in Tamale. Individual decisions coupled with later chain migration gave rise to the clustered migration pattern so typical of the Yoruba in Ghana as a whole, and to the geographical extension of Yoruba enterprise throughout the area. And it is to the nature of this enterprise that we turn in the next two chapters.

4

THE YORUBA TRADERS

The previous two chapters concentrated on migration. This chapter and the next examine in greater detail the role of the Yoruba in the labour market and particularly in trade. The development of the Ghanaian economy and the social background of entry into trade have already been discussed in some detail, so the emphasis in these two chapters is, rather, on the individual level of analysis – the careers and decisions of individual traders. This chapter starts with a description of the residential and domestic organisation of the Yoruba migrants in Tamale in 1969 which provides a setting for the case studies which follow. The purpose of these is three-fold. Some of them focus on individuals already mentioned in previous chapters and serve to continue the narrative. The second aim is to give a more rounded impression of the trading activities and strategies of the Yoruba traders in the period immediately prior to the exodus and the relationship between trading and other aspects of their social lives. The third aim is to focus on some of the recurrent problems facing the Yoruba traders in general. The five men and two women selected, range from the well-established and relatively prosperous traders to the younger traders with or without the support of their senior relatives and the marginal traders struggling to make ends meet.[1] The career of each trader was, of course, unique, and these case studies by no means exhaust either the range of problems which were encountered in the market or the strategies evolved to deal with them. Nevertheless, most of the Yoruba traders in Tamale acted as links in the distribution of manufactured goods between the larger European, Levantine or African firms on the one hand and the Ghanaian consumer on the other. The range of goods in which they dealt was fairly narrow and they operated for the most part with limited capital. It is natural, therefore, that the careers of many of the traders should have shown a good deal of similarity, as did the problems they faced and the strategies with which they attempted to solve them. But first it might help to set the scene, with a sketch of Yoruba living conditions in Tamale on the eve of the exodus.

HOUSES AND HOUSEHOLDS IN TAMALE

The Yoruba population of Tamale in 1969 stood at over 2,000, nearly 90 per cent of which originated from the four towns of Ogbomosho, Igboho, Igbetti and Shaki (Table 4.1). Though there was no exclusively 'Yoruba quarter' of the town, there was a degree of residential concentration in particular wards (Table 4.2). The majority of Yoruba in the town lived in the Sabon Gida,

Table 4.1: Yoruba population of Tamale in 1969 by town of origin.

Town	Number	Percentage
Ogbomosho	680	32.9
Igboho	386	18.7
Shaki	380	18.4
Igbetti	371	17.9
Otu	46	2.2
Irawo	27	1.3
Offiki	19	0.9
Shepeteri	19	0.9
Other towns	139	6.7
Total	2,067	100.0

Source: Registration forms, Ministry of Economic Planning and Rehabilitation, Ibadan.

consisting of wards G and H. However, in addition a number of Igboho and Shaki migrants had houses in the area between the Mossi Zongo and Aboabo (Ward I). Many of the Igbetti had built houses in Tishigu (Wards B and K). The British had established their administrative headquarters near a group of Dagomba villages which were gradually engulfed by the rest of the town as it expanded. The result was a situation in which the rectangular compound which made up the bulk of the housing in the town surrounded clusters of traditional round Dagomba huts which appeared to have been little affected by the processes of urban development going on all around them. A series of

Table 4.2: Residence by ward of Yoruba men in Tamale, 1969, by town of origin.

Ward	Ogbomosho		Igboho		Igbetti		Total	
	no.	%	no.	%	no.	%	no.	%
A	2	2.8	4	13.3	2	3.9	8	5.3
B	12	16.9	0	0.0	22	43.1	34	22.4
CH	2	2.8	0	0.0	0	0.0	2	1.3
D	0	0.0	0	0.0	4	7.8	4	2.6
E	2	2.8	0	0.0	5	9.8	7	4.6
F	4	5.6	0	0.0	1	2.0	5	3.3
G	4	5.6	3	10.0	0	0.0	7	4.6
H	28	39.4	6	20.0	7	13.7	41	27.0
I	3	4.2	14	46.7	4	7.8	21	17.8
K	8	11.3	0	0.0	2	3.9	10	6.6
M	1	1.4	0	0.0	0	0.0	1	0.7
Villages	3	4.2	2	6.6	2	3.9	7	4.6
Not known	2	2.8	1	3.3	2	3.9	5	3.3
Total	71	100.0	30	100.0	51	100.0	152	100.0

Source: Male interviews.

layouts had been planned by the township authorities, and the plots had been allocated to anyone who had applied for them irrespective of ethnic origins. The earliest of these were the Mossi Zongo (Ward A) and the Hausa Zongo (Ward F), and, slightly later, the Sabon Gida. The earliest Yoruba in Tamale had gravitated to the last of these. In the 1932 map of the town, this is still partly shown as an area of irregularly shaped Dagomba compounds. However, the area was being gradually transformed with the demolition of the older houses to make way for the typical single-storey rectangular buildings with a central courtyard. Apart from the main roads, a network of passages and open ditches ran between the houses, and in places these opened onto open spaces with latrines and rubbish dumps for the houses around. There were communal water taps at various points to serve the older houses with no water supply of their own. By 1969, many of the houses had both water and electricity, but the older houses often had none, the main source of illumination being kerosene lamps. Most of the roofs were by this time made of corrugated iron or aluminium, though thatched roofs were still fairly common.

Some of the earliest Yoruba traders to settle in Tamale acquired houses in the Sabon Gida, and they included Alhaji Karimu of Ile Isalẹ Alagbẹdẹ in Ogbomosho and his relatives. Since then it remained the main concentration of Ogbomosho migrants. Three of the earlier Yoruba chiefs had had houses there, as well as the former Yoruba Imam. To the Yoruba the Sabon Gida was also known as 'oke ọba' – the 'chief's hill' (the Yoruba word implies no great degree of steepness). After 1945 other areas of the town were laid out, including Tishigu and the areas on the Kumasi and Damongo roads. The Yoruba who built during this period tended to put their houses up there, though in some cases they stayed living in the Sabon Gida themselves, renting their new houses out to others. In 1969 three of the four large descent groups within the Ogbomosho community still lived in the Sabon Gida: the fourth, Ile Isalẹ, was concentrated in Rahimi's house in Tishigu.

DOMESTIC ORGANISATION

The rectangular compounds in which most of the Yoruba in Tamale lived could contain anywhere between six and thirty rooms arranged round the courtyard. One side would be taken up either partly or completely with the 'bathroom', a small room with a hole in the wall at ground level to allow water to drain out. It also usually included a latrine (if any), the tap (if any) and a communal kitchen in which were stored the mortars and cooking pots belonging to the residents. Many of the houses lacked some or all of these amenities. In some newer houses the bathroom was a proper room with a shower, but in others it consisted of a grass mat hung across an empty space within the surrounding wall of the compound. The bathroom was also used for urination. The latrines in houses which had them were of the bucket type, their contents being collected each night by the municipal night-soil men, but in houses without, the residents had to walk to the nearest public latrines. The routes to these were among the main foci of social interaction, especially in the Sabon Gida where most of the houses lacked their own latrines. The rent for houses like this was also lower – three cedis a month per room compared with the five charged in the newer parts of the town. At least part of the courtyard in each house was covered by the roof, and in many compounds a low wall and gate separated the areas adjacent to each room. It was here that most of the food preparation, cooking and other domestic work were carried on. Usually at least some of the rooms leading out of the house had doors set in a verandah. The courtyard and verandah were the main areas of shade, and so many people spent most of their time out there on grass mats on the floor. In the hot season, many people slept in the open as well.

Patterns of Yoruba residence in Tamale varied considerably.[2] Many lived in compounds completely occupied by Yoruba, while others were the only Yoruba in houses full of members of other ethnic groups. There were all gradations between the two extremes. In the case of the Yoruba-owned houses, the allocation of rooms was made by the owner, and followed closely the pattern to be found in the home towns in Nigeria. The landlord usually had a sitting room or 'parlour' for himself, and a bedroom as well as additional rooms for each of his wives. He usually had the largest rooms in the house, with access both to the verandah outside and the courtyard inside. Married sons usually had a single room for themselves and their wives.

The younger children slept with their mothers, while the two groups of teenage boys and girls usually had a room each, with up to five or six people sleeping in it. Rooms left over could be used for storage, allocated to other relatives, left empty for visiting strangers, or rented out to tenants. Some were reserved for relatives who lived outside Tamale but who paid regular visits to the town. Yoruba who did not own their own houses rented rooms from others unless they had a senior relative with a house who was prepared to give them a room for nothing. The general rule was that 'family members', especially junior relatives working for the landlord, did not pay rent. However, the situation with regard to more distant relatives was not as clear cut. An Igbetti man with a house in Tishigu had rented a room to his mother's brother, which was considered something of a joke by the others: he had a reputation for eccentricity and miserliness.

In those compounds which contained related migrants and their families, the allocation of domestic work approximated closely to the Nigerian model. Yoruba social organisation places considerable importance on the order in which children are born into the compound, or in which wives marry into the compound. The general pattern is that senior members of the household organise, while the heavier and more disagreeable tasks are delegated to the junior members. The subservient position of wives in their husbands' houses partly derives from the fact that they are junior not only to wives who have married into the house before them, but also to children born in the house before their arrival. These rules of seniority traditionally applied within large compounds comprising a large number of men and their families. With the breakup of these larger compounds into a number of smaller units in the northern Yoruba towns, the degree of surveillance by senior relatives has been reduced and room for independent initiative as a result has increased. The tension between rules of seniority based on membership of a large compound and a more restricted model in which members of different polygynous families were largely independent of each other was visible in Tamale, and was complicated as well by the factor of house ownership. Limata (who features in one of the case studies below) lived in a house which had formerly been owned by Mustafa Iyanda and which was now owned by his sons. Here, there was tension between the wives of the sons and the wife of Mustafa's brother who still lived there. This woman saw herself as the most senior wife in the house and acted accordingly. The other wives felt that the house was really theirs, and that they were only allowing her to live there as a favour. There was also tension between the sons and their father's brother over the running of the house and the collection of the rents. After Mustafa's death, the brother had collected the rents for a time, but Mustafa's sons became dissatisfied with this, and eventually insisted on being paid directly by the tenants.

In compounds which consisted of unrelated men, there was less cooperation between the women, and they tended to work on their own. Where a man had more than one wife, the pattern again followed the Nigerian model: the women cooked for themselves and their children each day, and cooked for their husband on a rotational basis. There might be more cooperation if the wives got on well with each other, but this was not always the case. Yoruba inheritance patterns have traditionally meant that property is divided between groups of full siblings by the same mother, then equally among individual children. A woman is therefore often forced to assume the role *vis à vis* her husband and co-wives as protector of the interests of her children as against those of the children of other wives. Most polygynous husbands go out of their way to demonstrate that they are treating wives and their groups of children equally, but with resources like money for subsistence, education and trade at stake, tensions are almost impossible to avoid completely. If relations between wives were really bad, one solution was to find a room for one of the wives in another compound. The wives might also be separated when a man married a second wife and there were no spare rooms in the house in which he himself was staying.[3]

Much of the food the family consumed was prepared by outside foodsellers. Tamale had a substantial cooked-food industry, and there were numerous women selling various types of food in addition to the many chop bars around the town. Breakfast for most people in the town consisted of beancakes and porridge bought from a local seller, and most of the Yoruba who spent all day in the market would eat there as well, sending a child to bring food to them from a chop bar. The evening meal was normally prepared by the wife, but if she was trading as well she might also buy food from a chop bar instead. One of the reasons given by Ogbomosho women for their success in trade was that their husbands did not expect them to spend so much time on domestic chores, leaving them free to attend to their enterprises. Their relatively greater independence might also have been related to the larger contribution many of them were able to make to the household budget, compared to the wives from other towns, because of their larger turnovers.

The three major items of expenditure within the household were food, clothes and education. The division of the financial load varied greatly, depending on the relative wealth of the spouses, the number of children, and the total income of the polygynous family. In general, men earned more than women, and when the wife was trading on a small scale, the husband had to provide nearly everything. Polygynous men tended to be wealthier, but their households were correspondingly larger. In order to maintain good relations between their wives, it was important that the husbands should be seen to treat the groups of children by each wife evenly, for instance paying for the same number of children of each wife to go to school, but leaving the mother to pay for any of the others.[4] It was expected that the husband would provide certain items for all the children such as new clothes for the Muslims festivals, or for Christmas. It was also expected that each parent would assume complete responsibility for children helping them in trade. But however the expenditure was divided, there would still be a certain amount of flexibility. For instance, if a man had no money on him in the morning to give his wife, or chop money for the children, he would leave early for the market, leaving his wife to provide the money from her own pocket. He would then pay her back at the end of the day out of his takings. As the first case study makes clear, even the most respected members of the Yoruba community had their financial problems, and their domestic responsibilities tended to expand with their trading enterprises.

MEN AND TRADE
Alhaji Lasisi

Alhaji Lasisi from Ile Olowo, Igbetti, was in his mid-fifties at the time of the exodus. He was by all accounts a relatively prosperous member of the Yoruba community. In 1969 he owned two houses in Tamale. One of these he had built himself, and the second he had taken over on the death of his junior brother the previous year. He was renting out three rooms in his own house and all seventeen rooms in the brother's house, which brought him an income of around NC100 a month. The combined value of the two houses was in the region of NC12,000.

By 1969, Lasisi had been selling manufactured cloth exclusively, as he had been for some years. With increased duty, exchange control and the rise of a

Plate 4.1: Igbetti trader, wearing a Ghanaian wax print, with his daughter.

local weaving industry in Tamale, Yoruba cloth had become unprofitable and he had stopped selling it since Ghanaian independence in 1957. After this, he bought goods in the south, like most of the other Yoruba, but gradually started to make more and more use of the large wholesale firms in Tamale itself, acquiring passbooks for four of them in the 1950s before they became difficult to obtain. He had access to any cloth that came into the Tamale stores, and before the 1966 coup he could sell this relatively quickly. His main sales were to other Yoruba traders who had run out of particular lines before they had the money for a trip to the south, and to Ghanaian women who bought cloth from him in 12-yard pieces for subdivision. They were generally unable to obtain cloth direct from the stores, and Yoruba wholesalers were their main local source of supply.

Before the coup Lasisi had been relatively successful, and the high point of his career was when he was able to send his father and half brother to Mecca. He paid for this in 1965, though they did not actually make the trip until 1967. Until the coup, Lasisi's eldest son used to take the car to Bolgatanga to sell wax prints on market day. On a good day he could sell up to NC600 worth of cloth there. Tamale market day produced similar sales, but the average had slumped to NC100 by 1969. Sales had also slumped in Bolgatanga, and Lasisi's son had begun to use public transport to go there after the car had started to give trouble. Later he stopped going completely.

Conditions in the market had deteriorated in other ways after the coup. Lasisi had been a prominent member of the CPP: it was rather ironic therefore to see on his wall a photograph of himself and some of the other Yoruba leaders holding anti-CPP banners and presenting a cow and a load of yams to a visiting army commander after the coup. Despite all these efforts to get on the right side of the new administration business still suffered. The cutback in government expenditure meant that sales of consumer goods, including cloth, were badly hit. Also, relations between the Yoruba traders and the authorities were disrupted by the change of leadership, and there was a wave of arrests of traders for selling smuggled goods and for infringement of the price control regulations.

This affected Lasisi directly. In 1967 he took out a bank loan, using his house as security, ostensibly to start a rice farm. Half of the money he kept for himself and the rest he gave to the eldest son. The accounts of the two of them differ on what happened next. According to the son, Lasisi sent him to Togo to buy cloth and smuggle it back. Lasisi said that it was the son's idea and not his. However, the fact was that the load of cloth was seized by the police at Bolgatanga and confiscated. No further action was taken, but the loss of several hundred cedis put Lasisi into difficulties repaying his loan. The bank threatened to take him to court, but he managed to reschedule the payments. He was helped by the death of his junior brother in 1968, which enabled him to start collecting the rent from the brother's house. He was also helped by advice from his friend Luke to try his hand at rice farming. He put NC1,000 into the farm, NC250 of which Luke supplied, and he used a piece of land he had obtained from a chief in a village just outside Tamale. All the supervision was done by himself and his driver. The 1969 crop came to 400 bags of rice, ninety of which he gave to Luke. Had he been able to store the rice until the end of the dry season and sell it when the price was at its highest his financial problems would have been solved, but the compliance order intervened. In December 1969 he sold his brother's house and paid off the bank loan, and in 1970 he sold the rest of his assets in Ghana and returned to Nigeria.

Lasisi's life-style, like that of most of the older Yoruba Muslims in Tamale, was outwardly austere, and had grown more so as a result of his financial problems. He had numerous dependents. In addition to his own two wives and eighteen children, there were his senior son's two wives and three children, a brother's son and his wife, the driver, and the son of his junior sister, all dependent on a single enterprise. The wives were trading on a small scale. One of them had taken over the market stall left vacant on the death of the brother, while the other sold from a stall attached to the side of the house. A lot of trade went on from the houses in Tamale. There were wealthy women traders among the Yoruba, but most of them were from Ogbomosho. Few women had the capital to do their own buying in the south. Lasisi's senior wife sold provisions and pomade, plus a few basic medicines. The junior wife with the stall at home sold provisions and bread to the residents of the surrounding houses. Other popular lines included chewing sticks, *kenkey* prepared by a Ga woman in a nearby house, cigarettes, matches, soap and detergents. Although the wives earned enough to keep themselves and their younger children in clothes and to pay for some of the food, the sheer size of their families meant that much of the expense still fell on Lasisi.

Lasisi had a large house, but only occupied two rooms of it himself, with an additional two for his wives. Most of the rest were occupied by the other members of the family. The senior son qualified for two rooms, as, in addition to his own wife, he had married one of the widows of Lasisi's younger brother. The driver was unmarried, but qualified for a room on account of his seniority. Another was reserved for the brother's son and his wife, while the teenage boys shared a room between them. The younger children slept with their respective mothers, and the three rooms which were not occupied by the family were let out to non-Yoruba: a Wangara from Mali who helped with the small mosque which Lasisi had built on the side of the house, and two government workers from Ashanti. The other house which had belonged to the junior brother was rented out to non-family members, including an Ewe fireman and his Fanti friend, an Efutu plumber, a Mamprusi nurse and his junior brothers, and a Yoruba clerk from Offa with two wives and an unmarried junior brother.

The furnishings of Lasisi's room were relatively simple. They included an armchair with foam cushions and torn plastic covers, a large wall clock of uncertain age and reliability, a large cracked mirror on top of a dressing table, and the ubiquitous Nigerian almanacs dating from the days of party politics, featuring the photographs of Chief Akintola and Sir Ahmadu Bello.[5] The exterior of the house was painted in pink and green and the inside of the living room had also once been green, but had faded to a brown long since. To the right was Lasisi's bedroom containing a double bed with a box under it, a collection of hooks along the door for clothes, a mosquito net with poles and little else. The only concession to a higher life-style was the electric fan which pursued its eccentric course overhead. Of the gadgets which were often found in the rooms of the younger Yoruba who had money – refrigerators, record players and tape recorders – there was no sign. Lasisi's major item of prestige expenditure in the early 1960s had been an Opel stationwagon which was now rather old. It was still used on ritual occasions, and one of the most common sights on the road outside was the car being propelled by a crowd of small boys to get it started. Minor repairs on the vehicle were a constant source of worry, and Lasisi usually cycled to market, unless he had to go on to the farm or attend a meeting.

He used to set off for the market every morning about 8 a.m. or so, one of the boys having been sent on in advance to open the stall and sweep it out for the day's business. He was helped by the two senior sons, the son of his brother and the son of a junior sister. Lasisi did most of the buying himself as most of the stores from which he bought were on the main street, only a few yards from his stall. The sister's son could be sent out with messages to the stores or to other traders. The senior son had been trading with his father since the debacle with the smuggled cloth, though for three years he had been trying to branch out on his own as an agent for the pilgrimage to Mecca. So far he had only received NC80 commission a year from this, though he was hoping to sell the fifty tickets during the following year which would entitle him to a free one for himself. He felt that he was being hampered by his father's unwillingness to help him become established in this, by providing him with an office for instance. After the cloth incident, Lasisi had no particular trust in his son's commercial ability, neither had he any capital with which to help him.

On market days, in addition to the usual Tamale buyers, there were the traders from the surrounding villages who came into Tamale to buy cloth for re-sale in their own areas. Lasisi normally sold cloth in twelve-yard pieces only, and would only sell in units less than this as a special favour, to customers he knew well. All the purchases would be noted down by himself or one of the boys in a school notebook kept under the counter, underneath the transistor radio usually tuned in to the Ghana External Service. Lasisi had learned to read and write in Yoruba in 'night school' – lessons from other literate Yoruba – some years previously. Though he could read and write reasonably fluently himself he preferred to dictate to one of his literate sons if they were around.

He was one of the earliest of the Igbetti Muslims to educate his children. The first and second sons had not gone beyond the first two years of primary school, but the third and fourth had both gone on to secondary school, and the eldest daughter had taken a secretarial course. The second daughter had completed primary school and had worked for a time as a housemaid in Lagos. In 1969 she was helping her mother in her stall in Tamale market.

In addition to his two Yoruba wives, Lasisi had at one stage married a Dagomba woman. For a time she had lived in his house with the others, but had produced no children. Then came the deaths of the two Ile Olowo men in the same year. Lasisi's brother died of illness in Tamale and Ahmadu died in a road accident at Damongo. The Dagomba wife was accused of witchcraft and was thrown out of the house by Tijani, Lasisi's half-brother, over on a visit from Damongo.[6] Lasisi continued to visit her, however, and on leaving Ghana he handed his market stall over to her. Her influence was blamed by the other members of the family for the decline in his trading fortunes. Despite this, Lasisi was able to retain at least an air of prosperity by making use of the considerable wardrobe he had acquired during his better years. He gave up drinking and smoked less, but whereas in the past he had had several suits of new clothes made for himself each month, by 1969 his clothes were starting to show signs of wear. He cut back on food expenditure as well, and no longer killed two chickens every Friday as he had done formerly.

Outside his immediate family and the rest of the Yoruba community, Lasisi maintained a wide network of contacts in Tamale from the days in which he had been more involved in local politics. He knew most of the local political leaders and civil servants, and maintained regular contact with other leading Yoruba, but he had a few particularly close friends. One was Alhaji Sani from Ile Isalẹ Alagbẹdẹ in Ogbomosho. A second was Alhaji Mustafa Iyanda from Ile Iyanda, also in Ogbomosho. After Iyanda's death in 1967 Lasisi remained on good terms with his sons and was still asked for advice at family meetings. His other close friend was a Dagomba, the Chief Driver in Tamale who was also the father of the Progress Party candidate in the 1969 general election.[7] Other contacts with Ghanaians came from his Dagomba wife, while he was also well known to the Tamale Muslims leaders through his attendance at the Central Mosque. His network of contacts made easier his relations with the authorities and the bureaucracy. It smoothed his troubles with the bank, enabled him to obtain land for his farm, made sure he received help from the agricultural extension services, and helped ensure a steady supply of goods from the local stores. Maintenance of these contacts required the expenditure of a good deal of time, as did the meetings of the Igbetti *parapọ*, the Yoruba *Ilupẹjọ* and the Nigerian Community Committee where his advice was respected because of his knowledge of the local scene.

Lasisi was typical of a particular group of established Yoruba traders in Tamale. In the 1950s and early 1960s he had achieved a large measure of success, acquired a house and a car, produced numerous children through two fertile marriages, and had managed to send his father and his brother to Mecca. After the coup his reserves were depleted and his domestic responsibilities became increasingly onerous. His difficulties were compounded by the incident with the smuggled cloth and the decline in sales. His problems would have been even more acute had it not been for the acquisition of his brother's house and his political contacts. The next case is that of a trader much earlier in his career, for whom these responsibilities had not yet arrived.

Ahmadu Bawa

Ahmadu was 24 years old in 1969 and came from Modeke, Igboho. He had married at the start of the year, but was still trading in partnership with his senior brother, Bukari, They were the sons of a former Yoruba Imam in Tamale who had died in 1962. In 1969 they were selling cycle parts. Bukari was about 40 and had been trained as a tailor by his father. He started trading on his own in 1952 with £30 he had accumulated from this. He bought cycle parts up from the south and took them to the rural markets around Tamale, but he was able to increase his capital by taking on tailoring jobs as well, sewing at home in the evenings on his return from the markets. As the business grew, he brought a father's brother's son over from Igboho to help him. However, the boy stole money from him and was sent home. Ahmadu was in primary school at the time. Both the brothers had received a Koranic education, and Bukari could read and write Arabic fluently. Though his father had been unwilling to allow Ahmadu to attend primary school, he eventually relented, and after his father's death, Ahmadu completed middle school, helping his brother with trade in the evenings and at the weekends. After leaving school in 1966, he worked in the market full-time. Though there were a few Yoruba traders in the market with middle school education or above, most Yoruba school leavers tended to look for other work. Ahmadu was willing to trade, but his real aim was to become a Koranic teacher when he could accumulate enough money to devote himself to the full-time study of Arabic. In any case, business was going well, even since the 1966 coup.

Their buying was done in the south, Bukari travelling down three or four times a month, depending on the market, taking between NC600 and 800 with him each time. Thus, assuming a 10 per cent profit margin on the goods, their income was in the region of NC250 or 350 a month. (It increased after the compliance order when they were about the only Yoruba in the market to stay in business.)

Like many of the other Igboho traders, they did most of their selling in the rural markets around Tamale. The Tamale market cycle consisted of six markets held on successive days. They were located in Tamale itself, Sankpala, Savelugu, Nyankpala, Kumbungu and Katin Daa (Tolon).[8] In the period before the compliance order, upwards of 100 Yoruba traders, both men and women, used to travel to these. On Tamale market day, both the brothers stayed in Tamale together, Ahmadu selling while Bukari sewed. For Sankpala, Nyankpala and Kumbungu, Ahmadu went to the market while Bukari stayed in Tamale. Both brothers travelled to the two largest markets at Savelugu and Tolon where they set up separate stalls at opposite ends of the market to maximise their sales. They usually arrived there at about 10 am and stayed until 6 pm. After this the remaining goods were loaded back onto the lorries, and they arrived back in Tamale at around 8 pm. In addition to the cycle parts, the brothers did a smaller trade in cloth, mainly drills and khakis. When he was on his own, Ahmadu took orders for clothes to be made with the cloth, together with the measurements and the money. Bukari made up the clothes in his market stall or at home in the evenings, and Ahmadu took them back to the customer on the following market day. Some of the cloth was bought in the south along with the cycle parts, but if they ran out Ahmadu was able to obtain more from an Ogbomosho friend in Tamale. Much of the brothers' business was done with local Dagomba wholesalers or cycle repairers to whom the brothers sold parts in dozens at reduced prices. They were willing to advance credit of up to NC25 until the next market day to the traders they knew well. On average they took between NC40 and 60 in each stall in each of the markets that they visited.

In the rural markets they were assisted by a father's junior brother's son who had also completed middle school, and by a couple of Dagomba farmers from Tolon who came regularly to help them at Kumbungu, Katin Daa and Save-lugu during the dry season. These men had been working with them for some time. They cycled to the markets where they met the brothers and helped them to unload the goods and set up the stalls. They were not paid a regular amount, but might be given a few shillings at the end of the day. It was recognised that they kept any money that they could extract from the customers over and above the regular prices while the two brothers were away from the stalls. Ahmadu thus had opportunities to maintain his social contacts in the local villages, including other Yoruba living in the area, old school friends who had become teachers, dispensers and agricultural extension workers, and his girlfriends.

Despite the nominal control of the business by the senior brother, the two brothers still got along well together. Apart from their financial success, another factor holding them together was their mother, who lived in Tamale with them. In 1969, Bukari had organised a lavish wedding for Ahmadu, and they were also sending money home as fast as possible to build a house in Igboho. Ahmadu gave the money he collected each day to Bukari, keeping as much as he needed for food and other expenses, and Bukari did not demand an account of every penny. Ahmadu lived with his wife in a single room in the house which their father had built in the Sabon Gida of Tamale. He owned both a radio and a portable record player which his friends called in to listen to at all hours, whether he himself was in or not. There were few other signs of affluence, apart from rather more comfortable chairs than one usually found and a double bed with a spring mattress. His main expenditure was probably on food: apart from his breakfast of *ẹkọ* and beancakes he ate most of his meals in chop bars.[9] He usually ate 20p worth of guineafowl and stew before setting off for the markets, and his normal evening meal consisted of a leg of fowl, a portion of rice, two fried eggs, and salad, costing altogether about 50p. He ate this at the chop bar run by an old colonial-trained cook where the lorries unloaded, one of the best eating places in Tamale. In the evening he would go out with some of the younger and more sophisticated Yoruba to the films: he was especially fond of Italian westerns. Alternative entertainment could be found at the dances at the Ghana Legion or the Cafe de France which took place several times a week,[10] where he sometimes arranged to meet up with one of his girlfriends. His wife, he maintained, was 'not jealous'. He had several close male friends, also with middle school education, and with a similar range of interests.

Thus although Ahmadu was not independent, he had come to a satisfactory working relationship with his brother which was to their mutual benefit. Unlike most of the traders in Tamale they had been doing relatively well since 1966 when Ahmadu was able to join his brother in full-time trade. Their success was based on their ability to exploit the market both in Tamale and the rural areas and to combine trade with tailoring. Relationships between the two brothers remained amicable in a household presided over by their mother. Eventually, when Ahmadu had a family of his own, they might have decided to separate, but for the time being their cooperation was continuing to be profitable. The problems of younger traders struggling to become established on their own without this support are well illustrated by the next case.

Rahimi Sule

Rahimi had had to cope with many of the difficulties which Ahmadu had so far managed to avoid. He was a trader from Ilorin in his thirties, though his background was similar to that of many of the Ogbomosho who had come up to Tamale from the south. He had been taken to Kumasi initially to join a father's sister and had later moved to the north to join another father's sister, one of the wealthiest Yoruba women in Tamale. His father had been a yam trader in Ogbomosho and Ilorin, and Rahimi had helped him until his father's death. After this he spent two years as an apprentice fitter, and then came to Ghana to join his aunt who made *adirẹ* cloth in Kumasi. He worked for her for two years, and then spent nine months as a shoeshine boy, during which he saved enough money to start selling bread. His aunt was apparently not able, or not willing, to give him any starting capital. With his savings he apprenticed himself to a potter, but the potter went out of business shortly after.

Rahimi had now lost all his money, but he was able to persuade a Yoruba trader in the market to let him have pens, stationery and sunglasses on credit to sell. Initially he walked around the town to sell: later he sold his goods outside the Central Post Office with the tacit agreement of the postal officials. This arrangement lasted until the arrival of a new postmaster who cleared away all the traders. Later, Rahimi went back to the same site and tried trading again, but he was arrested and had to pay £10 to the police to get his goods back. It was then that his aunt intervened and suggested that trade in Kumasi only seemed to be getting him into trouble. Her senior sister was on a visit from Tamale at the time, and said that he should come and join her instead. He sold what was left of his stock, paid his debts, and with the aid of a loan of £30 from his aunt in Tamale he got a job as a worker in a Lebanese bakery, earning 3/- a day. He found conditions there difficult, and, after an argument with the foreman over whether or not he had arrived late for work, he stopped going. This led to an argument with the aunt who refused to give him chop money, and he was forced to look for another job. After a month at the labour office he had an interview with the local cigarette distributor who gave him a job as a sales boy. At first he was selling on a cycle, and later was sent with a van to sell in the Yendi and Bimbilla areas. By 1967, he had saved £100. Then he had an argument with the area manager which he put down to the fact that 'he was not of the same tribe'. At this point, he left and decided to trade on his own.

Despite the depressed state of the market after the coup, he was able to find a niche for himself. A number of the younger Yoruba traders without market stalls had taken to selling goods from barrows which they placed at strategic points around the town such as outside the market entrance and the lorry parks, or near the big stores on the main street. From these they sold a wide range of small, cheap, manufactured goods, collectively known as *worobo* and Rahimi found that he could fill a need by replenishing their stocks during the course of the day. He also sold to a number of smaller traders in the market, selling them goods in dozens. Most of his sales were on credit, with payment being made at the end of the month or when the customer had the necessary cash. Rahimi used to buy once a month in the south, and he thinks that he made £20 on his first load of goods. By 1969 he was taking several hundred pounds with him at a time. He was considering buying a small motor bike as with that he would be able to reach some of the traders in the villages around Tamale who bought goods from him. He always bought from the same Indians and Lebanese in Kumasi, and said that at times they had offered to give him goods on credit. They had confidence in him as they had seen his orders grow each month since he started trade. He said that he disliked buying on credit, however, as he thought that he would run into problems 'if the market grew cool'. This was probably a rational attitude in the light of his own difficulties in getting back the money he was owed by credit customers. Most of his growing difficulties in 1969 stemmed from this. He had built up a business by exploiting a particular niche in the market in a period of recession, but as the recession deepened he found the traders to whom he usually sold increasingly unwilling to pay, as their own customers defaulted in increasing numbers. One customer owed him NC96 and had been unable to pay, so he had given Rahimi his tape recorder instead. This was a large machine and Rahimi would have been able to sell it at a good price had it been working. However, it was not, and so he had taken it to Kumasi for repairs. The parts were difficult to get hold of, and so for several weeks he had been anxiously telephoning Kumasi to find out what progress had been made. He had also acquired a broken camera for the same reason.

There were other expenses. His Kotokoli girlfriend had become pregnant, and after the baby was born the question of the naming ceremony arose. Rahimi's aunt was putting pressure on him to have nothing to do with the child, but Rahimi felt that he ought at least to hold a naming ceremony. But for the attitude of the aunt, he said he would have married the girl. He was able to name the child with the help of his Ogbomosho friends who lived in the same house. They bought a goat, arranged for mallams to preside over the prayers,[11] and helped him with the preparation of the food. He also felt obliged to make frequent visits to the girl's parents, giving them a cedi or so as a gift every time he went.

Unlike Ahmadu, therefore, Rahimi had no senior relatives with whom he could work or who were willing to provide him with capital. He eventually became established with the money he had been able to save working as a cigarette salesman, and had been able to establish a niche for himself in difficult market conditions. Apart from mobility, the only other strategy available to him to build up his clientele was credit, and this proved risky for a trader with limited experience and limited resources. On top of all this came the expense of his girlfriend's pregnancy. Underlying his difficulties was his alienation from the only member of his family in Tamale with the means to help him.

Isaac Ogundiran

Isaac Ogundiran of Ile Oke, Ogbomosho, by contrast, was one of the most conspicuous members of the Yoruba community in Tamale. He was the UAC cycle dealer in Tamale, and he operated from a store on the main street, opposite the market. He was also a prominent member of the First Baptist Church, the largest of the three Yoruba churches in the town. To the church members (which included the majority of the Igboho and Ogbomosho Christians) he was known as *Alaga* because of his chairmanship of the church committee.[12]

Isaac had arrived in Tamale in 1937, after completing primary school in Ogbomosho. Few of his contemporaries had formal education, and this increased his prominence. Before and during his schooling, he had been

helping to weave Yoruba cloth in his home compound. He was taken to Ghana
by Joseph Ade, the son of his father's senior brother, who had already taken
Luke with him some six years previously. They went along the coast with cloth
from Ilorin and Abeokuta. Until 1953, he worked with Ade, who arranged his
marriage in 1950. During this time the trade in Yoruba cloth continued, with
Isaac coming back to Nigeria to buy between £300 and £600 of cloth at a time.
Most of it was bought in Okeho where he would take a sample of the patterns
required, wait three or four weeks until the cloth was completed, and then take
it back to Ghana. In Ghana, they made daily trips to Savelugu and the other
markets around Tamale. During the war, they had continued to take cloth to
Ghana using bicycles.[13]

On his retirement to Nigeria, Ade left Isaac with substantial capital and
passbooks for the UAC and CFAO stores in Tamale. Isaac began to trade in
provisions and cloth between Kumasi, Tamale and Upper Volta with the help
of his junior brother, John, who came over from Nigeria in 1950. The travelling stopped after Ghanaian independence: Isaac was involved in a serious
lorry accident in which he lost the lower part of his right leg. With an artificial
leg and with undiminished enthusiasm, he put down a deposit of £700 with the
UAC to open the cycle shop in Tamale. In the 1960s, when the supplies of cycles
became erratic, he started to deal in provisions as well.

By this time, business was going less well. After 1961 imported goods
became more difficult to get, and Isaac suffered two further setbacks. First, he
sent £500 into Togo to buy goods to bring back to Ghana, but his goods, like
Lasisi's, were confiscated at the border and he lost the money. Then there was
the affair of the younger brother who had become a daily contribution collector, and who ran off with the funds, leaving Isaac to pay off the creditors and
keep the matter out of the hands of the police. John spent some time in
Ogbomosho until the affair had quietened down and then returned to Tamale.
He found a job working for a Lebanese merchant as a shop assistant while Isaac
relied on the help of his junior half brother. One heard a lot of criticism of Isaac
for letting John continue to work in this way and for not providing him with the
capital to start on his own, but after what had happened the relations between
the two were still strained. Despite these losses, Isaac maintained the appearance of prosperity with the aid of his wife, one of the wealthiest of all the
Yoruba women in the town. The two of them pooled their money to an unusual
extent. Together they bought a house on the road to the cemetery, and Isaac
started a rice farm after the 1966 coup.

In understanding Ogundiran's career and his position in the Yoruba community one has also to consider his relationship with his older relative, Luke.
According to informants, there was little love lost between the two. It was
commonly said that much of Isaac's energy went into trying to compensate for
Luke's age and seniority with achievements in other fields. Ogundiran had had
schooling, and while his primary education was derided by the younger and

more sophisticated members of the Baptist Church, many of whom were at secondary school, he still had a higher level of literacy than any of his peers. Luke could only read and write a little Yoruba but nothing else. While Luke's social life revolved around the Yoruba elders and the Dagomba community in Tamale, to which he was linked through a Dagomba wife, Ogundiran mixed with the civil servants and the literate businessmen in the town. His closest friends were Solomon Ayoola, the CFAO cloth dealer, also from Ogbomosho, and J.A. Oladokun, the secretary of the Igboho Parapo, who worked as a storekeeper with the Workers Brigade. Luke had five wives, while Isaac had only one. Luke belonged to the Ogboni lodge in Tamale: Isaac joined the Loyal Order of Oddfellows, a quasi-masonic lodge with a mainly educated, élite membership.[14] While Luke was a leading figure in the Ogbomosho *Parapo*, Isaac became a leading figure in the First Baptist Church. As there was no regular pastor, he effectively ran it, doing the major part of the preaching himself and deciding the main aspects of church policy with the help of a compliant committee. He maintained this position with considerable rhetorical ability in the pulpit. People who crossed swords with Alaga found themselves the object of oblique references the following Sunday, the meanings of which were easily grasped by the close-knit congregation.

What is important from our point of view is not Isaac's wealth – he was a good deal less wealthy than Luke, for instance – but his style of life and his methods of business. He had much in common with Ayoola. Both of them were educated and yet had gone into commerce. They operated from proper stores by the street rather than from corrugated iron stalls in the market. This was the type of intermediate commerce to which many of the younger Yoruba traders aspired, symbolised by a shop on the main street, an account with one of the large firms, and a telephone. Both men had wide-ranging friendship networks with others in the town who had a similar educational and occupational background. Indeed, Isaac often seemed to be using his education, his style of trade and his contacts with the educated Ghanaians in the town to increase his standing in the Yoruba community, particularly in relation to Luke. Isaac was regarded, for all his faults, as a man with *ilaju* – understanding of the outside world[15] – and as a useful intermediary between the Yoruba migrants and the authorities, both in Tamale and further afield. But his style of life, and his membership of the Oddfellows, involved him in expenses beyond his means in the difficult trading conditions of the 1960s, and in reality he was only able to maintain the image of the prosperous middle-level trader with the help of an enterprising and wealthy wife.[16]

Caleb Olawole

Caleb had, in common with Isaac, a leading position in the Yoruba Christian community in Tamale, but there the similarity ended. Caleb was about sixty years of age in 1969. He had come to Ghana first in 1947, at the suggestion of one of the Igboho migrants from Ile Balogun, his father's sister's son. Before this, he had been a farmer and then a labourer in Epe, near Lagos. He had married with his savings and was able to gather together £16 to trade in Ghana. He travelled to Ghana on foot, taking woven cloth from Igboho to sell. Until 1964 he had been going out to the rural markets, but after this he stayed in Tamale.

A significant feature of Caleb's trading career was the frequent changes he had made in his selling lines over the years. He had started off selling cloth for a few months, and then moved into the trade in foodstuffs between Tamale and the south. This also did not pay, and so he went back to selling cloth. Finally, after trying beads and jewellery for a time, he ended up with a tiny stock of singlets and children's clothes. In 1969 he was one of the poorest Igboho traders in Tamale, though he said that business had been better before the coup. Unusually he did the bulk of his buying in Tamale itself, from the Lebanese stores and from the local branch of Chellerams, where his son worked. At times friends would buy some goods for him in the south, but he never had the money to go for himself. Some of his friends were able to let him have goods on credit, and they did not press him for repayment when he was in difficulties. He bought small amounts of stock every three or five days, all the sources of supply being within a few minutes walk of the market.

If Caleb had never been successful as a trader, he was, all the same, well known and respected in the Yoruba community as an elder in the Second Baptist Church. His whole life revolved around this. He had been converted to Christianity in his teens by a senior brother and had learned to read and write while still in Igboho through bible classes. He had been one of the founders of the Second Baptist Church in Tamale, and he was one of the most frequent preachers there.[17] Most of the other members of the church were also poor. The leader was a tailor whose trading had failed twice. The secretary was a part-time driver, and the choirmaster was a teacher in the small school attached to the church. The only noticeably wealthy member of the church was the storekeeper from the large army barracks on the Bolgatanga Road. The tone of the two Baptist churches differed markedly. The Second Church congregation was much smaller than that of the First Church, and dress was less ostentatious. The first sermon I heard there was, appropriately, on the theme of the poor expecting their reward in the kingdom of heaven.

Caleb and his friends found a degree of solace in their church membership while they struggled to make ends meet in their every-day lives. He was helped by his son, a middle-school graduate who worked in the Tamale branch of Chellerams, but who could only provide limited assistance on his small salary. Caleb's wife was also trading on a small scale. He had never been able to afford a trip back to Igboho in twenty-two years, but he had not lost contact with home. The two youngest of his seven children were in Igboho with his father's junior brother.

Unlike Isaac Ogundiran, therefore, who came from a wealthy family and who, for at least part of his career, had been relatively successful, Caleb had only managed to muster limited capital at the start of his trading career, and his business had never got off the ground, despite frequent changes of selling line. Lacking the capital either to buy in bulk from the stores in Tamale or from the south, he was unable to buy cheaply and his profit margins were low. Thus there appeared to be no way out of his financial difficulties. He could expect only limited support from his wife and son and in the final analysis it was probably only the friendships which he had built up within his church which prevented him from returning to Nigeria to farm.

WOMEN IN TRADE

So far, little has been said about Yoruba women in Tamale, despite the fact that they were the majority of the Yoruba traders. This is not simply sexist bias in the analysis, but reflects the fact that in many aspects of migration and trade women really did have a subordinate role. As far as migration was concerned, very few women went to Ghana on their own initiative: most were taken there by their husbands or senior relatives. The fact that the age of marriage was generally higher for men than for women meant that while many men in their twenties and even early thirties could move around as single individuals, the women could not. This had implications for the accumulation of trading capital as well. While some men had the opportunity to build up their trading capital for several years before their domestic responsibilities multiplied, this was rarely true for women. They were dependent on their husbands or senior relatives for capital, and often in the early stages of trade they had to cope with pregnancy and young children, which not only consumed their time and energy, but also involved spending money which might otherwise have been ploughed back into business. A few Yoruba women in Tamale became wealthy despite this, though trading opportunities were more limited than for their counterparts in Kumasi and Accra, and a small élite group had even managed to invest in property. Others, like Limata below, ended up living and trading on their own, after divorce or at the death of their husbands, and these women were particularly isolated. The subordinate role of women extended to the formal associational structure of the Yoruba community. The town *parapo* and the churches had their women's associations, but they were fewer in number and less highly organised than those of the men, and they played less part in formal decision-making. They were probably less important for the women in the formation of their friendship networks than they were for their husbands: if men drew most of their closest friends from the same church association or home town *parapo*, the women relied more on informal networks of kin and friends in the neighbouring houses, and the friendship networks often included members of different ethnic groups. For some of the more isolated women, trading on their own, such as Limata, these networks could be

Plate 4.2: A woman trader from Ogbomosho and her daughter.

extremely important as a source of support. Her career and lifestyle make an interesting contrast with that of Raliatu, one of the most successful of all the Yoruba women traders in Tamale.

Raliatu Sani

In 1969, Raliatu was in her mid-thirties: she had been married to Alhaji Sani, one the Ile Isale Alagbede traders from Ogbomosho, for sixteen years, and had five children. Before her marriage, she had been trading with her mother in Onitsha. Her success in Ghana may have had something to do with this early training in one of the most competitive of all West African markets. She was taken to Ghana by her husband who gave her £13 to start trading, and by 1969 she was established as one of the leading Yoruba women traders in Tamale, and was one of the ones who had managed to acquire a house. The other Yoruba landladies included Rafatu, the daughter of Alhaji Karimu the Yoruba chief, and thus, like Raliatu, connected to the richest Yoruba family in Tamale; Ogundiran's wife Mary; Rahimi's aunt from Ilorin; and Alhajiya Dogo, the wife of a wealthy Ogbomosho fishnet seller. Thus, three of the four were from Ogbomosho, and of these Raliatu and Rafatu were both the youngest and the wealthiest. Raliatu's house, completed early in 1969, probably cost at least NC6,000. I only found out about her housewarming party after the event as it took place soon after I arrived in Tamale, but by all accounts it was a lavish affair. Both women had wealthy relatives. Although Rafatu's husband was relatively poor, she had been able to start trade with a loan from her father, and to get passbooks for the Tamale stores through her brother. Raliatu's UAC passbook had come from her husband, and she used to buy most of the goods that she obtained in Tamale. Both women dealt in provisions, both wholesale and retail, and both had large stalls in the market unlike many of the women traders who had to make do with a makeshift table outside their houses or in front of their husbands' market stalls.

The two women also shared a mixed reputation within the Yoruba community. There was admiration for their wealth, but the means by which they might have acquired it were popular subjects of gossip and speculation. The usual explanations were in terms of ritual and sex. There were a large number of ritual experts in Tamale who could be consulted about financial problems, and even Ogundiran had been heard to talk of Raliatu's 'spiritual powers'. The alternative rumours told of late-night and early morning visits to the managers and storekeepers in return for reduced prices and access to goods in scarce supply. As one informant acidly put it: 'They are better known to the managers than to their husbands.' They were also said to keep out of trouble with the police and customs officials in the same way. Underlying these suggestions were the double standards of sexual morality common throughout West African society. Whereas most men regarded a varied sex life as normal and desirable, they were unwilling to grant the same autonomy to the women. How much substance there was to the rumours about Rafatu and Raliatu was unclear. Rafatu was separated from her husband, but Raliatu was still living with Alhaji Sani, apparently on the best of terms.

Whatever the truth of the matter, there is no doubt that to have accumulated enough money to have built a house from starting capital of £13, Raliatu must have been an extremely shrewd trader, as well as having the support of a wealthy husband. Her main selling line was provisions. She had a passbook and said she bought twice a month in Tamale, about NC200 on each occasion. In addition she was one of the few Yoruba women in Tamale who made regular trips to the south on her own account, taking NC400 each time she went. She also took orders for a number of the other Ogbomosho women who could not afford to go themselves, and this helped pay for her transport and increase her bargaining power with the Kumasi traders. According to her, her turnover was probably between NC800 and 1200 a month.[18] However, it is very likely that her own account was not the whole story. First, when goods were short in the 1960s, anyone with privileged access to them would be able to increase their profit margins, and Raliatu's good relations with the storekeepers were undoubtedly important. Second, she could spot other trading opportunities as well. At one point, she was a frequent visitor to the office of Bosco, a salesman with the State Distilleries. This fact caused more rumours to circulate, as Bosco himself had a reputation as a womaniser. He was from Offa and, in addition to having two wives, he had also had a child by a girl from Ogbomosho who sold cigarettes outside the Rivoli cinema. He was also a tenant in one of the houses belonging to Raliatu's husband's close friend, Alhaji Lasisi of Ile Olowo. Despite rumours that Raliatu had been prepared to leave her husband for Bosco, had she not been warned off by senior relatives while on a trip to Nigeria, the relationship could also have been simply economic. Bosco's firm used to write off a number of bottles each month for breakage during transit, and Raliatu probably disposed of the surplus bottles in the market on his behalf.

Her success was primarily due to ability and effort, but other factors helped. Her husband was wealthy and had junior wives, which lessened her domestic commitments and expenses, making it possible to plough more money back into the business. In addition she was able to participate in what Sudarkasa has called the 'network of fostering' (1973), allowing her to dispense with some of her family responsibilities at an early stage in her marriage, and to obtain help from relatives in her trade later on. She took her younger children to the market, and the older ones were at primary school. The eldest one had gone home at the age of three, and now lived with Raliatu's sister in Lagos. She was helped in her trade by a father's brother's son from Nigeria, and he was able to keep records of credit sales for her, as she was illiterate herself. A final factor was the tolerance among the Ogbomosho migrants of an extremely independent economic role for their wives, a tolerance which drew unfavourable comment from migrants from the other towns, often with specific reference to Raliatu or Rafatu. There was undoubtedly a measure of envy and sour grapes in this: as one Igbetti woman admitted while talking about Raliatu, 'the other women criticise her, but they are the ones suffering while she is enjoying life'.

Limata Aduke

Limata, on the other hand, was completely on her own. She was from Ilorin and lived in Tamale Sabon Gida in a house belonging to the sons of Mustafa Iyanda, where she sold bread and a few provisions. Her husband had been from Ogbomosho but after their divorce and his death several years before, she had not remarried. She first came to Ghana as a girl with her father's sister and they stayed together at Nsawam. From there they used to trade in the Accra area, and the father's sister was wealthy, owning buildings. They sold cloth and provisions. She returned to Ilorin to get married just before the Second World War, and stayed there to have her first child. The child died. While she was expecting her second child she left her husband and came back to Ghana while the husband stayed in Ilorin. The marriage eventually broke up and she joined her father's sister again. This time they settled in Kumasi. They dealt in the same goods as before, and from time to time they came up to Tamale to sell cloth and buy foodstuffs to take back down to the south. Limata married an Ogbomosho man in Kumasi, had two more children, and then divorced him as

well. At this point she came to Tamale to settle. She had a variety of connec-
tions there. Her mother's father had spent some time in Kishi and had married
a Kishi girl. He had also spent some time in Igbetti and, being a Muslim, came
to know Alhaji Raji. Raji was Limata's landlord when she first came to Tamale,
and he sent one of his daughters to stay with her and help her with trade when
she first settled there.

In 1969 Limata's trade was not going at all well. She was several months
behind with the rent for the shop and the single room behind it where she lived,
and Iyanda's sons were getting fed up with the situation. She paid NC4.50 a
month rent, and an additional NC2.00 a month towards the electricity. There
was a single meter in the house and the bill was divided up according to the
number of electric points used by each person. Limata had a fluorescent light
in the shop and formerly she had had another light outside, but she found that
the bulbs were being stolen and had taken it down. She had formerly sold
provisions and had had a passbook with GNTC, but she had run into trouble
with the price control officials and had also found that she had had to bribe the
storekeepers to get any goods at all. So in 1969 she was concentrating on the
sale of bread, together with small amounts of milk and sugar which she bought
from other Yoruba women.

Another problem was her ill-health. She needed treatment, but preferred to
go to the hospital at Damongo, rather than be treated in Tamale. This meant
additional travelling expenses. Her working capital was now dwindling fast.
She had in stock in the middle of 1969 only about NC 13 worth of goods,
including some rather old Ghanaian coffee and bottles of ink, mementos of her
more prosperous days. The items which she was still selling included milk,
sugar, Fanti *kenkey*, cigarettes and bread. There were three types of local
bread, most of which was consumed for breakfast together with dilute tea or
coffee by government workers living in the surrounding houses. 'Sugar bread'
and 'tea bread' were very sweet and were baked by Dagomba women in the
Sabon Gida. 'Butter bread' came from a local Lebanese bakery. For the sugar
and tea bread she was allowed credit by the baker because she was an old
customer: she received 12 loaves for a cedi and sold them at 10p each. For the
Lebanese bread she had a passbook, and, in addition to the profits on the sales,
she received a commission at the end of the month. Her income was in the
region of NC15 to 20 a month, depending on sales.

This meant a long working day. It started at five in the morning when either
she or one of the girls working for her set off to collect the bread from the
Lebanese. The sugar and tea bread were brought by the children of the women
who baked it. Limata had two girls working for her: the daughter of a Gurunsi
nurse who was married to a male nurse from Ilorin, and the daughter of a
Dagomba friend from a nearby village who wanted her daughter to learn how
to trade. Both the girls were 10 years old. They helped with the housework and
food preparation and also ran errands, like going to fetch the kerosene which

Limata sold. This was collected in a two gallon bucket and poured into Star Beer bottles for sale.[19] The customers paid 10p a bottle, but had to bring their own containers. There was a profit of 20p a gallon, depending on the amount spilt during the trip up the road and the care with which it was poured into the bottles. In return for their help, Limata fed the girls, and this cost between 15p and 20p a day, which represented a third of her monthly income.

She tried various other ways of making money, including making sugar candy which she sold for a pesewa a lump to the passing school children. A more ambitious project was when, together with the Gurunsi nurse and an Ogbomosho woman from a neighbouring compound, she tried to bake her own bread. They made over 100 loaves, with ingredients costing NC7.50. However, the oven was too hot and many of them were burned. In addition, the Dagomba woman who had been supplying her with bread previously refused to sell to Limata when she found that she was trying to compete with her. Then Limata had to go back into hospital and there was no further baking.

Social obligations were another constant expense for Limata. Her social network included women from Ilorin, Ogbomosho, Igbetti and Kishi, and she was constantly being called on to help with the preparations for weddings and naming ceremonies involving women in these towns. A wedding not only meant that she would have to spend two days or more away from the shop, helping with the preparations at the bride's house, but that she was expected to contribute a gift, usually of cloth or money, worth two or three cedis.

A final set of problems stemmed from her relations with the others in the house. She felt that the other women were making things difficult for her because of the rent she owed. There was trouble over the use of the oven at the side of the house. The woman who actually owned it was away in Ogbomosho on a visit, and although Limata had mentioned to her before her departure that she wanted to use it, the most senior wife in the house tried to prevent her from doing so. The other bone of contention was the water supply which was very bad. One night early in the rains, Limata got up when the rain started to fall and made sure that all the containers in the house were full. There had been no water in the taps for a couple of days. She overslept the next morning, and got up to find that all the water had been used by the other women in the compound.[20]

Faced with these difficulties, Limata was thinking seriously of retiring to Ilorin. The people there had been telling her to come home for years, as, with the exception of an elder classificatory sister, she was the oldest member of her natal compound. In more prosperous times she had been able to visit Nigeria every two years, staying for a couple of months in Ogbomosho, Ilorin and Kishi before returning to Ghana. Lately however she had not been able to go home at all. Her only remaining savings were NC147 which she had deposited with Ghana Airways some years before towards a trip to Mecca, and she was negotiating with the clerk in the Tamale office to get the money back. She had already tried to get it back through a local mallam who was also a part-time agent for the Hajj, but had only wasted time and effort. By the end of 1969 she had finally collected her money and would probably have left Ghana in any case, had not the exodus occurred.

THE DILEMMAS OF TRADE

The people described in this chapter range from some of the most prosperous Yoruba traders in Tamale – such as Lasisi, Isaac, the Bawa brothers and Raliatu – to some of the most marginal – such as Caleb and Limata, both of whom faced chronic financial problems and were seriously considering returning to Nigeria. Not that the wealthier traders did not experience difficulties of their own. Both Isaac and Lasisi lost considerable sums in their forays into Togo and through the activities of their junior relatives, but at least they had resources on which they could fall back such as houses or, in Isaac's case, an enterprising wife. Only Raliatu and the Bawa brothers had been at all successful since the 1966 coup. Raliatu's ability to accumulate capital must have been helped by her husband's relative wealth, while Ahmadu Bawa's profitable partnership with his brother was in marked contrast to Rahimi's less successful efforts to become established on his own.

Within the constraints created by the Ghanaian economy, therefore, individual traders had variable access to a variety of resources, both economic and social, on which they could rely. But their eventual success or failure depended not only on these constraints and resources but also on the particular trading and investment strategies which they decided to adopt. Three sets of problems appear to be particularly crucial. The first relates to mobilising sufficient capital to enable an enterprise to become viable. 'Sufficient' is of course a relative term. A sum of money which may be sufficient for an unmarried man or a woman with a wealthy husband and no children to become established will not be sufficient for an older migrant who arrives with a wife and children to support. And while a trader might be able to lead a hand-to-mouth existence for a while with limited capital, a sudden misfortune such as a period of illness, a fire in the market or an arrest could almost immediately render the enterprise unviable. Various options were open to the trader whose capital was rapidly diminishing. Assuming that no additional capital or loans were available from relatives or friends, a change of selling line, a change of location from, say, the market to a lorry park, or even a move to another town might be enough to revive the trader's fortunes. These decisions over time resulted in the gradual diffusion of the Yoruba throughout Ghana and into new areas of trade. More radical alternatives were to look for other kinds of work or to return home to Nigeria, probably to farm. If a migrant was more successful in another type of work, he might eventually accumulate enough capital to try his hand at trade once more. If not, he might in any case decide to return to Nigeria.

When and if the enterprise began yielding a steady surplus, a second crucial set of decisions had to be taken over how to use it. For many traders, rising incomes were gradually absorbed in higher costs of living as their families grew, as their children went to school and married, and as their assistants required trading capital of their own. But assuming that there was a surplus, a variety of options were available, ranging from building a house in Ghana or Nigeria or starting a rice farm, to going to Mecca or (for men) marrying more wives. The major options will be examined in more detail in the next chapter, but the question here is what effect these decisions had on income and viability. Building a house in Tamale could be a safe and lucrative investment: conspicuous consumption or building a house in the home town in Nigeria yielded less immediate benefits, whatever their long-term implications. Occasionally, an investment decision could involve such a substantial drain on the trader's resources that it could seriously undermine the trading enterprise as well.

The final crucial decision was when to return to Nigeria, if at all. Migrants in many parts of the world say they intend to return home, but seldom do so (Plotnicov, 1967). The Yoruba in Ghana usually meant it. Apart from the results of infant mortality or misfortunes such as road accidents, there were few deaths among the Yoruba in Tamale. Most of the elderly migrants died at home, whether or not they had been successful in Ghana. Unsuccessful migrants often returned home quickly, though a few like Caleb clung on in Ghana for years with the help of friends. Successful migrants looked forward to returning home to retire in a house built by their remittances from Ghana and to a position of seniority or a chiefship title. However, the sense of shame at returning empty-handed which seems to have been a significant factor in the permanent exile of so many Hausa or Mossi (Schildkrout, 1978; Olofson, 1974) does not seem to have been so acutely felt by the Yoruba. Sometimes it was actually relatives in Nigeria who took the initiative, urging migrants like Limata who had fallen on hard times to return home.

SUCCESS AND FAILURE IN TRADE

As we have seen in the previous chapter, the Yoruba traders, both men and women, were constantly being faced with decisions. In the case of the less wealthy traders, the options available within trade were usually limited: the main decision to be made was very often whether to remain in trade at all, try another job or return to Nigeria. For the wealthy traders, there was the question of how to invest a trading surplus most profitably. Some of the decisions, like Lasisi's rice farm, could be very successful, while others, like his (or his son's) decision to enter the smuggling trade could be expensive failures. But so far we have seen only a small sample of case studies. This chapter therefore will look more systematically at the 'opportunity structure' within which the Yoruba traders in Tamale worked, and the kinds of options which were available to them at each stage of their careers.

ACQUIRING CAPITAL

For the men there were two main sources of capital: gifts from senior relatives, or savings acquired from previous work. The sources and amounts of trading capital of the men from each of the three towns whom we interviewed are shown in Tables 5.1–5.3. There are small differences between the groups. In general the Igbetti men started with less capital than men from the other towns, while the Igbetti and Igboho men were more reliant on their own savings as their major source of capital than the men from Ogbomosho. The median starting capital rose from £20 in the pre-war period to £75 in the 1960s, but in real terms the increase was minimal.

Table 5.1: Principal sources of starting capital of Yoruba men trading independently in Northern Ghana, 1969, by town of origin.

Source	Ogbomosho		Igboho		Igbetti		Total	
	no.	%	no.	%	no.	%	no.	%
Relatives	19	47.5	15	48.4	30	51.7	64	49.6
Savings	11	27.5	13	41.9	23	39.7	47	36.4
Loans	0	0.0	1	3.2	2	3.4	3	2.3
Inheritance	4	10.0	2	6.5	1	1.7	7	5.4
Friends	2	5.0	0	0.0	2	3.4	4	3.1
Other	4	10.0	0	0.0	0	0.0	4	3.1
Totals	40	100.0	31	100.0	58	100.0	129	100.0

Table 5.2: Size of starting capital of Yoruba men trading independently in Northern Ghana, 1969, by year of starting independent trade.

Capital (£)	Pre-1939	1940–50	1951–60	1961–69
0–10	3	1	2	1
11–25	3	14	10	3
25–50	1	3	12	8
51–100	2	2	5	13
101–250	1	2	1	6
251–500	0	0	1	3
500–1,000	0	0	2	1
Over 1,000	0	0	0	2
Total	10	22	33	37

Some of the largest amounts of starting capital were acquired on the death or retirement of a senior relative. On retirement to Nigeria a trader usually took enough money to satisfy his immediate needs such as starting a farm, building a house or setting up in trade on a small scale.[1] The rest of his assets were usually divided between the junior relatives remaining in Ghana. The death of a trader in Ghana usually resulted in the transfer of all his assets to other close relatives there. There were three recent cases on my arrival in Tamale. Lasisi had taken over his brother's house and market stall as he was his only full sibling in Ghana and there were no adult children. The brother's wives married other Ile Olowo men in Tamale, Damongo and Igbetti. After Mustafa Iyanda's death, his sons took over the houses jointly, while the stall in the market, together with £800 worth of stock, went to his fifth son, who had been working most closely with him before his death. The more senior sons had their own stalls or other jobs already. However, the brothers still regarded themselves as

Table 5.3: Size of starting capital of Yoruba men trading independently in Northern Ghana, 1969, by town of origin.

Capital (£)	Ogbomosho		Igboho		Igbetti		Total	
	no.	%	no.	%	no.	%	no.	%
0–10	0	0.0	6	10.3	1	3.2	7	5.4
11–25	8	20.0	10	17.2	12	38.7	30	23.3
26–50	7	17.5	10	17.2	7	22.6	24	18.6
51–100	7	17.5	10	17.2	5	16.1	22	17.1
101–250	2	5.0	8	13.8	0	0.0	10	7.8
251–500	1	2.5	3	5.2	0	0.0	4	3.1
501–1,000	3	7.5	0	0.0	0	0.0	3	2.3
Over 1,000	1	2.5	1	1.7	0	0.0	2	1.6
Not known	11	27.5	10	17.2	6	19.4	27	20.9
Totals	40	100.0	58	100.0	31	100.0	129	100.0

working together, and they carried out a joint stock-taking every month and pooled the rent from their father's houses. Iyanda's wives returned to Ogbomosho and did not remarry. Iyanda had a brother in Tamale, but he received nothing, all the assets going to Iyanda's own sons. In a third case, after the death of another Igbetti migrant, his two eldest sons took over the business. The older one had been at secondary school, while the second had been helping his father in the market. In this case, as in that of Iyanda's fifth son, the result was a well-educated trader established in the market with substantial starting capital.

A direct gift or inheritance from a senior relative was not the only source of starting capital. A further source which was talked about little but which must have been a factor in the success of many traders was money that they had been able to pocket while working for senior relatives. It was accepted by many of the senior traders that some money did go into the pockets of their young assistants, though a few tried to stop it by searching their pockets at the end of each day. Provided that they could avoid being caught with the money actually on them, the assistants found this an easy source of income, in the absence of fixed prices and accurate written accounts. Among the younger Yoruba, the exploits of assistants in ripping off their elders were the subject of gossip and myth-making. It was even said that some of them in Kumasi, where the wealthiest Yoruba traders operated, had made enough to buy themselves taxis. But, perhaps more factual, one of my assistants said that he had been able to rent a room and furnish it out of the earnings from buying goods for his mother: he and his friends used it as a place to relax, imbibe cold drinks and listen to music in their spare time.

Most of the Yoruba in Ghana had had some experience of trade at some point during their careers, either through their own trade or working for senior relatives. For Yoruba children, learning to trade was a regular part of socialis-ation:[2] trade was one of the main themes of children's games, and even a comparatively young child could be useful in the market, either carrying messages or sweeping out the stall in the mornings. Older children were regularly sent off round the town with trays of goods for sale on their heads, and they became used to the responsibility of handling small amounts of money. Some of the teenagers working for wealthy traders regularly travelled to the south with several hundred pounds in cash to buy goods. Initially they would be sent with friends of their parents, but later they would be allowed to go on their own, and were sometimes able to make a good deal of pocket money out of the trip. Other children were taken or sent to the rural markets to help out with the transport and to keep an eye on the stall while the owner was absent. The children of successful traders were well grounded in trading techniques by the time they reached adulthood. Prices from the wholesale suppliers were not fixed, and it was easy for assistants who knew the normal range of prices to say that they had had to pay above the actual price, and to pocket the difference. With some assistants handling more than 1,000 cedis worth of goods at a time, considerable profits could be made. It was clearly in the assistants' interests to be able to start their own trade with as much capital as possible, even if their employers resented it. In general, the master–assistant relationship appears to have become more exploitative in the post-war period with the fragmentation of the cloth trading groups. This is in contrast to the more relaxed relationship between traders more equal in age before the Second World War. Some of those who were assistants in the later period said that the chop money their employers used to give them was nowhere near enough, and they would have gone hungry if they had not been able to make something on the side.

Credit from suppliers does not seem to have been an important factor in establishing Yoruba traders in Ghana, in striking contrast with the situation elsewhere in West Africa.[3] Most Yoruba traders said that they preferred to buy with cash rather than on credit, even though they had been offered credit by wholesalers. Some said that wholesalers would only offer goods on credit which they were finding it difficult to sell. In the 1960s, goods which were really in demand (e.g. smuggled goods) were never sold on credit and the supplier was in a strong position. Among the men, only traders who were really hard up like Caleb made extensive use of suppliers' credit. Even the passbook holders had ceased to be credit customers, as usually their deposits with the firms were worth more than the goods they were advanced. They were in fact giving the large corporations a substantial interest-free loan.

Loans within the Yoruba community were more common, and many Yoruba traders were able to secure loans from close relatives on top of their starting capital, some of which were never repaid. Lasisi was careful to say that some of his junior relatives had been given loans rather than gifts, but even after they had become established they had not paid him back: after so many years the matter had been dropped.

Apart from providing capital, a senior relative could help a young trader in other ways – by providing him with a stall in the market, with rent-free

Table 5.4: Main sources of starting capital of Yoruba women trading in Tamale, 1969, by town of origin.

	Igboho (n=32)		Ogbomosho (n=45)		Igbetti (n=63)		Total (n=140)	
	no.	%	no.	%	no.	%	no.	%
Husband/father-in-law	25	78.1	42	93.3	36	57.1	103	73.6
Own relatives	13	40.6	16	35.5	8	12.7	37	26.4
Loans/credit	0	0.0	4	8.9	1	1.6	5	3.6
Own savings	5	15.6	0	0.0	23	36.5	28	20.0
Trading with husband	0	0.0	0	0.0	2	3.2	2	1.4

Note: More than one response per trader has been tabulated.

Table 5.5: Size of starting capital of Yoruba women trading in Northern Ghana, 1969, by town of origin.

Capital (£)	Ogbomosho		Igboho		Igbetti		Total	
	no.	%	no.	%	no.	%	no.	%
0–10	17	36.2	49	62.0	20	33.3	86	46.2
11–15	13	27.7	14	17.7	14	23.3	41	22.0
26–50	6	12.8	8	10.1	15	25.0	29	15.6
51–100	3	6.4	0	0.0	4	6.7	7	3.8
100–250	5	10.6	0	0.0	4	6.7	9	4.8
251–500	1	2.1	0	0.0	0	0.0	1	0.5
501–1,000	1	2.1	0	0.0	0	0.0	1	0.5
Not known	1	2.1	8	10.1	3	5.0	12	6.5
Totals	47	100.0	79	100.0	60	100.0	186	100.0

accommodation in his house, with capital for his wife, or with short-term loans to enable a trip to the south.

In the case of a woman trader, the main source of capital was her husband who normally gave her capital around the time of their marriage (Table 5.4). The majority of women received money only from their husband or his father on marriage, and the percentage seems to have been higher in Ogbomosho than in the other two towns. The amount of capital (Table 5.5) varied with the means of the husband, but was generally smaller than that of the men, reflecting their greater dependency. There is a striking difference between the towns in the amount of experience women had in trade prior to their marriages (Table 5.6). Only a minority of the women from Igbetti had been traders before marriage, compared with the vast majority of the women from Ogbomosho. The Ogbomosho women in Tamale claimed that they had taught the other women to trade, and many of them had experience of trade in the large markets of Kumasi, Accra and northern Nigeria. Most of the wealthy Yoruba women in Tamale were from Ogbomosho. In contrast, some of the Igbetti women said that they had only started to trade when the local women, hearing that they were 'Lagosians', came to buy from them. There were other possible sources of capital. Many women had been trading with other relatives before marriage, and had received substantial gifts in the form of cloth, jewellery or money. Some were able to secure loans, passbooks or guarantees of credit from their husbands or parents to increase their turnover. Some husbands bought goods for their wives on their own trips to the south, or sold them goods on credit from their own stock.

The main point about trading capital therefore was that it was generated almost entirely within the Yoruba community. Initial capital for both men and women usually came from a relative or spouse, and was often substantial. Even if it was not, many traders had the training and experience to make the best use

Table 5.6: Occupations of Yoruba women trading in Tamale, 1969, prior to marriage.

Occupation	Igboho		Ogbomosho		Igbetti		Total	
	no.	%	no.	%	no.	%	no.	%
Farming	1	4.0	0	0.0	6	9.5	7	5.0
Housegirl	5	15.6	1	2.2	20	31.7	26	18.6
Trade	14	46.9	41	91.1	22	34.9	77	55.0
Crafts	12	37.5	3	6.7	15	23.8	30	21.4
Totals	32	100.0	45	100.0	63	100.0	140	100.0

of it, and could augment it with small loans and other help from friends and relatives. Thus with good luck and by restricting expenditure, the trader would be able gradually to accumulate capital. The adult male migrant, on the other hand, without prior experience, was in a more difficult position. He would have a network of friends to advise him, but would have to learn how to trade while risking his own capital. Many traders in this position sooner or later were forced to turn to other occupations. Some younger traders with more sophisticated tastes were unable to restrict their expenditure for long without spending their capital. I came across one case in which the junior brother was given three lots of capital before his brother suggested that he might try another type of work, but this was unusual: many traders only had the one chance. If a trader had been given capital by senior relatives and had lost it, there would be a family meeting to decide what to do. If the relatives decided that he had been unlucky, and if they could afford it, they might give him another chance. If they decided that he had been spending too much on himself, they would probably give him no further help in trade, but would suggest another job or send him back to Nigeria.

Other ways of accumulating capital were available. Many of the traders made use of rotating credit associations (*esusu*) or daily contribution collectors (*alajo*) to save. In the *esusu* a group of migrants contributed a regular sum, and after each round of payments, the entire amount collected could be given to a single contributor. The payments continued until each contributor had received a lump sum.[4] *Esusu* often operated within the church *egbẹ* and town *parapọ*, and a trader who was just starting would save as much as possible. Payments could amount to NC150 or more. Others preferred to save with the daily contribution collectors, and a few Yoruba had made this their main work. They collected regular contributions from their clients and, in return for looking after the money, kept the first round of contributions each month.[5] Obviously the safety of the money depended on the honesty of the individual running the operation. There had been cases of default, but in Tamale the longest established collector was the secretary of the Ogbomosho Muslim *parapọ* who combined the collection with the work of the association. The system was convenient for the traders. The collector came round to their stalls each day, and the entire amount that they had invested could be withdrawn on demand. These institutions were preferred by the Yoruba to the post office and the savings banks. Service in these was very slow, and the interest received was not considered worth the time expended. If anything, the use of the banks by the Yoruba had decreased over time. In the early days of trade, when Ghana and Nigeria had used the same currency, the banks had been useful for transferring money to Nigeria to buy cloth, but with the imposition of exchange controls it became impossible. Some traders also said that they were afraid that bank accounts would be used by the tax officials for income tax assessment. A few Yoruba still used bank accounts for specific purposes, such as building a house or starting a farm, but for most of the Yoruba the activities of the banks were peripheral.

A final source of loans were the Yoruba associations in Tamale. The Igbetti Muslim *parapo* in Tamale was collecting money to rebuild the central mosque in the home town. The money they had already collected was lent out to the members in sums of NC100 at the start of each month. The traders could use the money for the month, but had to give it back at the end with 5 per cent interest added. Each trader normally retained the use of the money for three consecutive months before handing it over to another member of the association. In this way, over the course of time, most of the members seemed to have had access to it. The results were impressive: the fund had increased from a few hundred pounds in 1966 to over NC6000 in 1969.

SALES LINES

After acquiring capital the next decision faced by the Yoruba trader was what to sell. Most of the Yoruba traders in Ghana sold a relatively restricted range of goods: provisions, *worobo*, cloth, clothes, shoes and cycle parts, each of which had its own requirements in terms of starting capital and methods of trade (Table 5.7). The most important of these were provisions which included tinned food, matches, soap, candles, batteries, insect spray, toilet paper and thread for tying hair. Provisions were sold by 15 per cent of the men, who usually sold them wholesale, and by nearly all the Yoruba women, who usually sold them retail. Most women also stocked a few packets of cigarettes of different brands and a few 'native medicines' such as antimony (*tiro*), sulphur and potash (*kaun*).[6] The provisions came from wholesale firms in Tamale and the south, while the native medicines came from Hausa traders in Tamale or Egba women in Kumasi.

Only a couple of Yoruba traders in Tamale still sold Yoruba woven cloth in 1969, though several others sold *adire* made in Ghana. With the decline in the woven cloth trade, many of the men had turned to the sale of other types of cloth. By 1969, most cheaper types of cotton cloth were produced in Ghana including bafts, shirting and wax prints. The main sources were the large firms

Table 5.7: Goods dealt in by Yoruba men trading in Northern Ghana, 1969.

	Ogbomosho (n=44)		Igboho (n=64)		Igbetti (n=40)		Total (n=148)	
	no.	%	no.	%	no.	%	no.	%
Provisions	7	15.9	12	18.8	3	7.5	22	14.9
Worobo	13	29.5	12	18.8	18	45.0	43	29.1
Cloth (European)	11	25.0	24	37.5	10	25.0	35	23.6
Cloth (Nigerian)	4	9.1	2	3.1	2	5.0	8	5.4
Clothes	7	15.9	8	12.5	11	27.5	26	17.6
Shoes	8	18.2	4	6.3	11	27.5	23	15.5
Cycle parts	2	4.5	7	10.9	7	17.5	16	10.8
Fishnets	3	6.8	0	0.0	1	2.5	4	2.7
Foodstuffs	1	2.3	3	4.7	2	5.0	6	4.1
Drugs	0	0.0	4	6.3	1	2.5	5	3.4
Other	2	4.5	7	10.9	0	0.0	9	6.1

Note: More than one response per trader has been tabulated.

which still imported a small amount of cloth, but it was nearly double the price of the local fabrics. However, most of the Ghanaians regarded imported cloth as being of better quality, and they were prepared to pay more for it, so a lot of it was smuggled into the country. Also smuggled in were more expensive types of lace, suitings, and synthetic fabrics. The Yoruba men usually bought and sold cloth in 12 yard pieces, selling mainly to Ghanaian women traders who retailed them in shorter lengths.

Along with provisions and cloth, the other most important category of goods dealt in by the Yoruba traders was *worobo*. The source of all of these were the Indians and Lebanese in the south, and many *worobo* traders sold them together with clothes, underwear and cosmetics from the same sources. Some clothes were also smuggled in, such as the popular knitted tee shirts from *ile Ferensi* ('French' territory).

Most of the shoes sold in Tamale market were also sold by Yoruba. In earlier years, several of the Yoruba migrants had been shoemakers, but when the market was flooded with manufactured shoes they had turned to shoe repairs or trade. The main sources of shoes in Tamale were GNTC and Bata.

A few of the Yoruba men sold drugs and cosmetics. The drugs ranged from the usual patent medicines for toothache, headaches, piles and diarrhoea, etc., to antibiotics and birth control pills. The sale of prescription drugs was technically illegal, but widespread. Two of the firms dealing in cosmetics and non-prescription drugs, Patterson Zocchonis and A.J. Seward, had Yoruba agents in the market who sold wholesale to the other traders.

Cycle parts were one of the most stable selling lines, and some of the traders had been dealing in them for nearly thirty years. The original sources of parts had been the expatriate firms, but later the Lebanese and Indians had started to import cheaper parts from China, Taiwan and Eastern Europe.

Nearly all the fishing nets in Tamale were sold by a small group of Ogbomosho traders, who worked in adjacent stalls. Most of the demand here came from Ewe, Hausa and Dagomba fishermen. In addition, one of the Igbetti traders cycled round the rural areas selling nets which he had bought from the Ogbomosho dealers direct to the fishermen.

Despite the importance of the trade in staple foodstuffs (known by the Yoruba as *oja apo* – 'sack trading') few Yoruba in Tamale were actually involved in it, though some with cash to spare during the harvest would buy up grain, hoping to sell it at a profit in the dry season. The only Yoruba I interviewed who were full-time foodstuffs sellers had only sold them since 1966: they had sold cloth previously but had been in trouble over control prices. Several older informants spoke of buying and selling foodstuffs in the years after 1945, but with the expansion of the market for consumer goods in the 1950s the sale of foodstuffs had been left to other ethnic groups. According to one informant, Ibadan and Oshogbo traders had been coming to Tamale to buy foodstuffs at one time, but the trade had been taken over by Dagomba who had worked as porters for them (cf. Garlick, 1956).

A number of factors appeared to influence the choice of a selling line. Some lines like cloth, wholesale provisions and fishing nets, required greater starting capital and were unsuitable for newly established traders with limited means. Clothes, on the other hand, had low unit costs and higher profit margins, and a stall could be made to look impressively full with only limited capital. But the usual line taken up by the younger traders was *worobo*. These small items were both cheap and portable. They could be sold from a tray or barrow, enabling the trader to seek customers outside the market. Many of these goods were not subject to price control, and profits were higher since the consumer was less likely to know the cost price. The younger trader selling these goods was largely dealing with people of his own age, and could predict which lines would sell.

However, the distribution of selling lines can also be seen as the result of a developmental process. Most of the senior members of the larger groups of traders had been dealing in Yoruba cloth initially, and had moved from that into the sale of European cloth. Most of them were still selling cloth in 1969. Their junior relatives who had separated in the post-war period had moved into other lines, particularly *worobo*.

There was also the factor of personal networks. The Yoruba traders in the market included several clusters of friends and relatives selling the same types of goods. The trade in fishnets is a good example. The first Ogbomosho trader to sell nets was Rahimi from Ile Isalẹ. He was followed by three of his friends, but by the late 1950s he found that the goods were no longer moving as quickly as they had done. He changed to selling shoes, and was followed by a number of his junior relatives. The three friends were still selling nets in 1969.

Trade of this type is labour-intensive and involves a quick turnover of capital. This allows rapid changes of selling lines. A trader who finds that the goods he is selling are going slowly can make a change the next time that he goes to the south to buy, and he is most likely to try a line that one of his friends or relatives is selling more successfully. A trader who makes a successful innovation is likely to be imitated by friends and relatives, and the market may soon be saturated as a result. If this happens, the most marginal of the traders will probably try yet another selling line, and so on. In each period it was the younger traders with more limited capital and less experience who were forced to look around for new opportunities, and the general trend was a move away from standard selling lines to new types of *worobo* with which they could exploit the growing sophistication of the local consumers.

The fact that nearly all the Yoruba women were selling provisions has to be seen against the constraints under which they operated. Many of them were able to cope with both trade and housework by selling from the house goods for which there was a demand in the neighbourhood. Many of the women, particularly from Igbetti, had very limited capital, but they could at least enter the market by buying a few popular items for resale. If they bought at the 'dozen price' this would give them a small profit margin. Buying goods by the case increased profits, but required more capital. The women sold goods on which profit margins were low and fixed, but the margins could be increased by selling in very small units. Matches from a 3.5p box were sold in bundles of ten matches for 1p, a profit of 1.5p on the box. Candles costing 25p a dozen were sold for 3p each. Sugar was usually sold at 1p for five lumps, or three lumps if it was in short supply. This produced a profit of 12p a box over and above the control price of 28p. The women could carry on with the housework and deal with the customers as and when they appeared. Thus, although the women traders outnumbered the men, very few of them had permanent market stalls. The others sold from the house, from headloads, or from tables set up in front of their husbands' stalls. Those that rented stalls of their own were the wealthier women like Raliatu who combined wholesale and retail trade, and who made their own trips to the south to buy. In 1969, 236 of the 700 stalls in Tamale Central Market were registered in Yoruba names, but only forty-three of these were women. Some women operated from stalls officially rented by their husbands. There was also a difference between towns, reflecting the larger scale of trade of the Ogbomosho women (Table 5.8). Thus one option for the trader in difficulties was to change selling lines to those which required less capital. The normal direction of change was away from cloth and the wholesale trade in provisions and towards clothes and *worobo* or the retail trade in provisions, which required less capital.

The availability of capital also dictated sources of supply. Most of the Yoruba men in Tamale went to the south to buy most of their goods (Table 5.9). Fewer women went to the south: most of them either bought in Tamale or sent orders down with their husbands or other traders. The usual sources of

Table 5.8: Selling places of Yoruba women trading in Tamale, 1969, by town of origin.

	Igboho (n=32)		Ogbomosho (n=45)		Igbetti (n=63)		Total (n=140)	
	no.	%	no.	%	no.	%	no.	%
Headload	3	9.3	3	6.7	8	12.6	14	10.0
House	10	31.3	2	4.4	25	39.7	37	27.0
Market stall	9	28.1	32	71.1	28	44.4	69	49.3
Market circuit	12	37.5	9	20.0	1	1.6	22	15.7
Villages	3	9.4	1	2.2	4	6.3	8	5.7

Note: More than one response per trader has been tabulated.

goods in the south were the expatriate firms and the Lebanese, Indian and Yoruba merchants of Accra and Kumasi. The availability, the range and the prices of goods were all better in the south, and most traders went down at least once a month to buy. Few of the traders did the bulk of their buying in Tamale. They included Lasisi and Caleb, but they did so for different reasons. Lasisi's contacts in the Tamale stores were such that he could get all the cloth he wanted there, while Caleb never had the money to go to the south at all.

INCREASING DEMAND

Other options for the trader in difficulties were to look for new sources of demand, either by trading in a different place or by offering goods on credit to their customers. In the early days of Yoruba trade in Tamale, the majority of traders had been going on foot round the rural areas, and later they travelled by lorry or cycle to the major rural markets. In 1969, most of the traders still doing the rounds of the rural markets were from Igboho. Others had done so previously (Table 5.10), but had found it more profitable to stay in Tamale

Table 5.9: Sources of goods of Yoruba men trading in Northern Ghana, 1969, by town of origin.

	Ogbomosho (n=44)		Igbetti (n=40)		Igboho (Tamale) (n=22)		Igboho (Other) (n=42)		Total (n=148)	
	no.	%	no.	%	no.	%	no.	%	no.	%
Accra	36	81.8	28	70.0	13	59.1	24	57.1	101	68.2
Kumasi	31	70.5	32	80.0	14	63.6	27	64.3	104	70.3
Tamale	9	20.5	11	27.5	4	18.2	6	14.3	30	20.3
Rural areas	1	2.3	1	2.5	2	9.1	1	2.4	5	3.4
Other S. Ghana	0	0.0	2	5.0	0	0.0	7	16.7	9	6.1
Outside Ghana	3	6.8	3	7.5	0	0.0	3	7.1	9	6.1
Other	2	4.5	0	0.0	2	9.1	8	19.0	12	8.1

Note: More than one response per trader has been tabulated.

Table 5.10: Involvement of Yoruba men trading in Northern Ghana in rural
markets, by town of origin.

	Ogbomosho		Igbetti		Igboho (Tamale)		Igboho (Other)		Total	
	no.	%	no.	%	no.	%	no.	%	no.	%
Going in 1969	1	2.3	6	15.0	10	45.5	18	42.9	35	23.6
Stopped before 1969	13	29.5	18	45.0	8	36.4	10	23.8	49	33.1
Never went	30	68.2	16	40.0	4	18.2	14	33.3	64	43.2
Totals	44	100.0	40	100.0	22	100.0	42	100.0	148	100.0

every day. As communication had improved, their main customers from the
villages started coming into Tamale to buy on Tamale market day. The trader
with assistants or partners, like the Bawa brothers, could get the best of both
worlds by exploiting both markets. An alternative to the market cycle around
Tamale was to have a junior partner travelling even further afield. One of
Mustafa Iyanda's sons was going to Yendi and Bolgatanga to sell until 1969,
and Lasisi's son had been making regular trips to Bolgatanga until the coup.
But generally the larger towns and villages in the north gradually acquired
their own resident Yoruba traders, and the Tamale traders concentrated more
and more on the growing market in Tamale itself. The situation was rather
different in the other large northern towns where demand was not as great. A
higher percentage of Yoruba male traders travelled to the rural markets in
Bawku than in Tamale, and in some cases their wives helped look after their
stalls while they were away.[7]

Another way of changing location was to use a barrow to display and
transport goods. Most of the growing number of barrows in Tamale belonged
to younger Yoruba men who had initially sold in the lorry parks but who had
spread to other parts of the town as well. Their favourite locations were on the
main street outside the large stores or the post office, where an Ogbomosho
trader did a substantial trade in ballpoint pens and stationery, and at the
entrance to the market itself, probably the busiest thoroughfare in the town.
By 1969 the best locations had all been taken, and some of the traders had taken
to cycling round the outlying parts of the town in order to find new trade. At
least one trader had found a profitable niche on Education Ridge, selling goods
on credit to students and teachers at the secondary schools and training
colleges there. His case is a good illustration of the problems of credit sales, as
by the third week of each month his money was tied up in this way, and he had
to borrow from his wife in order to stock up for the remainder of the month.
After pay day he could recover the bulk of his money and go down to the south
where he bought most of his goods. He charged higher prices for the goods
sold on credit, up to 50 per cent more, but the students in particular had
few alternative sources of goods as they were rarely allowed off the school

compounds, and the Ridge was some distance from the rest of the town. Another captive clientele was exploited by the Ilesha trader who had a store at the army barracks six miles out of town on the Bolgatanga road. He bought goods in Tamale to sell to the soldiers on credit, and his sales had steadily increased since the military took power. He had sent over NC4,000 back to Nigeria since the coup.

Whether or not a trader sold on credit was a function both of the size of the available capital and the types of goods sold. Poorer traders were in a dilemma. They had to be prepared to sell on credit in order to generate sales, especially if they were selling from their houses rather than the market, but credit sales also tended to tie up too much of their capital for too long. The retailers who sold goods to monthly paid wage earners had to sell on credit as their customers ran out of cash soon after the start of the month. The risk of default was covered by higher prices. The wealthier wholesale traders and dealers in smuggled goods did not have to sell on credit at all. Some even had money deposited with them in advance by their customers against goods in short supply.

For the trader on credit, there were two main problems. One was assessing the credit rating of customers, and the other was getting the money out of them at the end of the month. Most traders tried only to give credit to customers that had been coming to them for some time, and they built up the amount they were willing to advance them gradually, from a few shillings to a maximum which depended on the resources of the trader and his perception of the customer's solvency. With most of the lower grades of clerical workers only earning NC30–40 a month and with the daily minimum wage set at 75p in 1969, most of the debts were small. There was still a risk of default, but this was reduced by careful selection of credit customers. It was also true that for many workers the market was the only source of credit, and customers tried not to throw away a credit rating which they had taken some time to build up.[8] There was thus an equilibrium point in many transactions: the minimum payment which would both satisfy the trader and allow the customer to continue his credit relationship.

The second problem was enforcing payment. The trader whose customers refused to pay up was in a relatively weak position, but he could strengthen it by putting pressure on the customer both where he worked and where he lived. There was an occasion in my own compound when a trader turned up to demand the money owed him by a nurse. She refused to pay and a noisy scene ensued. After the trader had left, the other residents began to put pressure on her to pay at least some of the debt in order to avoid further trouble in the house. Another trader owed money by several students at the nursing school went to see the Principal: she was worried by the threat of her girls being taken to court over their debts, and helped him to obtain the repayment. Legal action in the local court was a last resort for the trader unable to get his money in any other way and the court records are full of cases of this sort. Occasionally when

Table 5.11: Education and literacy of Yoruba men trading in Northern Ghana, 1969, by town of origin.

	Ogbomosho		Igboho		Igbetti		Total	
	no.	%	no.	%	no.	%	no.	%
Illiterate	12	27.3	17	42.5	22	34.4	51	34.5
Literate in Yoruba	21	47.7	19	47.5	33	51.6	73	49.3
Primary school	3	6.8	1	2.5	2	3.1	6	4.1
Middle school	7	15.9	2	5.0	4	6.3	13	8.8
Above middle school	1	2.3	1	2.5	3	4.7	5	3.4
Total	44	100.0	40	100.0	64	100.0	148	100.0

Note: Middle school includes standard 6 and 7.

a debtor defaulted, he would give the trader some other item to cover the debt, and, if the trader thought it unlikely that he would ever get the money, he had little option but to accept it.

THE HAZARDS OF TRADE

Credit sales raise the general question of how traders who usually lacked formal education dealt with problems of calculation and accounting. In fact, a fluency in the performance of complex mental arithmetical calculations was one of their most noticeable talents, and this was the result of long practice. During the long period of service which many traders underwent, they would encounter dozens of calculations each day: these involved the basic price of each of the items in the stall, and various common multiples – all the numbers up to a dozen, and then two dozen, three dozen, a gross, a case, and so on. Through constant repetition, these calculations became a reflex response to a customer's request, but it made it difficult for the traders to change their habits when the currency changed, as it did twice in the 1960s. In 1969, the Yoruba traders still calculated in pounds, shillings and pence, two years after the introduction of the New Cedi. In fact, outside the larger stores, it seemed as if decimalisation had bypassed Tamale completely. It was usual, when buying 2p worth of

Table 5.12: Method of recording credit sales by Yoruba women trading independently in Tamale, 1969, by town of origin.

	Igboho		Ogbomosho		Igbetti		Total	
	no.	%	no.	%	no.	%	no.	%
Books (self)	2	6.3	6	13.3	2	3.8	10	7.2
Books (others)	8	25.0	10	22.2	17	27.9	35	26.5
Memory	22	68.8	16	35.6	28	45.9	66	50.0
No credit sales	0	0.0	13	28.9	14	23.0	27	20.5
Totals	32	100.0	45	100.0	61	100.0	138	100.0

goods, to give the trader 5p (i.e. the old 6d) and to receive 4p change. On the other hand, the traders would demand twelve 1p pieces for an item costing 10p (the equivalent of the old shilling).

Another problem was keeping track of the money owed by each credit customer. First, credit tended to be given only to well-known customers. Second, traders tried, where possible, to give credit in round sums which would make the task of remembering easier. Third, as one trader explained, there was the question of motivation. When a man was owed money and his living depended on it, he had considerable reason not to forget credit transactions: traders who did so tended to go out of business. Many of the Yoruba men in Tamale were literate enough to jot down names and the money owed to them, even if they had no formal education (Table 5.11). Many of those with no formal education had learnt to read and write Yoruba in informal classes held by literate Yoruba, either in Tamale or in their home towns. Fewer of the women were literate, but some were helped by junior relatives who had formal education and who could keep records for them, if they could not do so for themselves (Table 5.12). Literate traders had a variety of simple procedures for keeping track of what they were owed. Some used to issue their regular customers with small notebooks in which details of their sales or deposits could be noted. Others kept a single record themselves in an exercise book. Only a few appeared to keep a record of daily sales, and nobody, apart from those who was agents for the larger firms, were operating on a large enough scale to require the use of more complex accounting techniques.

But exact written records in this type of trade were not usually necessary. A rough calculation of a trader's position could be made at the time of a buying trip, usually at the same time in each month. At this point, the value of the goods left in stock could be assessed and added to the value of the cash in hand. This would give a rough idea of how trade had been going since the last trip. The trader travelling south to buy would normally take every available penny, spending it all on goods, and travelling back on credit.

In the 1960s, the hazards of trade multiplied. Insolvent credit customers were a perennial problem, but now their numbers were steadily increasing. Since the coup many traders had lost money by getting into trouble with the authorities. Others simply found business going into a steady decline. The danger sign for most traders came when they had to use more and more of their trading capital to live between buying trips, and as a result were able to buy fewer goods. With reduced turnovers, traders were more vulnerable to other problems which regularly occurred.

Many goods especially manufactured ones, were breakable and a single defective item in a carton would mean the loss of the profit on the whole carton. The Kintampo road, on which most of the traders travelled, was in such an appalling state in 1969 that careful packing was essential. In addition, the process of taking goods in and out of the stall each day to display them caused wear and tear. In the case of clothes, too much exposure to sunlight caused rapid fading, particularly with cloth made in Ghana, and there was also the possibility of rain damage if a sudden leak appeared in the stall, staining cloth, ruining paper and cardboard, and making metal goods rust. Most traders preferred to sell their stock as quickly as they could while the goods were still in a good condition, but by the late 1960s goods in general were moving more slowly.

In addition to the increasing risk of spoilage, slow turnover also meant that capital was tied up for longer periods and profits consequently reduced. A trader who had savings to fall back on could afford to keep a supply of slow-selling goods or even to buy goods intending to store them until a shortage forced the price up. However, the trader just starting and with no savings might be left with little alternative but to sell the goods off at cost price or at a loss.

It was also quite possible for traders, especially those with little experience, to be cheated by the wholesalers. In one instance, a boy bought batteries from a Lebanese in Accra for his mother, costing NC200. Batteries were scarce at the time and he thought he had a good buy until they opened the cases and found that many of the contents were corroded. He went back to complain, and the Lebanese unwillingly gave him back NC70, mainly because there were other Yoruba customers in the shop. Some of the batteries were salvaged and this reduced the loss to NC20, but for a trader just starting a loss of this size would have been a serious matter.

Fluctuations in supplies produced additional risks. If a trader was lucky enough to be left with stocks of goods in short supply, he might be able to make a greater profit than usual, but the opposite situation could also arise. It was possible for a trader who bought goods at a high price when they were in short supply to be left holding them when new supplies arrived and the price dropped. He would then have to decide whether to hang onto them in the hope that there would be a further shortage, or to sell them at a loss.

The large firms supplied most of the standard selling lines, and it was their supplies which were often erratic. Most of the large firms had branches in Tamale, but the supplies of goods allocated to the north were never sufficient. Some goods were only available to some of the passbook customers, and the allocation of both goods and passbooks provided the storekeepers with endless opportunities of making money. Traders who knew the storekeepers well would be informed in advance when the goods were expected, and supplies would be reserved for them. It was common for the storekeepers to charge extra for the goods but to issue receipts for the control price only. This meant that many of the goods were purchased by the traders at above the retail control price, and they were forced to sell them at an even higher price to make any profit at all. There was always the risk of arrest. Meanwhile, the risk for the storekeeper with his official receipt was nil. Information on the exact date of arrival was also important. If a consignment was expected the following week from Kumasi, the storekeepers would advise the traders to go to the south in the interim, as they would be able to sell most of the goods before the consignment arrived. If it was expected in the next couple of days, the traders would be told to hang on and save the lorry fare. More information could be gathered from Luke and Ayoola, both of whom had telephones.

Another of the main hazards which faced the traders in the period after the coup were the price control regulations and the agents who were enforcing them. Prices of many of the goods which the Yoruba sold – provisions, cloth and many other manufactured items – were controlled, though such legislation is difficult to enforce effectively where so many small-scale traders are involved and where supplies are so erratic. For the traders in Tamale, a complicating factor was the poor communications between them and the authorities. Details of adjustments in control prices were usually sent to the police and to the firms, but often got no further. The first news that traders had of a change in the control price was often when they were arrested for selling goods at the old one. A further complication which arose in one of the court cases which I attended was the inability of the police to distinguish between similar articles, for instance local and imported cloth, which had quite different control prices.[9]

The irony in Tamale in 1969 was that the new price control officer was himself a Yoruba, a relative of the Yoruba chief in Accra. He came to Tamale determined to make an impression, and there was a wave of arrests in the market soon after his arrival. Normally, however, matters could be sorted out before this happened. One of the good things about the Tamale police, according to one informant, was that they usually came and warned the traders when a new man had been transferred to the town. On one occasion, this trader had just been arrested by an officer newly transferred from Kumasi, when the regular Tamale police came to tell him of the new man's arrival. They told the Kumasi officer that they would look after the case for him, took the trader to the outskirts of the town in a police car, asked him how much he would give them, and let him go.

TURNOVER AND PROFIT MARGINS

We are left with the question of the scale of operations of the Yoruba traders, and of their incomes from trade. The figures for the approximate monthly turnovers of both the men and the women are given in Tables 5.13 and 5.14. Most traders bought goods at regular intervals and tended to buy similar amounts each time. These figures were gathered in Nigeria after the exodus, and obviously they have to be treated with extreme caution, but they are broadly consistent with the rest of the data. The figures suggest, once more, that the Ogbomosho traders were operating on a rather larger scale than those from Igbetti, with the Igboho traders somewhere in the middle. A majority of the traders said that conditions in the market had been much worse since the

Table 5.13: Approximate monthly turnover of Yoruba men trading independently in Northern Ghana, 1969, by town of origin.

Monthly Turnover (NC)	Ogbomosho no.	%	Igbetti no.	%	Igboho no.	%	Total no.	%
0–300	4	10.0	7	22.6	11	19.0	22	17.1
301–700	16	40.0	10	32.3	16	27.6	42	32.6
701–1,700	7	17.5	11	35.5	10	17.2	28	21.7
1,701–2,700	5	12.5	1	3.2	6	10.3	12	9.3
2,700–3,900	1	2.5	0	0.0	6	10.3	7	5.4
3,901–	2	5.0	0	0.0	2	3.4	4	3.1
Not known	5	12.5	2	6.5	7	12.1	14	10.9
Total	40	100.0	31	100.0	58	100.0	129	100.0

1966 coup, and some claimed that their sales in 1969 were as little as a quarter of the 1966 level. Many of the women said that they bought in very small quantities at frequent intervals, and could not give a figure for their monthly sales. Presumably most of these were at the bottom of the scale as far as turnover was concerned, and a high percentage of Igbetti women fell into this category.

The Yoruba traders in Tamale generally had limited capital, and made their money out of quick turnover rather than high profit margins. In the case of provisions and cloth, margins were fixed by the price control legislation. The difference between the price paid to the wholesale firms and the retail price averaged about 10 per cent of the wholesale price.[10] However, in some cases the goods passed through the hands of three traders before they reached the consumer, and each of them would receive a margin of much less. A cloth

Table 5.14: Approximate monthly turnover of Yoruba women trading in Northern Ghana, 1969, by town of origin.

Monthly Turnover (NC)	Ogbomosho no.	%	Igbetti no.	%	Igboho no.	%	Total no.	%
Not known/fixed	21	44.7	38	48.1	25	41.7	84	45.2
0–20	0	0.0	4	5.1	0	0.0	4	2.2
21–50	0	0.0	9	11.4	2	3.3	11	5.9
51–100	3	6.4	9	11.4	10	16.7	22	11.8
101–200	7	14.7	9	11.4	6	10.0	22	11.8
201	8	17.0	7	8.9	7	11.7	22	11.8
501–1,000	7	14.9	3	3.8	7	11.7	17	9.1
Over 1,000	1	2.1	0	0.0	3	5.0	4	2.2
Totals	47	100.0	79	100.0	60	100.0	186	100.0

Note: 'Not known/fixed' includes mainly women buying in small quantities on a daily basis, as required.

trader noted that he used to buy 700 cedis worth of cloth a month and that he would be lucky if he managed to make 30 cedis on it. Given the control price, the transport costs to Kumasi and his intermediate position between the wholesalers in the south and the Ghanaian women retailers in the north, this might not have been far from the truth. He said that he sometimes dealt in smuggled goods, but that he would take an even lower margin on these in order to get rid of them quickly. In the case of small manufactured goods where the customer was unlikely to know the cost price, the margin would probably be higher than on standard lines, perhaps as high as 50 per cent. The margin for goods sold on credit could be higher still, but this was realistic in the light of the way in which credit sales tended to tie up capital, and given the high risk of default. Generally, however, profit margins appear to have been low, and they were kept low by the control prices, the level of competition in the market, and by the lag between the rise in the cost of living and the level of wages in Ghana in the 1960s.

A common complaint made against market traders in West Africa is that they hoard goods until the price rises. Certainly there were Yoruba women traders in the markets and back streets of Tamale selling sugar at 45p a box when the control price was 28p, but they were probably not the ones making the large profits. Usually they would have had to pay well above the control price to get the goods from the store, and the storekeeper was the one who would have benefited. Second, storing goods against a price rise tied up capital, which would have otherwise rotated during the same period. Few traders in the Yoruba community could afford to hoard goods on any scale, as the opportunity costs were too high. Nevertheless, the equation of market trading with hoarding persisted after the departure of the Yoruba, and provided the state with one of its rationales for its assault on the markets and the market traders in 1979 and after.

SMUGGLING

If the road to success lay not through exploitative prices but through quick turnover, the ideal goods were those for which there was a constant high demand, and which could be sold quickly for cash rather than on credit. In 1969 the goods which fitted this description best were those smuggled into Ghana from the neighbouring Francophone countries. This was just one area of trade in which the activities of the traders were of considerable interest to the Ghanaian state and its agents.

In 1969, many of the goods smuggled into Ghana were sold by Yoruba. In the early 1960s smuggling had flourished: levels of employment, government expenditure and demand all remained reasonably high, but the shortage of foreign exchange and the import restrictions meant increasingly that essential goods were in short supply. The Yoruba were very adept at using their contacts in other countries to make good these shortages.

The reasons for smuggling varied over time and between goods of different types. First there were instances in which the consumers preferred imported items to those produced in Ghana, even though the latter were readily available. Second, there were cases in which imported goods were temporarily in short supply within Ghana due to import restrictions and trading bottlenecks. Third, there was the case of luxury goods which were either unobtainable in Ghana or subject to a prohibitive import duty. As far as the north was concerned, the third type of goods was of little importance. One heard of spirits, wigs, perfumes and electrical goods being smuggled into the south of the country but there was little market for these types of goods in the north. The main items smuggled into the north of Ghana and sold in Tamale were more mundane, and included cloth, drugs, provisions, clothes, cosmetics and cigarettes.

The irony was that most of these had been produced in Ghana for some time, but there was a strong consumer preference for the imported items. 'State Express' cigarettes imported from 'French' had a smoother taste, according to informants, and could be distinguished from the local variety by their firmness, the numbers on the packet, the numbers on the cigarette paper, the brightness of the lettering and so forth. A common sight at any cigarette stall in Ghana was buyers testing for these signs before parting with their money. Similarly, imported aspirin tablets were believed to be more potent than the locally made ones, and would fetch twice as much in the market. Local cloth faded and wore out more quickly than imported cloth, while local nail polish wore off more quickly. In addition to these goods, for which there were local substitutes, the supply of many other types of goods was irregular, and shortages could occur at any time. The Yoruba had contacts in Togo and Upper Volta to fill the gaps. There were large groups of Shaki traders in both countries, and they were also numerous in Yendi and Bawku, the two largest smuggling centres in the north. In Tamale, the acknowledged leaders of the smuggling trade were also from Shaki. The trade flowed both ways, as when goods were available in Ghana they were much cheaper than those available outside, owing to the low black market value of the cedi. One of the main results of price controls therefore was to create an export trade in essential goods.

Smugglers operated on varying scales. Some of the biggest operators in the south had the capital to bring in lorryloads of goods at a time, and the contacts at the border posts on the main roads to get away with it. Most of the goods came in via Aflao and were distributed by Zabarima and Yoruba traders in Accra. Most smugglers in the north operated on a smaller scale. The most usual method was to buy goods in Togo, leave them on the Togo side of the border and cross into Ghana by lorry. The goods themselves were transported into Ghana by cycle along the bush paths at night, loaded onto lorries, and taken to Tamale, Yendi or Bawku. On their arrival in Tamale they were taken to the house of one or other of the Shaki traders and the regular customers were told that they were available. The goods were then distributed extremely quickly, to reduce the risk to the smugglers of being detected. Smuggled goods were usually kept in the house or the back of the market stall, and were never on open display in case of spot checks by the CID. Demand always exceeded supply, and the goods could be sold very quickly for cash. Some traders even paid in cash in advance for goods to ensure that they got part of the next consignment. Informants agreed that as long as you were not caught in actual possession of smuggled goods, it was virtually impossible to lose money as a middleman in the smuggling industry.

A key factor in the trade was the availability of CFA francs with which most of the buying was done. There were various sources. First, there were the proceeds from trade in commodities like fruit and kola with the francophone countries. Most of the kola was handled by Hausa and much of the money used by Yoruba smugglers was purchased from Hausa dealers in Kumasi and Accra.[11] Another important figure in the trade was the lorry driver on the international routes. He was a specialist with both a knowledge of the border conditions and contacts with the guards in the border posts. Most of the traders who had money to be taken over the border relied on the driver to do it for them, in return for a 10 per cent commission. On the way back into Ghana drivers had to make sure that the goods in the lorry were not too closely investigated. The roads of Ghana since the 1969 coup had been liberally sprinkled with police road blocks, any one of which could spell trouble for the bearer of smuggled goods. The drivers knew all the tricks for disguising smuggled goods, such as packing them into cartons from identical locally produced goods and resealing them. If the driver saw that the tape on the cartons had been tampered with, he would demand NC10 or more extra for the transport. Not all of this was retained. If a lorry was stopped at a road block and had no smuggled goods on board the standard 'dash' for the officer on duty was 20p in 1969. If the police decided to inspect a lorry carrying smuggled goods, the driver would have to give them NC5 or NC10 to make sure that they did not look too closely.

Most Yoruba traders in Ghana probably dealt in smuggled goods at some time or another. For the wholesaler, they could be got rid of quickly, and this speeded up turnover. For the retailer, they were important in attracting a loyal and regular clientele. Provision sellers in the streets had to keep a couple of packets of the 'better' cigarettes for their regular customers. They made little or no profit on the cigarettes themselves, but their customers would come to them for other goods, on which they would make a profit. Similarly, the clothes and cosmetics sellers in the market who did a lot of business with the local prostitutes stood to lose customers unless they could supply the 'better' nail varnish, cosmetics and imported cloth which the girls required.

One of the major difficulties which the Yoruba traders faced after the coup stemmed from a police move against smugglers throughout the country. Despite their generally good relations with the police, the smugglers could still fall foul of the law. The last line of defence in the Yoruba community were the 'big men' who could go and beg the *oga* ('boss') at the police station. In Tamale, the man most often seen down at the police station to plead on behalf of his fellow townsmen was Alhaji Salami, a meat contractor to the army and one of the leading brokers in smuggled goods. On one occasion two Shaki traders from Upper Volta were arrested with NC2,000 worth of CFA francs in the spare-wheel compartment of their car. Alhaji Salami and other prominent Shaki traders were constant visitors at the police station until the men were finally released a few days later. One of the requirements for a smuggler to stay in business was to have the right contacts with officialdom to stay out of trouble, and this meant, ironically, that at the time of the compliance order it was the wealthier smugglers who found it easiest to remain in Ghana and stay in business.

ALTERNATIVE STRATEGIES

For a variety of reasons, a trader might find it difficult to stay in market trade in Tamale, and he would be forced to look for other opportunities. There were three options normally open. These were (a) to go elsewhere to trade, usually to a smaller town or village, (b) to find another job in Tamale, or (c) to go home to Nigeria, usually to farm. The first of these options was taken over the years by a number of traders, and it resulted in the gradual dispersal of the Yoruba all over the country. Moving out of the town to the 'bush' had a number of advantages. First in many villages the trader had little if any competition, and this meant that profit margins could be higher. Second, the trader would be less likely to be bothered by police, customs and price control officials. Third, overheads were less: the trader would have to pay little, if any, stall rental, and the cost of housing would also be lower than in the town. The early Yoruba traders in the north of Ghana had a number of contacts in the rural villages, and their junior relatives often settled there permanently. A successful Yoruba trader in the rural areas would often form the nucleus for a small community of later arrivals, usually from the same Yoruba town. Some of these traders in the villages became relatively wealthy, at least in comparison with the rest of the villagers, and they branched out into farming and milling. Having numbers of wage earners resident locally helped. The construction of the Kintampo road attracted Igbetti traders to both Buipe and Yapei. The trader living at Buipe had gone there in 1955 as a last resort after his stall in Tamale market had been destroyed in a fire, but had stayed there once the road was under construction.

The second option was to find other work. Yoruba migrants tended to move into other work at two stages of their careers: as a means of accumulating capital for trade after having failed to obtain it from senior relatives, or after failure in trade. Some of those who took on other jobs as a way of raising trading capital found that they preferred them to trade and so never returned to the market. These alternative occupations can be classified according to the qualifications needed for them, and the training required.

First, there were the jobs that required no formal education, but did require an apprenticeship. These included tailoring, driving, carpentry and so on. Second, there were the unskilled jobs such as washing clothes and government labour. The prestige of these types of work was very low in the Yoruba community, but they were not regarded as degrading if they were seen by the individual as a means of acquiring the capital to start trading. Third, there were occupations that required unusual qualifications, such as those of drummers and mallams, for which not everyone was suited. These tended to be concentrated in particular families, such as the migrants from Ile Onilu (literally 'The Drummer's Compound') in Igbetti who moved between Nigeria and Ghana as ceremonies and annual festivals dictated.

A Yoruba's range of options was determined by previously acquired skills, age and ability, education, and often the availability of friends and relatives willing to teach the job. In general the Yoruba valued the independence given by some occupations such as trade and craft work. 'Government' work was also favoured because of its relative security and the short working hours. Work for private individuals was less favoured, and the most negative evaluations that I heard concerned the two individuals employed by Lebanese. For Yoruba migrants with no other skills, trade was to be preferred because of the independence it gave: as a trader one could hope for 'improvement' in one's condition, even though a labourer might be making more money than many of the traders in the market. Tailoring had a particular attraction in that it could be carried on at the same time as trade, and it was probably the most popular alternative to trade among the Yoruba migrants in the 1950s. Many tailors in the market also sold goods, usually cloth. At least one Yoruba tailor in Tamale in 1969 had got a job with the government, sewing uniforms for the Workers Brigade. Government jobs were highly valued: they not only ensured a regular income, but the working hours allowed the individual to run his own business in his spare time. Similar opportunities were open to mechanics, carpenters and fitters, and there were a number of Yoruba working for the Public Works Department in Tamale in similar jobs.

Another craft which could be combined with trade was cycle repairing. Several Yoruba had learned to repair cycles in Nigeria and used their skills in Ghana. The wear and tear on machines in the rural areas was considerable, and spare parts were an essential commodity. Many of the repairers built up a substantial trade in parts to other repairers, in addition to buying for their own needs. An Igbetti repairer in Damongo said that by 1969 he was buying NC600 worth of parts a month for his own use and for sale.

In the 1960s, driving began to rival tailoring in popularity as an alternative to trade. Being associated with a vehicle, even if only as a lorry mate, had a certain

Table 5.15: Education of children of Yoruba migrants, 1969, by town of origin.

	Number of children of school age		Percentage ever attended primary school		Percentage ever attended post-primary school	
	m	f	m	f	m	f
Muslims						
Ibgetti	50	45	58.0	37.8	22.0	4.4
Igboho	85	84	81.2	54.8	31.8	8.3
Ogbomosho	67	66	86.6	54.5	38.8	19.7
Total Muslim	202	195	77.2	50.8	31.7	11.3
Christians						
Igbetti	31	39	90.3	79.5	41.9	25.6
Igboho	47	45	87.2	82.2	44.7	20.0
Ogbomosho	15	16	93.3	81.3	53.3	31.3
Total Christian	93	100	89.2	81.0	45.2	24.0
Total	295	295	81.0	61.0	35.9	15.6

attraction for many of the younger men who were fed up with trade. They usually started as apprentices, hanging on the back of the lorry and collecting fares from the passengers, as well as helping with the loading and unloading and with any breakdowns which occurred on the road. In time they would learn to drive, and eventually they would be able to raise the money to bribe their way through the driving test and obtain a licence. Then it was a question of finding an owner willing to take them on to drive his vehicle. Most of the drivers aspired to owning their own vehicle, but few of them achieved this. The only major exception among the Yoruba in Tamale was an Igbetti lorry owner who used to run a regular service to Nigeria through Yendi where he had made his base. Even this man had only become established after several accidents, trouble with the police and a spell in jail. In 1972, after the exodus, he was again in difficulties after his lorry had overturned in 'French', and in 1973 he had not been seen in Igbetti for some time, probably because he still owed a number of people there money.

EDUCATION AND THE LABOUR MARKET

Finally, there were the clerical or other types of jobs that required formal education to middle school or beyond. Those with the qualifications for these were unlikely to trade, except under special circumstances, and rising rates of education in the Yoruba community after independence meant a steady drift of the younger people out of the market.

Table 5.15 gives details of the education of the children of the migrants that we interviewed. Compared with other migrant groups such as the Hausa, Mossi and Frafra, the rates were very high, as they had been in Western

Nigeria since the 1950s.[12] Not surprisingly, the rates were higher among Christians than among Muslims, and higher among boys than among girls. Some Muslims had been reluctant at first to send their children to school, perhaps on the grounds that they might be converted to Christianity, a common enough occurrence in British West Africa where education was initially dominated by the missions.[13] The following is the account of an Ogbomosho clerk of his attempts to obtain education in the late 1940s in the face of parental opposition:

> I was attending evening classes until I found that I was interested in it [i.e. education]. Then I applied to the head of the United Primary School near the cemetery in writing. By that time it was a very new school . . . by then we were paying fees. My school friends would add my books to their lists when they got their parents to buy them and when it came to the school fees, sometimes the Fathers [i.e. the Catholic priests who had been running the literacy classes he had been attending earlier] would pay. The uniform too I couldn't get so often I went to the school in tattered clothes. I would be attending classes for six months and then sometimes for three months I would have to stay away for lack of money. My brothers [i.e. senior agnatic relatives] didn't want me to go to school. My mother too had by that time left my father so I was the only unwanted child in the house. I spent two and a half years at school and then I was promoted to Standard Three.

Finally he found a job with an expatriate geologist and was able to make enough money to get himself through Standard Six. However, despite his experiences he had not cut off relations with his family or the other Ogbomosho migrants. In 1969, his quarters were 100 yards down the road from the house in which most of his relatives in Tamale lived, and he often called in to greet them, as well as regularly attending the meetings of the Ogbomosho Muslim *parapọ*. Neither had he lost all his entrepreneurial drive. In 1969 his staff quarters were full of chickens he was rearing for the market.

By 1969, after the expansion of the Ghanaian education system in the 1950s, most of the Yoruba had at least some children who had attended school, and increasing numbers were going on to secondary education and training colleges. The result was an ever-increasing diversity of occupations among the second-generation migrants. Education among girls was less common, especially among Muslims. Girls without formal education helped their mothers in the market until they married, usually at around eighteen years of age.

The middle-school graduate was most likely to try to get clerical work of some sort, unless he could get a place in a secondary school or training college. Children unable to get into either often went to one of the private commercial colleges which had sprung up all over Ghana in which they could learn typing, book-keeping and other office skills, perhaps enough to pass one of the recognised examinations. The next step was to find a friend or relative with the right contacts to find them a job and to provide the bribes necessary to secure it. Recruitment relied more on personal contacts than formal qualifications, and so there was a certain amount of clustering of Yoruba migrants in, for instance, the stores, the Public Works Department and the State Transport Corporation. Finding a job could take several months and could involve travelling to other towns in Ghana. These examples are fairly typical:

Bello was an Ogbomosho from Bibiani. He graduated from middle school and came to Tamale where his sister was married to the eldest son of Mustafa Iyanda. He attended typing school and got a job as a clerk in Gambaga, but he disliked the town, resigned and came back to Tamale at the suggestion of his brother-in-law, who started to look for a job for him locally. The brother-in-law had started a farm and had contacts in the Ministry of Agriculture, and eventually Bello secured a job there.

Sule's parents were from Ogbomosho and lived in Prang, on the road from Kumasi to Tamale. Sule left school in Kumasi and was unable to find a job there. He learned to type and stayed with other relatives in Takoradi and Accra, but had no success there either. Finally he arrived in Tamale and stayed with his mother's sister's senior co-wife's son. He located a job through contacts in the Yoruba community. GNTC wanted him, not because of his typing, but to join their football team. This job fell through, however, but another job was eventually found in the Ministry of Health, through an Ogbomosho man who worked for the Ministry of Finance. After six months looking for a job, Sule was employed as a messenger there.

What was evident in both these cases was the time which relatives were prepared to expend to locate and secure jobs. The quicker they could find a job for an unemployed relative, the shorter the period during which they would have to support him themselves. In addition, a relative in a bureaucratic position could be a useful resource later on, either in providing an extra contact with officialdom, or in finding a job for somebody else.

Attitudes to trade as an occupation among the younger educated Yoruba varied. Some of them regarded it as an occupation only for the elderly and the illiterate, while others aspired to become traders, even though they had clerical jobs, because of the possibility of 'improvement'. But the sort of trade they usually had in mind was the sort associated with Ayoola and Ogundiran – a commercial enterprise run from a permanent shop on the main street, rather than from a corrugated iron stall in the market. A few managed this with the aid of their senior relatives. I came across a young trader from Kishi who had given up teaching after his brother had put down a deposit of NC4000 with GNTC for him to open a provisions store in Bawku. This was a rare instance. Few of the younger Yoruba had relatives with capital on this scale, and over time there was a gradual movement of the children of traders into other occupations outside the market.

By the time of the exodus, an increasing number of second-generation migrants had formal education and had moved into jobs outside the market. In this respect the Yoruba differed from groups such as the Mossi among whom rates of education were much lower. The implications of this for the maintenance of Yoruba identities in Ghana will be considered in the next chapter.

ALTERNATIVE INVESTMENTS

For the successful trader, a time would come when the enterprise was generating enough of a profit to allow alternative investments, either in Ghana or the home town. The most logical step for the trader in this position to take was the expansion of the business. This could be done in a variety of ways. One was to move into a more capital-intensive form of trade. The other was to recruit more assistants and to continue in more or less the same way as before. Some of the wealthiest of the Yoruba traders in northern Ghana had become registered stockists or agents for the large firms, the earliest being Luke in Ile Oke. The largest operator of this sort that I came across was the Igboho man who owned the UAC store in Navrongo. He had more or less retired himself, and he left the running of the store to his son, another secondary school graduate. In 1969, sales were running at about NC10,000 a month. However, there were various factors inhibiting the development of these larger enterprises. First, there was the question of the initial large deposit needed to set up the store, usually a sum which very few of the traders were able to raise. In most groups, trading capital had been divided among junior relatives long before it accumulated to this extent. A comparison of the Ile Oke and Ile Isalẹ groups, both of which have been discussed above, will bring this point out.

In a sense, these two descent-group histories represent polar ideal types. The history of the Ile Isalẹ group is more typical in that it resulted in a proliferation of traders in one part of the market selling a similar range of goods. The history of Ile Oke was marked by a greater degree of innovation. Luke was the first Yoruba trader in Tamale to become a licensed agent for the large firms, and the first to see the potential of grinding mills and rice farms as alternatives to trade. While the Ile Isalẹ group were forming a series of one-man labour-intensive enterprises, Ile Oke produced more diverse investment patterns. Obviously, one of the most important factors here was the differing ability of Luke and Isaac, but other differences in the two histories might also have contributed. First, there was the difference between the point at which fission occurred in each case. Luke and Rahimi were both married around 1940, but while Rahimi was given capital and started on his own in 1948, no split took place in the other group until 1953, by which time Luke had been able to finance his own CFAO store. By that time, Braimah's original capital in the other group was already divided between four people: himself, Rahimi, and his own two sons. Second, there was the difference in response to the expansion of the market in the 1950s. The Ile Isalẹ response was to recruit large numbers of junior relatives who could cope with the demand in the rural areas. Thus, when the market contracted in the 1960s, the capital of the Ile Oke group was still in the hands of only two men who could shift it into the investments they considered to have more potential. For the Ile Isalẹ group capital remained fragmented. The only person who did attempt to diversify did so when there were other demands on his resources (the house his father was building) and in an area which was ill chosen. The legacy of the recruitment of assistants in the 1950s was a number of impatient young men in the 1960s who were expecting marriage arrangements and trading capital from their masters in a time of reduced prosperity.

The other main factor inhibiting the growth of larger trading enterprises was simply that the market was getting overcrowded. The number of towns and larger villages in the north which could support enterprises of this type was limited. It is noticeable that in the 1960s Luke moved out of an association with the large firms and started on his own again, and that Ogundiran, though retaining his association with UAC, was not the most successful member of his family. The Navrongo store mentioned above did particularly well because of the business it received from the Navrongo Secondary School and the large community of Catholic priests stationed in the town. But the fact remained that in many cases expansion of trade in the 1960s did not represent the most profitable use of capital, and many of the Yoruba were able to obtain higher returns in other ways.

From time to time some of the traders in Tamale had experimented with the ownership of taxis, lorries, and other forms of transport, usually without success. The main problem lay in selecting and supervising the driver, which was either time consuming, or, if entrusted to another, resulted in loss of revenue. In Tamale in 1969, Yoruba transport ownership consisted of a battered old taxi run by a young Ogbomosho man with the appropriate legend on the side 'WHY WORRY?' The Igbetti lorry owner mentioned as previously based there had moved to Yendi. Several other people had tried to run vehicles for a time, but had decided in the end that it represented a high-risk investment with a low return, compared with other possibilities. The ownership of grinding mills presented similar problems. Significantly, Luke's nephew, the only Yoruba to own machines on a large scale, had made it his main occupation. For the part-time owner, there was the same problem of the supervision of assistants.

But by far the most significant form of investment for most migrants with money to spare was in housing. In the larger Ghanaian towns housing was a profitable and secure investment. The first Yoruba-owned houses in Tamale were in the Sabon Gida where many of the Yoruba, especially those from Ogbomosho, still lived in 1969. In the 1950s some of the migrants had started to build elsewhere in the town, and later a few of the wealthier ones had started to buy up houses as a commercial investment. Some who owned houses in other parts of the town continued to live in the Sabon Gida to retain links with friends and relatives there. Luke was a good example. He owned six houses in Tamale, but continued to live with his Ilorin landlord. In the 1960s, house ownership represented an asset which could be used as security in getting a bank loan. A final factor encouraging Yoruba building in Ghana was the increasing difficulty of sending money to Nigeria. Building in Nigeria became steadily more expensive, and housing represented the best means of investing the money in Ghana.[14]

Another type of investment becoming more popular by 1969 was farming. Land around Tamale was plentiful and suitable for rice cultivation.[15] Food prices were high, especially in the dry season, and trading conditions had deteriorated. Loans were available from the government and the banks for establishing rice farms, and a small group of Yoruba started to make use of them. Luke seems to have been the first and he was soon followed by Isaac, Lasisi and the sons of Mustafa Iyanda. By 1969 even the Yoruba Imam, Alhaji Bello, was to be seen visiting Lasisi to investigate the possibilities. In the 1970s, after the exodus, rice cultivation spread even more rapidly, and Tamale became the agricultural boom town of the north (Shepherd, 1978).

Finally there were a variety of short term investments which the Yoruba with cash to spare could consider, including money-lending, grain speculation and cattle ownership. Many migrants owned cattle which they entrusted to local Fulani herdsmen, and at least two Yoruba owned herds of twenty or more.

By the late 1960s, therefore, the decline of trade meant that some migrants now derived much of their income from other investments. For instance, by 1969 Lasisi was only selling NC800 worth of cloth a month, which probably gave him an income of NC60 or NC80 a month at the most. In comparison he received around NC95 a month in rent from the two houses, and in 1969 he made over NC1,000 from his rice farm. It is not difficult to see the attractiveness of investments outside trade during this period.

Trade, farms and houses were not the only substantial investments open to migrants, though some of the other possibilities yielded less tangible and immediate economic benefits. Major items of expenditure included marriages and, in the case of Muslims, the pilgrimage to Mecca. A minority of wealthier migrants were polygynous (Table 5.16) – Luke had five wives, two of them Ghanaian, and one of the Igboho migrants had seven – but by 1969 the cost of arranging a marriage could amount to NC400 or more, the equivalent of several months' income, even for a wealthy trader.[16] In addition, there were the junior relatives working for most of the larger traders who required help with their marriages. The pilgrimage represented an outlay of similar magnitude. But the biggest drain on the resources of many migrants was the construction of a house at home in Nigeria. In most instances this generated little income as many of the houses built by migrants remained virtually empty until their owners' retirement, or were lived in by close relatives who paid no rent. But

Table 5.16: Number of wives of married Yoruba men living in Northern Ghana, 1969.

Wives	Ogbomosho		Igboho		Igbetti		Total	
	no.	%	no.	%	no.	%	no.	%
1	48	69.6	35	44.9	27	58.7	110	57.0
2	12	17.4	31	39.8	14	30.4	57	29.5
3	6	8.7	7	9.0	5	10.9	18	9.3
4	2	2.9	4	5.1	0	0.0	6	3.1
5 or over	1	1.4	1	1.3	0	0.0	2	1.0
Total	69	100.0	78	100.0	46	100.0	193	100.0

they involved considerable expenditure, particularly as much of the money used to build them had to be bought on the black market. (Migrants in the CFA zone were much more favourably placed in this respect.) Until the currency restrictions of the 1960s it had been customary for migrants to build at home before building in Ghana. This changed in the 1960s. Ownership of a house in Nigeria proved to be particularly valuable after the 1969 exodus, and the first thing that many migrants did on their arrival home was either to complete or to start building a house before looking for economic opportunities elsewhere. Houses at home were not only places to which the migrants could eventually retire. They symbolised and served to reinforce their commitment to their home town, and acted as valuable reminders to the rest of the town of their success abroad. Those who also regarded them as a source of security were, in 1969, proved right.

CONCLUSION

The wealthy Yoruba in Ghana occupied an intermediate role in the trading hierarchy between the larger firms and the Ghanaian consumers. Yoruba enterprise had done much to create a distributional structure for the large firms which they could not afford to create for themselves. It had also done much to extend the market economy from the larger central markets to the rural areas which, by the late 1960s, had acquired their own resident Yoruba traders. The Yoruba migrants were able to achieve this with resources of capital, skill, labour and information generated within the community and which were, at least in the earlier stages of migration, unavailable to members of other ethnic groups to the same extent.

The Yoruba had relied extensively on family rather than wage labour and its low cost had been a major factor in their success. The more fortunate traders were able to accumulate, but their savings were invested not in capitalistic expansion of their enterprises but by diversifying into property or, increasingly, rice farming. Despite their emphasis on self-employment and self-reliance as desirable, they remained largely dependent on the multinational trading firms and the state, both formally and informally. In the first place, they provided the large firms with a retailing infrastructure, helping to expand their turnover without proportionately expanding their costs, while the pass-book system gave the firms, in effect, low interest loans. The firm's employees also benefited from the payments that the traders made to them to ensure supplies of goods. This type of trade and dependency on the firms had a further corollary. The Yoruba traders could no longer control the supply of goods or entry to the market as they had been able to do in the trade in Yoruba cloth in the pre-war period. Unlike the Hausa described by Cohen, there was little vertical integration of trade among the Yoruba in Tamale. Their position depended on their comparative advantages in access to capital and other factors of production rather than a monopoly of access, and by 1969 local Ghanaian traders were competing increasingly effectively with them. Meanwhile most of the younger educated Yoruba were increasingly turning to other occupations. The exodus probably only served to accelerate dramatically a process of Ghanaianisation in many sectors of the market which, in the long run, would have taken place anyway. Had the Yoruba stayed in Ghana during the 1970s, there is a fair chance that they would have retained an important stake in the rice industry which was just starting to develop as they left the country.

The resources which the Yoruba derived from their fields of social relations and which contributed to their success in the market have been clearly spelt out already – capital, skill, information and labour. But the advantages of member-ship of the Yoruba community went beyond these. If traders ran into trouble with the authorities, the big men in the community would be called on to act on their behalf through their informal contacts with the bureaucracy and the police. The associational structure of the Yoruba community, described in more detail in the next chapter, allowed rapid settlement of many of the disputes arising between Yoruba traders in the market, saving them both time and expense. The positive advantages of involvement in community affairs tended to reinforce the cohesiveness of the Yoruba traders as a group, just as the recruitment of junior relatives as assistants in trade served to renew and strengthen links with home. Migration and labour recruitment remained kinship-based until the exodus, in marked contrast to Yoruba enterprises in other parts of West Africa where more open patterns of recruitment had developed.[17] In the case of the migrants from the northern Yoruba towns to Ghana, earlier patterns of social relations had not yet been eroded to this extent.

It is against this background that career strategies and individual investment decisions have to be seen. Most of the Yoruba traders thought of themselves as sojourners, and many of their decisions reflect their eventual goal of retirement to their houses and kin groups at home. This helps explain the priority given to building at home, even though it might result in a serious drain on capital and the delaying of more immediately profitable ventures in Ghana. And even

Plate 5.1: An ornate 'upstairs' house (centre) built in Ogbomosho by a wealthy trader in Tamale.

these ventures were along familiar lines – housing, trade, occasional excursions into transport or mill ownership, and, towards the end, rice farming. Housing was the most popular: it yielded a substantial income at comparatively little risk, allowed the owner to retain personal control, and was an asset which could easily be realised when the moment for retirement came.

By the time of the exodus conditions were changing rapidly. Both Ghana and Western Nigeria had seen the rapid expansion of education in the 1950s, and a growing number of younger migrants had moved into occupations outside the market. This raises the questions of how far the boundaries of the Yoruba community and the strength of Yoruba identity were being eroded, and these questions form the theme of the next chapter.

6

THE YORUBA COMMUNITY IN TAMALE

It will have become clear by now that the nature of social relations both within the Yoruba community and between the Yoruba and other groups was largely shaped by the pattern of migration and the changing economic roles of the migrants. This brings us on to the widely discussed yet still extremely contentious subject of ethnicity, which is the central focus of the present chapter. How did the Yoruba function as an ethnic group, both in terms of internal organisation and articulation with the other residents of the town?

ETHNICITY AND MIGRATION IN WEST AFRICA

As a starting point we might take two previous studies of ethnicity and migration in West Africa which have several points of contact with the situation of the Yoruba, those of Cohen and Schildkrout.[1]

Cohen worked among Hausa migrants in the Sabo area of Ibadan in Western Nigeria. While Hausa migrants had settled throughout the city, he was most interested in the migrants that controlled the transport and distribution of livestock and kola nuts, a group which remained resolutely separate from the majority Yoruba population, not only in terms of occupation, but also residence, religion, politics, language and culture. Not only were these migrants not assimilating, despite their loss of contact with home, but they were, if anything, becoming more segregated. Cohen linked this separation to their economic role. Their control over the cattle and kola trades had been maintained only after bitter struggles, and an important resource in these was their ability to mobilise politically. Ethnic groups, like the kinship and religious groups into which they sometimes merge, provide an excellent basis for the solution of practical political problems: maintaining distinctiveness, communication, decision-making, authority, ideology and discipline.[2] In his later work, Cohen went on to develop these ideas into a more general political anthropology of symbolism.[3] Ethnic groups are symbolically differentiated informal interest groups involved in struggles over power and resources.

Although Schildkrout was also dealing with northern migrants in a southern West African town, the situation she describes was very different. The Mossi in Kumasi did not monopolise particular niches in the labour market, nor did they gradually develop greater cultural distinctiveness. If anything, what cultural distinctiveness the first generation migrants possessed was eroded among their children born in Ghana, the *'yan kasa* or 'children of the soil'. The *'yan kasa* spoke Hausa rather than More as their first language, and were scattered residentially throughout the zongo. By African standards they had high rates of intermarriage with other zongo groups, with whom they participated in religion and in inter-ethnic associations. And yet the category 'Mossi' remained salient in the recurrent political crises of zongo life, even if Mossi identity was expressed in zongo cultural forms rather than forms imported from Upper Volta.

Although the examples are so different, the difference is to some extent a function of the empirical concerns and theoretical models. Cohen is primarily concerned with economic struggles and sees Hausa social organisation and culture in Sabo as contributing to their economic success. When he looks at the cognitive dimensions of symbolism it is as a 'blueprint' for economic organisation. The reality described by Schildkrout at first appears to be more complex, but that is because she is describing an entire ethnic community, not just particular commercial subsections within it. Ethnicity to her is an ideology of shared kinship and provenance which persists despite residential separation, occupational diversification and even loss of language.[4] The problems dealt with by these two authors thus turn out to be different and even complementary: the role of ethnic mobilisation in economic success, and the maintenance of ethnic categories and boundaries despite the cultural changes resulting from life in a multi-ethnic setting.

Taken together, these two studies raise a series of questions which can form a starting point for the discussion of the Yoruba material as well. First, what was the relationship between Yoruba social organisation and their position in the market? Did they function, like Cohen's Hausa migrants, as an effective economic informal interest group, and what were the major differences between the two cases. Second, what was the role of religious organisation among the Yoruba migrants? Did it separate them from the rest of the town and allow them to function more effectively in the market, as Cohen argues was the case in Ibadan, or did it provide a framework for integration into a wider stranger community, as Schildkrout implies was the case in Kumasi Zongo? Third, given that the Yoruba maintained much stronger links with their home areas than apparently either the Mossi or the Hausa, what was the reason for this and what were the implications for the rest of Yoruba social life? Fourth, what were the main features of marriage choice within the Yoruba community, and what were the implications of these. Fifth, what effects did residential organisation have on Yoruba social behaviour? Finally, how did the Yoruba migrants fit into the local political system, and to what extent were they involved in local political issues as a group or as individuals?

The rest of the chapter explores these aspects of Yoruba identity in Tamale. First, I outline the institutional framework of the Yoruba community, and its links with the rest of the Yoruba population of Tamale, Yoruba migrants elsewhere in Ghana, and with the home towns in Nigeria. Second, I look at the more informal aspects of social organisation including friendship networks and marriage patterns. Third, I look at the ways in which these formal and informal links were mobilised to cope with the crisis of the compliance order in 1969. Finally I return to the broad theoretical questions raised here to see what light the Yoruba material sheds on ethnicity in West Africa in general.

ASSOCIATIONAL STRUCTURE

The associational structure of the Yoruba community in Tamale was similar to that described for Kumasi,[5] though on a smaller scale. The main organisations were the Tamale branches of the town unions or *parapọ*, religious institutions such as the churches and mosque, the *Ilu Pejọ* or Yoruba Community Committee which brought together representatives of all the Yoruba towns with migrants in Tamale, and the Nigerian Community Committee which provided a link with the Nigerian High Commission in Accra (Figure 6.1).

The Town *parapọ*

The Yoruba town *parapọ* are classic examples of West African ethnic-based voluntary associations, dedicated both to helping migrants in the places where they settled and promoting the development and 'improvement' of their town of origin.[6] Details of membership and organisation varied slightly between the four major towns represented in Tamale. Membership of the Ogbomosho, Igboho and Shaki *parapọ* was restricted to married men, while the Igbetti membership included a few who were unmarried. In addition to the general meetings, the Ogbomosho and Igbetti Christians and Muslims had separate organisations. There were two Igboho *parapọ*, one for migrants from the Modeke quarter of the town, and one for the rest. This division had its origins in a dispute between Modeke and the rest of the town over the siting of the Igboho Central Mosque in the late 1950s, and the groups had remained separate.[7]

Each of the groups had a regular meeting place which was maintained with funds provided by the members in the form of weekly dues. The Shaki, Igboho and Igbetti meetings were held weekly, while the Ogbomosho and Igbetti Muslims met every fortnight. The migrants from Modeke in Igboho met every six days, on the morning of Sankpala market, as many of them traded in the rural markets. If a meeting coincided with a naming ceremony or other celebration organised by one of the members it would usually be cancelled unless there was important business to discuss, and the members would attend the celebration instead. Each group had its officials: a chairman (*alaga*), secretary (*akọwe*) and treasurer (*akapo*), together with their deputies. The chairman was usually chosen on the basis of age and ability to control a meeting rather than on the basis of wealth. This was essential, as discussions often involved disputes between members and could become heated. The secretary and treasurer on the other hand had to be literate and they were often younger men. The Igboho secretary was a storekeeper with the Workers' Brigade, the

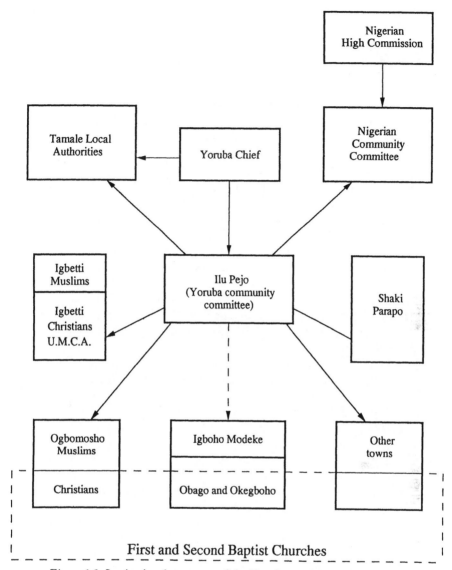

Figure 6.1: Institutional structure of the Yoruba community in Tamale.

Igbetti and Shaki secretaries were literate traders, and the Ogbomosho secretaries were a timekeeper at the airport site, a trader with middle school education, and the choirmaster from the First Baptist Church.

The associations kept registers of the names of the members together with their payments of dues. The size of the membership varied from 170 for the Ogbomosho *parapọ* to eighty-three for the Shaki *parapọ*.[8] There were rules and fines specified for certain offences: members of the Igbetti *parapọ* for instance were (in theory) fined 5p for failure to attend or for late arrival; 25p for smoking or chewing kola during meetings; and up to NC2 for causing a disturbance. In fact, only between a third and half the members attended most meetings, and the others sent their contributions with friends and relatives or paid in advance. Not all the members necessarily lived in Tamale. The Igbetti register, for instance, still included the names of migrants who had moved to Yapei, Buipe, Sawla and Daboya, but the migrants in Yendi and Damongo were numerous enough to have their own meetings. Some of the more recent Ogbomosho arrivals in Tamale were still officially members of the Ogbomosho *parapọ* in Kumasi. But the general pattern was for the vast majority of migrants to join the local branch soon after their arrival in Ghana.

The pattern which the meetings took was fairly standard. They opened and closed with prayers, and many of the members arrived early to pay their dues. Letters and messages from other branches were read, and announcements were made about forthcoming naming ceremonies, etc. To judge from the minutes a considerable amount of time was taken up with communications from home and branches elsewhere, and over the arrangements for the annual general meetings held in Nigeria and elsewhere in Ghana. After these general matters the floor was open and anyone who had a matter to discuss could address the meeting. These could include personal problems, disputes between members or matters of general interest.

First there were subjects of concern to all the Yoruba in the town. These were usually discussed by the Yoruba *Ilu Pejọ*, but there could also be a discussion by the town *parapọ* as well. Often these were concerned with trade. Early in 1969, representations had been made to the Tamale council over the cost of trading licences. The council wanted to charge each trader NC10 a year, including the women who sold from headloads and who had no stalls. The *Ilu Pejọ* took up the matter and reached an agreement with the council that the traders with market stalls should pay NC10, while those with headloads should pay 20p a month. A second issue concerned price control enforcement, and this was one of the meetings to which the women came as well. At the start of 1969 the government had made efforts to tighten up enforcement of the controls, and the police warned the Yoruba that those most likely to be arrested would be those selling provisions, the Yoruba women. Some of the women agreed to stop selling goods at above the control prices, but there was opposition from some of the wealthier women traders who had most to lose from doing so. The threat was made that their husbands would take away their passbooks unless they agreed to cooperate. There was another crackdown on the traders in June and July 1969, and this time it involved both men and women from all the Yoruba towns.

Second there were requests for assistance from individual members with particular problems. Early in 1969, an Ogbomosho schoolboy fell into a waterhole and drowned while he was away with his school camp at Savelugu. The Ogbomosho members contributed the money to bring the body back to Tamale for burial. Personal problems were usually handled by the town *parapo* rather than the *Ilu Pejo*. If they were short of funds they normally turned to other branches of the town *parapo* in Ghana rather than to migrants from other towns in Tamale. For instance at one meeting the Shaki *parapo* in Yendi wrote to the other branches in the north asking for contributions as they had a complex court case on their hands.

A third area in which the town *parapo* were involved was in questions of marriage and divorce. Nearly all Yoruba marriages, whether in Tamale or in Nigeria, were performed according to customary law, and to obtain a divorce in the home town one could normally go to the local court. Marital disputes in Tamale were kept within the community. As most marriages were between partners from the same home town, it was usually the town *parapo* which would consider marital disputes which could not be settled by the partners and their senior relatives. Cases would only be taken to the *Ilu Pejo* which involved adultery with a person from another Yoruba town. Pressure would be put on the parties to resolve their differences, or, if this was not possible, they would recommend a divorce. In some instances a couple would go home either to try and sort out their differences or to obtain a divorce, but in other cases they just separated. There were a number of cases in Nigeria in 1970 in which returned migrants who had been separated for some time while in Ghana went to the local courts in Nigeria to ask for a formal divorce.

Cases involving disputes between people from different towns, like disputes which the town *parapo* had been unable to resolve, were taken to the *Ilu Pejo*, though they might well be taken to the town *parapo* first, in order to obtain advice and the support of the other members. *Parapo* membership was also useful if a migrant was in trouble with the authorities. The senior members had links with the police and other officials and could intercede on the member's behalf. If a member was arrested, one of the 'big men' would be contacted and he would set off to the police station to try and settle the matter. Lasisi, Luke and Isaac were among the elders most frequently called in on these occasions.[9]

As well as helping to cope with some of the problems of migrants in Tamale itself, the *parapo* helped them retain links with home. They did this in a number of ways. First each of the associations rented a post office box, and it was through these that most of the migrants received their mail. The secretaries collected the mail daily and passed it on to the members directly or through friends and relatives. Second there were more formal links with the home town. Each of the associations held an annual general meeting at home, and delegates from all the branches in Ghana would be sent. In the case of the Ogbomosho *parapo* there was an annual meeting in Ghana itself. The members of each branch contributed to the fares of the delegates: in the Ogbomosho case this meant a contribution of NC2 from each married man, 50p from each married woman, and 25p from each unmarried man.

Third, as far as the home town was concerned, the main function of the branches of the town *parapọ* abroad was as fund-raising bodies for projects at home, as well as to provide the political leaders of the home town with the resources to lobby government and the bureaucracy effectively.[10] In the case of Igboho, for instance, each member in Ghana had to contribute an annual sum of NC4 for the men and NC1 for the women towards 'development' at home. They were expected to make additional contributions towards the costs of churches and mosques. By 1969 two large churches in addition to the two central mosques were under construction in Igboho, and the Tamale migrants had also helped pay for the Irepo Grammar School, a police station, two town halls, and two markets. In addition there were occasional emergency appeals, as when Igboho was hit by a freak storm and many roofs in the town were blown off. The funds collected could also be increased by loaning them to the members who returned them with interest.

The women from each town also had regular meetings, and made regular contributions. The Igboho Christian women gathered on Friday afternoons for a prayer and bible study session at which other matters could be discussed, and the Muslim women met on Thursday mornings for the same purpose. The dues were 5p a week with 2.5p fines for late arrivals. The money collected was redistributed to the members to buy cloth for the important religious festivals. When there were important matters to be discussed concerning market trade, women's representatives would be invited to the men's *parapọ* meetings, but the fact remains that the men's associations had the more elaborate organisation and took the more important decisions. At the level of formal decision-making at least, the women in the town associations, as in the areas of migration, capital accumulation, education and religion, tended to take second place.

Religious organisations

Overall, two-thirds of the Yoruba in Tamale were Muslims and the remainder Christians. Proportions varied between towns: nearly half the Ogbomosho migrants were Christian while the migrants from Shaki were almost entirely Muslim. Beliefs in witchcraft, sorcery, and the efficacy of prayer and ritual in trade and other areas of daily life remained strong among both Christians and Muslims. It was common for migrants to consult Ifa diviners in Nigeria either before they decided to migrate and on their visits home, and in Tamale they resorted to a wide range of religious specialists, including Islamic Mallams, northern Ghanaian diviners and 'herbalists' from the south. A Yoruba Ogboni lodge existed in Tamale, attended by Luke, despite his membership of the Baptist church.

Islam is strong both in areas of northern Ghana such as Gonja and Dagbon, and among migrant groups like the Hausa and Mossi, so generally the Yoruba Muslims were well-integrated into the religious life of Tamale. There were numerous small mosques attached to houses in every area of the town, as well as in the market, and the local Muslims would perform the daily prayers wherever convenient. It was only during Yoruba Muslim rites of passage that Yoruba identity assumed importance. These were presided over by the Yoruba Imam, Alhaji Bello from Offa. He had been Imam since the death of his predecessor, Mallam Bawa from Igboho, in 1962. As well as carrying out the duties of Imam, he also ran an Arabic school in the Hausa Zongo and kept the records of births, marriages and deaths in the Yoruba Muslim community. In the years that he was Imam before the exodus he had recorded over 1,000 births and only ninety-three deaths. The ceremonies he was asked to preside over were therefore usually naming ceremonies. These took place when the child was a week old, and Bello would be given a cedi and a portion of the meat for officiating. He would also collect a share of the money given in return for prayers by those present. If Bello was not able to attend, or if there were two ceremonies held on the same day, one of his two deputies, both from Ogbomosho, would attend instead.

There was a Yoruba mosque in the Sabon Gida, built on land which had belonged to one of the first Shaki migrants. The Yoruba Muslims were responsible for its erection in the 1930s and for the expenses of maintaining it, but members of other ethnic groups from the surrounding areas also made use of it. Most Yoruba preferred to pray at a mosque nearer home. Bello was officially the Imam of the Yoruba mosque, but he lived too far away from it to attend regularly. He used instead to lead the prayers at his own mosque in the Hausa Zongo. He had appointed a Dagomba Mallam to preside at the Yoruba mosque in his place. The Yoruba mosque therefore hardly provided the same sort of focus for the Yoruba Muslims that the churches did for the religious life of the Yoruba Christians.

For the Friday prayers, individual Yoruba migrants attended either of the two large Friday mosques. The older Central Mosque was near the Sabon Gida, while the newer Friday mosque, belonging to Alhaji Ajura, a leading Dagomba Mallam, was on the Bolgatanga road. This had been built after a long dispute between Ajura and the officials at the Central Mosque.[11] The Yoruba Muslims were little concerned with this dispute, which seemed to be a Dagomba affair, and the main factors determining which mosque they attended appeared to be where they lived or which mosque their friends used.

Towards the time of the exodus, however, there were signs that the Yoruba Muslims were trying to assert their identity more strongly. The main sign of this was the establishment by Bello's son of a Koranic school specifically for Yoruba children in the Sabon Gida. According to Bello himself, one of the reasons for this was to improve the standard of the Yoruba spoken by the children. Hitherto, all the Koranic schools in the town, including the two run by Yoruba Mallams, were attended by a cross-section of the Tamale Muslims, and Hausa or Dagbane had been the languages used there. There was no shortage of demand for the new school from the Yoruba. When it started, there were already 200 pupils enrolled, and another forty put their names down the day after the opening. As well as the children who attended the Koranic school each morning from 8.30 am to 1.30 pm, there was considerable demand for Koranic tuition from the Yoruba adults. Both the established Arabic teachers in the Yoruba community, Alhaji Bello and Alufa Lasisi from Ogbomosho, held evening classes, and they drew 180 students between them. In addition to these two, there were a dozen other recognised Yoruba Mallams in Tamale. They derived most of their income from divination, performances of ritual and prayers, and the preparation of amulets for their clients, both Yoruba and Ghanaian, who consulted them about sickness, misfortune or decisions. For day-to-day ritual, therefore, the Yoruba made use of the Muslim institutions in the town as a whole. It was only during rites of passage – namings, weddings and funerals – that the Yoruba Muslims emphasised their cultural identity, and even here the organisation of the celebrations involved the Muslim members of a particular town *parapo*, rather than the Yoruba Muslim community as a whole.

Unlike the Muslims, however, Yoruba Christians in Tamale had little contact through their religion with other groups in the town.[12] Three of the dozen or so churches in Tamale had almost exclusively Yoruba congregations and few of the Yoruba Christians worshipped anywhere else. The largest Yoruba church, the First Baptist, had a membership of round 400, half from Ogbomosho, a third from Igboho and the rest from Shaki and the minority towns. The Second Baptist Church had a smaller and more diverse congregation, from Shepeteri, Ilesha, Igboho and Ogbomosho. The total membership in 1969 was around 100. The UMCA had a total membership of around 200, all from Igbetti.

The first Yoruba Christians in Tamale had come mainly from Ogbomosho. They started to hold meetings in the late 1920s and Joseph Ade had been among the early leaders. By 1939 they had started to hold regular services in a rented room. They built their first church in 1947 and a larger one in 1963. The first pastor was D.A. Alasade who remained with them until after the Second World War. After a difference of opinion he left and founded a church on the Bolgatanga road. In 1969 this was run by the American Baptist Missionary in Tamale and had a mainly Ghanaian congregation. The pattern of a large Yoruba congregation coexisting with a small Ghanaian congregation in the same town was typical of the Baptist Church in Ghana. The foundation of the two other Yoruba churches in Tamale came rather later.

After an interval, Alasade was succeeded by Pastor Adeyemi, a graduate of the Ogbomosho Seminary. It was during his term of office that preaching stations were established in and around Tamale. A group of the younger men on the church committee took it in turns to go out to the villages to preach, as well as in the prison and hospital in Tamale itself. However, Adeyemi was not popular among some of the older members of the congregation from Ogbomosho and Igboho, mainly because of his opposition to polygynists serving on the church committees. Polygynous elders like Luke saw that this would undermine their influence. In the end, the issue caused so much trouble in the congregation that Adeyemi returned to the Seminary in 1956.

It was also during Pastor Adeyemi's time that the UMCA church was formed. The United Missionary Church for Africa, founded in 1922, was the oldest and largest church in Igbetti. At first the Igbetti Christians in Tamale had attended the Baptist Church, but they felt that Adeyemi was pressuring them into formal membership. They wrote to the United Missionary Society in Nigeria to ask if a pastor could be sent to Tamale, and they broke away to form their own church. Apart from a small congregation in Damongo this was the only UMCA church in Ghana, though in forms of service, doctrine and organisation the two groups of Yoruba Christians in Tamale were very similar.[13]

Adeyemi's successor, Pastor Ladele, got on better with the elders but less well with the younger men who complained to the mission when he decided to discontinue the preaching stations. They were suspended by the church elders. American and Nigerian mission officials, with some sympathy for the younger members, attempted to mediate, but more trouble erupted the following year when allegations of adultery by senior members of the church made matters worse. A split which resulted in the formation of the Second Baptist Church soon followed.

According to the First Baptist Church leaders the main argument was over polygyny. According to the Second Baptist Church leaders it was the issue of adultery. Having been suspended once they decided to form their own church. Many of the younger, more educated members of the congregation were in sympathy with them, but pressure was put on them by their senior relatives to remain in the main church, and only nine actually left. Soon after this the polygynous elders quietly retired from the church committees. Ogundiran, with his single wife, remained on it. Pastor Ladele stayed in Tamale until 1964. The Second Baptist Church, though small, survived and gradually increased in size, and in 1969 its members had just completed a new building.

After a year Ladele was succeeded by another evangelical pastor who fell out with Ogundiran almost as soon as he arrived. Ogundiran, as chairman of the church committee, had effectively been running the church since Ladele's departure, and he now refused to take any part. The new pastor, however, was having problems with his marriage and left in 1967. Ogundiran took over again as chairman, a position he held until the exodus. The church committee consisted of a chairman (Ogundiran), a secretary (Ayoola), a treasurer, and the members of both the Sunday school and pulpit subcommittees, the pulpit subcommittee being responsible for arranging the preaching. Ogundiran was also chairman of this, and his leadership in the church was now unassailable. During the summer of 1969 he was being helped by a student from the Seminary, but negotiations with the mission for another full-time pastor had so far come to nothing.

The organisation of all three of the Yoruba churches in Tamale was broadly similar. In the First Baptist Church, most of the congregation were members of one or other of the church *egbẹ* or societies. The boys and the younger men belonged to the Royal Ambassadors, an *egbẹ* found in every large Baptist Church in Ghana. The Baptist Mission organised regular meetings and camps for its members from all over the country. The other men were divided into five *egbẹ*, mainly on the basis of age. There were some anomalies: Egbẹ Ifeloju not only included men in their forties and fifties like Ogundiran but also literate clerks and teachers in their twenties and thirties who felt qualified by virtue of their education. On the other hand, the First Baptist Church choirmaster, an unsuccessful trader in his late forties, was a member of the most junior of the adult *egbẹ*, possibly because its members were expected to contribute less to church funds. A previous chairman of the Royal Ambassadors had been married with children before giving up the position.

The women were divided into three groups. The married women were members of the Women's Missionary Union, another *egbẹ* common to all the Baptist churches. The girls belonged to the Girls' Auxiliaries, the equivalent of the Royal Ambassadors. A third small *egbẹ*, Egbẹ Lydia, consisted of young educated unmarried women working as teachers and nurses in Tamale.

The collection of church funds was organised through the *egbẹ*, with the members of each paying a specified amount. In 1969 contributions towards the repair of the pastor's house amounted to between NC4 and 8 for the men, depending on the seniority of the *egbẹ*. The women paid NC2 each, and the Royal Ambassadors 50p. The men's *egbẹ* normally met after the Sunday morning service. They had their own officials, rules and regulations, including a system of fines. Most weeks the collection of dues was the only business, but other matters discussed could include quarrels between members and matters affecting the church as a whole. The members would be invited as a group to namings, weddings and funerals involving other members, and at Christmas or Easter some of the richer members would invite the whole *egbẹ* to their houses for a celebration. After the event the *egbẹ* members would contribute the same amount each as a present to the person holding the ceremony to help with the expenses. In return they would expect to receive special treatment, with food and beer being reserved for them. This led to trouble. Ogundiran, as the chairman of Egbẹ Ifeloju, tried to make it a rule that members of his *egbẹ* should contribute NC2 every time they attended a function. This was a considerable amount – the daily minimum wage in Ghana was still 75p. The younger men objected, broke away and formed their own *egbẹ*, electing Ogundiran's younger brother as their chairman, which did nothing to repair the strained relations between the brothers. It had also become customary for Ifeloju members organising a naming ceremony to slaughter a cow for the occasion. This came to a stop when a member bought a cow on credit and could not pay. It was decided that this threatened the reputation of the whole *egbe*, and that expenditure should be restricted in future in view of the deteriorating conditions in the market.

In addition to *egbe* contributions members were also expected to pay tithes (*idamewa*) to the church, in theory a tenth of their incomes. At the end of each quarter, the list of contributors and contributions was read out, which was felt to be necessary to put pressure on members to pay. It was generally felt that the wealthier traders were not paying enough. While the clerks with fixed incomes really were paying a tenth of their salaries, Luke, probably the wealthiest man in the church, was only paying NC6 a month.

The main church functions were the Sunday services, but there were also weekly prayer meetings, bible study sessions and choir practices. The more energetic younger members of the church often spent four or five nights a week in church activities. In addition there were other special events, such as the choir festival which took place in 1969, attended by choirs from all the other large Tamale churches. The purpose of this was to collect money for a church organ. One of the Baptist churches in Kumasi had recently acquired an instrument and Ogundiran was determined that Tamale should not be left behind. Offerings from the congregation were taken up at various times during the performance, and the platform was occupied by Tamale businessmen and school principals in addition to representatives of the Mission. Ayoola, perhaps the member with the most extensive local contacts, acted as chairman.

The town *parapo* and the Yoruba churches functioned as classic voluntary associations, very similar to those described elsewhere in the world. First they acted as adaptive mechanisms, allowing the migrants to enter into a ready-made social network on their arrival in the town, and they acted as supportive institutions for their members in a variety of ways. It was within the friendship networks that grew out of the organisations that the migrants spent much of their social lives.

Second, they helped the migrants maintain links both with home and with other migrants from the same town in other parts of Ghana. Along with this went the maintenance of Yoruba cultural identity. Whereas in Schildkrout's study of Kumasi the second generation Mossi migrants adopted zongo rather than Mossi associational patterns, the Yoruba in Tamale were involved in organisations which were modelled on, and which had close links with, the social institutions of the home town. Membership thus reinforced both cultural identity and links with home.

Third, these organisations provided a framework within which individuals could organise their social lives and compete for status and respect within the Yoruba community. It was this factor which led to the strains and stresses in the First Baptist Church in particular. Gradually the church had developed out of the informal meetings of the early Yoruba migrants in Tamale into a large formal organisation with a professional pastor. It was this development which brought about the clashes of values and personalities which were visible from the time of Pastor Alasade onwards. The clashes between church doctrine and traditional Yoruba values were most evident in the dispute over polygyny, but there were implications for the authority structure of the church which went beyond this. On the one hand, the 'big men' in the Yoruba community, the senior and wealthier traders, considered it their right to control the institutions which operated within the Yoruba community. For the younger members, the poor and the educated, church membership provided an alternative status system independent of the traditional Yoruba status determinants of age and wealth. These groups defined prestige in terms of doctrinal fluency, participation in church activities, and acceptance of Baptist teachings where they conflicted with traditional Yoruba practices. This was particularly so in their acceptance of monogamy, and the need to evangelise outside the Yoruba community. The older conservatives in the church were the wealthy traders, the heads of large family groups, who had been the original members of the congregation. In the town *parapo*, which they had also started, their influence and prestige were unchallenged. In the case of the church, however, they found their authority being undermined by much younger men, openly criticising the senior members with the apparent support of the pastor and the mission. The radicals of the 1950s were much younger men, many of whom were either unsuccessful in trade or not involved in trade at all: thus the importance for them of church membership as a framework for their social lives. It was these men who were enthusiastic about the preaching stations which the elders regarded as a waste of time.

This points in microcosm to the dilemma of the Baptist Church in Ghana. On the one hand it was trying to establish roots among Ghanaians and on the other the overwhelming majority of its members were Nigerian migrants. The Yoruba ran their churches in the same way and in the same language as they had done in Nigeria: membership of the Baptist Church was part of their Yoruba identity. In the case of the First Baptist Church this conflict of interests was reflected in the departure of the first pastor in the 1940s, in the opposition to the preaching stations in the 1950s, and in the split which led to the formation of the Second Baptist Church in 1959. It was, however, not only an issue in the Baptist Churches. The minister of the UMCA complained to me that his congregation did not appear to be interested in their own preaching stations which he himself was anxious to keep going.

The position of Ogundiran in all this was ambiguous. Like the leaders of the Second Baptist Church he was literate, monogamous, and an able preacher. But he was also wealthy and a member of one of the largest groups of Ogbomosho migrants. Thus he regarded his leadership of the church as

important for his own position in the Yoruba community, but was not particularly interested in evangelising outside it. It was this parochialism combined
with his steady refusal to play a secondary role which resulted in many of the
tensions visible in the church in 1969.

The *Ilu Pejọ*

In Tamale, as in the other major towns in Ghana, chiefs had been appointed by
the Native Authority for each of the major ethnic groups resident in the town as
part of the indirect rule system during the colonial period.[14] They were chosen
by the members of each community, though the choice also had to be ratified
by the local native authority. The first Yoruba chief in Tamale generally
recognised by informants was Olaosibikan from Ibadan (d.1934). He was
succeeded by Sani Offa (c.1954), Salami Ilorin (d.1957), Braimah Ilorin
(d.1960) and Alhaji Karimu from Ogbomosho (d.1970). In 1962, Alhaji
Karimu returned to Ogbomosho to settle and made only brief visits to Tamale
thereafter. Despite his retirement, a successor was not appointed, and in his
absence either Alhaji Salami, the next most senior of the Ogbomosho traders,
or Alhaji Bello, the Yoruba Imam, took his place when necessary, though by
this time the functions of the chief were much reduced.

In the early days, the Yoruba chief acted as the intermediary between the
Yoruba and the administration. He also sat with the other Tamale Chiefs in the
local Grade II Court. The local court was handed over to full-time magistrates
in about 1962 and the chiefs played no further part in it. About the same time,
Alhaji Karimu, the Yoruba chief, began to spend more time in Nigeria, and the
Ilu Pejọ became more important. It had started with informal meetings of
Yoruba elders at the house of the chief, but in the 1960s it developed into a
formal body with its own officials and representatives from each of the Yoruba
towns represented in Tamale. In 1969 these were: Ogbomosho, Igboho,
Igbetti, Shaki, Shepeteri, Abeokuta, Offa, Oshogbo, Ede, Ilesha, Iwo, Ilorin,
Otu, Ago Are, Iseyin, Ijebu and Offiki. Oyo and Ibadan had been deleted from
the list when the last migrants from the town left Tamale. The meetings
usually involved only the men, though in important discussions which concerned them women representatives could be called on as well. Ogbomosho
sent eight representatives, Igboho and Igbetti groups six each, Shaki four,
Shepeteri, Otu, Ilorin, Abeokuta and Ede two each, and the others one each.[15]

In 1969 the meetings were still held in the courtyard of Alhaji Karimu's
house, but in his absence they were chaired either by Alhaji Salami or Alhaji
Bello. The secretary was an Igboho photographer with a Standard 6 education,
and his assistant was the Ilesha trader from the army barracks who provided
useful links with the military after the coup. The rest of the representatives
were chosen mainly by virtue of their age, though the secretaries of the town
parapọ, many of them younger men, also attended. The older delegates
included some of the most experienced and respected men in the Yoruba

Plate 6.1: Igbetti drummers at a wedding: prior to 1969, the group did good
business playing in both Nigeria and Ghana.

community such as Luke and Alhaji Sani from Ogbomosho and Lasisi
from Igbetti. Normally meetings were held every two weeks, though like those
of the town *parapọ* they were suspended during the 1969 election campaign.
Emergency meetings could also be called. Like the meetings of the
town *parapọ*, the *Ilu Pejọ* meetings could deal with any matters which the
members wanted to bring up: in 1969 these included the political situation, the
situation in the market, and disputes involving Yoruba migrants from different towns.

Before my arrival in 1969 there had been a series of meetings to discuss the
situation in the market and the image of the Yoruba community as a whole,
particularly after the arrests for price control infringements and selling smuggled goods. The Yoruba felt insecure, and part of this stemmed from the
publication the previous year of the government's proposals for the indigenisation of market trade. There was also some concern over which of the parties the
Yoruba should support during the coming election. In the end, with typical
pragmatism, it was decided to support both the main contenders. Members of
the *Ilu Pejọ* joined both the Progress Party and the National Alliance of
Liberals, so that, whichever won, Yoruba interests would still be protected.
Officially as 'aliens' the Yoruba were not allowed to participate in the election,
so as a body the *Ilu Pejọ* remained strictly neutral. Approaches from both the

main parties for their support were sidestepped, and all official meetings were suspended during the campaign.

The more routine matters which the *Ilu Pejo* discussed were disputes between Yoruba from different towns. Disputes between Yoruba from the same town could usually be settled by the town *parapo*, though they might be taken to the *Ilu Pejo* if they proved intractable. If the police became involved in disputes between Yoruba, *Ilu Pejo* representatives went to ask if they could settle the matter within the Yoruba community. When a new police chief arrived a delegation was sent to welcome him and assure him of the continued support of the Yoruba in Tamale. The *Ilu Pejo* also arranged for Yoruba participation in events such as durbars for visiting dignitaries, dance festivals at the Cultural Centre in Tamale, symposia organised by the ministries on social problems, and so forth. It had funds available, gathered from the 10p contributions each member made at each meeting, and these were used for any 'gifts' to officialdom which the organisation considered necessary. If more money was required, special contributions could be levied from each of the town groups.

In some cases there was not enough time to call a formal meeting, and the senior members available would have to decide on a course of action. There was the case just after my arrival of a Yoruba fish trader from Techiman who was found dead, apparently murdered, in the Volta Lake at Yeji. The body was taken to Tamale by the CID and the police sent word to the Yoruba elders of what had happened. An informal meeting was called under a tree outside the police station, and it included both the relatives of the dead man and the Yoruba leaders from Tamale. They raised the money to bribe police to release the body quickly and to get it prepared for burial. The hospital workers demanded extra money as the body had been in the water for some time and was decaying. After the burial the police turned up at the cemetery and demanded the body back so that they could continue with their enquiries. Lasisi was sent down to the station with them to sort the matter out.

Thus not only did the *Ilu Pejo* provide a useful airing ground for matters of common interest and disputes, but it also provided a channel of communications between the Yoruba and the authorities. The local court officials commented that there was hardly ever a dispute between two Yoruba that came to their attention, and the court records that I was able to check bore this out. The absence of cases involving two Yoruba, considering the complex web of short-term financial obligations in which most of the traders were involved, was a tribute to the success of the *parapo* and the *Ilu Pejo* in keeping the peace between their members.[16]

THE NIGERIAN COMMUNITY COMMITTEE

Whereas during the colonial period it had been ethnic identity which formed the basis of urban administration, after independence the emphasis shifted to nationality. The Nigerian High Commission in Accra set up a series of regional Nigerian Community Committees through which it could communicate with Nigerians throughout Ghana.[17] The High Commission was anxious that all communications with its nationals should be dealt with through these. In 1966–7 the *Ilu Pejọ* in Tamale made a contribution to a rehabilitation fund set up after the troubles in Nigeria in response to an appeal from the High Commission. A sharply worded letter arrived back from Accra saying that in future all such contributions should be sent through the Nigerian Community as the High Commission did not recognise 'tribalistic associations'. In the early days after its formation in the early 1960s the Nigerian Community Committee in Tamale had consisted of members of all three of the largest Nigerian ethnic groups – Hausa, Yoruba and Igbo – though the three groups had had little in common. After the President, a driver from Offa, and the Secretary, a man from the Nigerian Midwestern Region, and left the town, the organisation went into temporary abeyance.

In 1968 it took on a new lease of life. This was due to the arrival in Tamale of Rev. Ayodele, a minister with an American Methodist church, who came from Oyan. Although Oyan migrants were one of the largest groups in southern Ghana, particularly in the diamond areas, there were very few Oyan migrants in the north. Ayodele had been involved with the Nigerian community in the south, and he approached Luke and Lasisi to see if they could revive the committee in Tamale. The impetus came from a planned visit of the High Commissioner to Tamale. A new committee was set up, including four Hausa and fifteen Yoruba, thirteen of them chosen by the *Ilu Pejọ*. As far as the Yoruba were concerned, the committee was reasonably representative. Luke was the president, Lasisi was the treasurer, and Ayodele became the secretary. There was a Hausa chairman. The committee also included the secretary and assistant secretary of the *Ilu Pejọ*, two representatives from each of the four main Yoruba towns, the UMCA minister and a secondary school teacher, also from Oyan, to help with the accounts and the administration. Rules were drawn up modelled on those of the other Nigerian associations in Tamale, including the usual fines for late arrivals and absences, and most of the meetings were held in Luke's front room.

In July 1969 the Ghanaian government informed the missions of foreign governments in Accra that they should issue all their nationals with passports. The Nigerian High Commission decided to register Nigerian nationals through the Nigerian Community Committees, and to have forms filled in for the issue of passports. This was to be organised by the secretary in each region, and Ayodele was put in charge of the operation for the Northern and Upper Regions. He made a trip round the north appointing secretaries in the main towns, including Navrongo, Bawku, Walewale, Yendi, Salaga, Wa and Bole. Committees had functioned in some of these towns before, though rather intermittently. At this point Ayodele ran into trouble: in order to facilitate the distribution of the registration forms, he called a meeting of the other town secretaries in the region without informing or inviting the other members of the Tamale committee.

The meeting was duly held. The discussions that took place showed that such a body could have served a very useful purpose. Ayodele reported on a meeting which he had attended in Accra at which had been discussed a number of aspects of life in Ghana which the Nigerians found troublesome, including exchange control regulations and the behaviour of the border guards at Idiroko, on the road from Accra to Lagos. It had been proposed that a delegation should be sent to Nigeria on behalf of the Nigerians in Ghana to complain about the situation, and that money should be raised to cover the cost of this. The other main item on the agenda was the distribution of the registration forms and their completion.

The meeting did not help relations between Ayodele and the rest of the Tamale committee. Luke was annoyed at not having been informed. There was also the issue of the amount which Nigerian nationals were being asked to pay for their registration and passports. The Tamale committee had suggested the sum of NC4 each – three of which would go to the High Commission and one towards the running of the Tamale committee. On his return from Accra, Ayodele announced that it had been decided that the fee would be NC5, of which he himself as regional organiser should keep NC2 towards the costs of registration. The rest of the committee appeared suspicious. Luke suggested that they should wait until they saw this in writing from Accra, and that for the moment, the Nigerians in Tamale should only pay four cedis. However, the registration went ahead immediately the forms were distributed, and the secretaries in Navrongo and Walewale quickly gave Ayodele NC560 in registration fees.

The use of this money caused further trouble between Luke and Ayodele. Luke went to Ayodele after the money had arrived and suggested a deal, as the High Commission had indicated that they would not be ready to receive the money for several months. It was against Luke's nature to leave funds lying idle, and as we have seen with some of the other Yoruba institutions in Tamale, the distribution of funds to members to use and increase was institutionalised. Ayodele however had his own problems. In addition to his mission work he was trying to start a business school in Tamale, under the auspices of his church. Assuming that the church would reimburse him later for his expenditure, he went ahead and rented a building, bought furniture and enrolled students. When Luke approached him about the deal therefore he had already spent the money himself.

Soon after this rumours began to spread through the Yoruba community that Ayodele had made away with the Nigerian Community funds, and he was forced to resign from the committee. The trader from the army barracks took over as secretary. Ayodele was bitter at the whole affair. He regarded his temporary use of the funds as legitimate and said he would have paid them back as soon as the money from his church had come through. Before the matter was settled, however, most of the Nigerian Community in Tamale had returned to Nigeria.

A number of points emerge from this brief history. First, there is no doubt that a role did exist for an institution such as the Nigerian Community Committee. There were a number of issues which could have been taken up at the national level between the two governments, including the scope of the Ghanaian indigenisation legislation, the problems of citizenship, the problem of passports and immigration, the problem of exchange control, and the question of trade between Ghana and Nigeria. When the interests of Nigerians were threatened, as happened at the end of 1969, such an institution could have been useful as a link between the Accra government and the Nigerians in Ghana to clarify the situation. But it was probably too much to expect that part-time, untrained and unpaid officials, however well-intentioned and efficient, would be able to cope with the registration of many thousands of Nigerians in the Northern and Upper Regions and adequately represent their interests in Accra. The whole episode pointed to the need for an adequate organisation to protect the interests of migrants in other West African countries.

ETHNIC STEREOTYPES

So far this chapter has been concerned with the associational structure of the Yoruba community and the formal organisations which existed within it. This has tended to emphasise the autonomy of the Yoruba community, isolated from the rest of the social life of Tamale and maintaining strong links with the migrants' towns of origin in Nigeria. This apparent isolation underlay many of the stereotypes which the Yoruba and their Ghanaian hosts held about each other. One of the most noticeable features of Ghanaian society is the deep cleavage – economic, social and cultural – between the north and south of the country.[18] Like many of the southern Ghanaians, the Yoruba often spoke of the northerners, or 'NT's', as unsophisticated people with low levels of education and sophistication and little knowledge of the outside world. In Yoruba terms they lacked *ilaju*. Many of the early accounts of trade and migration I was given emphasised how little knowledge people in the area had of money or manufactured goods until the arrival of the traders. However, some of the Yoruba were prepared to admit that since then many of the Dagomba had become shrewd traders and that their simple life-style had helped them when it came to capital accumulation.

The Yoruba image of the southern Ghanaians was very different. They were regarded as perhaps too sophisticated and many of the Yoruba traders commented on the way in which they preferred to spend money rather than save it. The other side of the coin was, of course, the image of the Yoruba held by the

northern and southern Ghanaians. In Tamale relations between the Yoruba
and the Dagomba, the largest ethnic group in the town, were relatively good.
After the announcement of the compliance order none of the incidents
involving intimidation of the Yoruba and other 'aliens' which appear to have
taken place in the south of Ghana seem to have taken place in Tamale, and
among most of the northerners that I talked to there was considerable sympathy for the position of the Yoruba. The effects of Yoruba trade were
regarded by many as beneficial, particularly in the rural areas, and the main
criticisms of them as a group were that they were 'too money-minded' and
'restrictive with their women'. The stereotypes held by the southern Ghanaians, particularly the educated, were more negative, often reflecting underlying competition in trade. In particular, there were complaints that Ghanaians
could not get goods at the stores because 'the Yoruba will have been giving
money out to the manager beforehand', and that the Yoruba were enriching
themselves at the expense of Ghanaians. Oyedipe's account of the Yoruba in
Accra, where he was himself a student, suggests that by the later 1960s the
general image of them was more negative than in the north.[19]

However, whatever the nature of the general stereotypes held, the situation
at the level of individual relationships was more complex, and was determined
by the interplay of factors such as residence, marriage patterns, education and
the links of the Yoruba with Nigeria in addition to their associational structure,
and these factors are examined in the next section.

RESIDENCE AND INTERACTION

The residential distribution of the Yoruba migrants in Tamale in 1969 has
already been described in Chapter 4. Several consequences for the life of the
Yoruba in Tamale flowed from the gradual development of the town and the
location of the migrants within it. First, apart from the encapsulated villages
within the town boundary, the population was extremely mixed. Even in the
Sabon Gida the Yoruba were by no means the only residents, and Dagomba-
owned houses were interspersed with those of the Yoruba throughout. As a
result of this diversity a considerable number of friendship links had developed
between the Yoruba and members of the other ethnic groups. Multi-ethnic
groups could be found relaxing in the open spaces between the houses and
visiting the *pito* bars scattered throughout the town. This trend towards greater
interaction between the groups was specially noticeable among the children.
Play groups often cut across ethnic boundaries, and, as the children went to
school, so did friendship networks. The younger Yoruba almost all spoke some
Hausa, Dagbane and Akan in addition to Yoruba and English. Many of the
compounds contained a mixture of ethnic groups. Thus, though most of the
Yoruba in Tamale lived in houses owned by themselves or other Yoruba
(often their senior relatives) the Yoruba landlords with rooms to spare let them
out to anyone who approached them for accommodation and who

seemed to be suitable, either because they knew them personally or because of a contact through a mutual friend, and there seemed to be no particular ethnic factors involved in the allocation.

Education resulted in similar mixing. Schools in Ghanaian towns, particularly at the middle and secondary level, are ethnically very mixed, especially in the northern schools which have always had a large proportion of southern students. Many of the Yoruba in Tamale had attended school in other parts of the country, and some of the cases of marriage between educated Yoruba and Ghanaians developed out of these school friendships.[20]

On the other hand, several sets of factors tended to reinforce interaction within the Yoruba community. One of these was the intensity of Yoruba associational life. In fact it was the group who might have been expected to assimilate most rapidly into Ghanaian social life, the younger educated Christians, who were most intensively involved within the Yoruba community through membership of the Baptist and UMCA churches.

The second factor was that of the links maintained with home. These were of several types. Those who could afford to made frequent visits home, particularly if they intended to build a house there, and every year delegations were sent to the annual general meetings of the town parapọ in Nigeria.

Another important set of links resulted from the pattern of child fostering which is common throughout West Africa.[21] In addition to their own children, many Yoruba were also responsible for junior relatives brought to Ghana from Nigeria or other parts of West Africa. This was only one side of a two-way process of fostering which meant a constant interchange of personnel between the migrant community and the home towns. This resulted from a number of factors. First, it was common in Yoruba society for children to be sent to live with their senior relatives, normally grandparents or people of similar age whose own children had left home. They would be able to help them with trade or domestic work. Second, fostering between full siblings either on a reciprocal or a one-way basis was also common when the siblings were separated. For the Yoruba migrants in Ghana, fostering served a double purpose. First there were the economic benefits of migration which could be spread more widely through the descent group. Second, many of the children born in Ghana could be sent home to Nigeria to receive primary education, learn Yoruba properly and get to know their home towns, in addition to helping out their relatives. There were also crisis situations where descent group members assumed responsibility for the children of close relatives who became sick or died. In such cases the younger children usually stayed with their mothers, but older children would usually go to the closest relative of the deceased who was in a good position to help them with education or with the acquisition of other skills. Thus many of the migrants in Ghana had sent some of their children to Nigeria. The children most usually sent appeared to be the senior ones, who were sent either to their father's or their mothers's parents. Perhaps the most common pattern was for a son to be sent to live with his father's father, and a girl to go to a mother's mother or mother's sister. In addition to learning Yoruba and helping relatives at home, a common reason given for fostering was that of discipline. Oyedipe lists a number of complaints commonly made in Accra by Yoruba parents about their children who had not been home – that they showed disrespect to their elders, that they failed to help in domestic work, that they asked strangers for money, and that they were 'morally lax'.[22] Similar comments were made in Nigeria in 1970 after the migrants' return. Some of the children were embarrassed to speak Yoruba because of their grammatical mistakes, and their inability to understand complex numerals, proverbs and greetings. They were also said to be irresponsible with money – a common saying was *o gọ bi ọmọ Ghana* – 'he's as daft as a kid from Ghana' – Ghanaian children having been spoiled by having too much money to play with. On the other hand, many children were sent to Ghana for secondary education which was much cheaper than in Nigeria, especially after the imposition of exchange controls.

Friendship networks

Some idea of the extent of interaction between the Yoruba migrants and Ghanaians can be gained from the material we collected on friendships.[23] In Nigeria we collected data on the best friends of the Yoruba migrants while they had been in Ghana. Information was obtained from forty-three men in Igbetti, ninety-one in Igboho and sixty-eight in Ogbomosho, who listed up to six of their best friends, together with their religions, ethnic groups and occupations, 897 responses in all. Tables 6.1–6.6 give details of the responses.

Many of the migrants' friends came from the same town of origin, as might have been expected. Between 46 and 55 per cent of the responses for each town fall into this category. The average man in the sample drew just under half his friends from the same Yoruba town, one in six from a different town, and two out of six from another ethnic group. Nearly 43 per cent of the population mentioned no friends from other ethnic groups at all. Around 60 per cent of the responses were within the Yoruba community which formed only 3 per cent of the Tamale population.[24] However, over half the sample listed at least one member of another ethnic group, and 18 per cent listed four or more.

Two other factors besides town of origin also seem to have been in important in the formation of friendship networks. Between 54 per cent and 65 per cent of responses from each town named friends in the same occupation.[25] Even more startling is the religious factor: over four-fifths of the friends named were of the same religion as the respondent, suggesting that the Muslims and Christians in Tamale were largely closed groups in terms of friendship networks.

If the responses are grouped in other ways the implications of the data are less clear. There seems to be little relationship between education and numbers of non-Yoruba friends, at least as far as migrants educated as far as middle

Table 6.1: Close friends of Yoruba men living in Northern Ghana, 1969, by place of origin.

Migrants' town	Same Yoruba town		Origin of friends Other Yoruba town		Non-Yoruba		Total	
	no.	%	no.	%	no.	%	no.	%
Ogbomosho	140	45.8	38	12.4	128	41.8	306	100.0
Igbetti	116	55.0	23	10.9	72	34.1	211	100.0
Igboho	178	46.8	59	15.5	143	37.6	380	100.0
Total	434	48.4	120	13.4	343	38.2	897	100.0

school are concerned. There is a U-shaped association between age and friend-ship links both within and outside the Yoruba community. The older and younger migrants both had more contacts outside their own towns than did the middle-aged migrants. Perhaps the most striking figure here is the large number of contacts which the older migrants had with Yoruba from other towns, as one would expect, given that the Yoruba community had been much smaller when they arrived in Ghana. Apart from these, there are few clearly visible patterns. Yoruba of all ages, religions and occupations found them-selves in settings which could lead to friendships either inside or outside the Yoruba community, and a full range of options – from having an almost entirely Yoruba network to having an almost entirely Ghanaian one – was found in all age groups and occupational categories.

Marriage

Another factor which reinforced the links between the migrant and his or her home town were the marriage patterns in the Yoruba community. The groups of migrants from individual towns were largely endogamous. Table 6.7 pre-sents data on the origins of the wives of the migrants we interviewed. The results are striking, and are partly a function of the way in which many partners were selected. The normal pattern was that the first spouse of a man should be

Table 6.2: Close friends of Yoruba men living in Northern Ghana, 1969, by religion.

Migrants' town	Religion of friends Same religion		Different religion		Total	
	no.	%	no.	%	no.	%
Ogbomosho	262	85.6	44	14.4	306	100.0
Igbetti	177	83.9	34	16.1	211	100.0
Igboho	318	83.7	62	16.3	380	100.0
Total	757	84.4	140	15.6	897	100.0

Table 6.3: Close friends of Yoruba men living in Northern Ghana, 1969, by occupation.

| Migrants' occupation | Occupation of friends | | | | | |
| | Same occupation | | Different occupation | | Total | |
	no.	%	no.	%	no.	%
Ogbomosho	165	53.9	141	46.1	306	100.0
Igbetti	137	64.9	74	35.1	211	100.0
Igboho	222	58.4	158	41.6	380	100.0
Total	524	58.4	373	41.6	897	100.0

arranged, and the expenses of the marriage paid for, by the parent or senior relative for whom he was working. The girl might be either from the home town or from a family from the same town already in Ghana. After the imposition of currency restrictions, girls who lived in Ghana already and for whom the marriage payments could be made in cedis were at a premium. Ahmadu Bawa said that his own wife had more than eighteen men trying to marry her, from Bawku, Walewale, Yendi and Tamale. The fact that marriages were often arranged by senior relatives tended to maintain the pattern of town endogamy: it was customary for the two families to look in detail at the background of the prospective partner, and this was easier to do if the partner came from the same town. Where the bride and groom came from different towns, there was usually a special reason for it.

Yesufu was from Ogbomosho, but his mother, divorced from his father, was from Shaki. He was brought up by his mother's sister for a time, and she was instrumental in arranging for his marriage to a Shaki girl.

Amuda's father was from Igbetti, but two of his father's closest friends were from Ogbomosho, and the marriage was arranged in Tamale with a classificatory daughter of one of them.

Table 6.4: Origins of friends of Yoruba men living in Northern Ghana, 1969, by educational level.

| Migrants' education | Origin of friends | | | | | | | |
| | Same Yoruba town | | Other Yoruba town | | Non-Yoruba | | Total | |
	no.	%	no.	%	no.	%	no.	%
Primary or less	380	49.5	93	12.1	294	38.3	767	100.0
Middle school	40	44.0	20	22.0	31	34.1	91	100.0
Above middle	14	35.9	7	17.9	18	46.2	39	100.0

Table 6.5: Origins of friends of Yoruba men living in Northern Ghana, 1969, by age.

| Migrants' age | Origin of friends | | | | | | Total | |
| | Same Yoruba town | | Other Yoruba town | | Non-Yoruba | | | |
	no.	%	no.	%	no.	%	no.	%
20–44	219	46.7	63	13.4	187	39.9	469	100.0
45–49	176	55.0	30	9.4	114	35.6	320	100.0
Over 60	39	36.1	27	25.0	42	38.9	108	100.0

Sunday was from Otu but was married to a girl from Ogbomosho. The Ogbomosho migrants had a reputation for being particularly exclusive with their women, and he was one of the first from his own town to marry an Ogbomosho girl. He had been to school in Kumasi where most of his friends had been from Ogbomosho, and he met the girl through them. They wanted to get married, but the parents were against it, so to force the issue she became pregnant. The parents then agreed.

In the first two cases, the marriage was arranged by senior relatives, even though the partners were from different towns. One of these was the result of a previous cross-town match, and the other a result of the father's friendship networks. The third case represents another common variation: the couple decide on marriage on their own, and force the issue against parental opposition. However, marriages between couples from different Yoruba towns were still quite rare in Tamale, little commoner than marriage with members of other ethnic groups. I gathered from informants who had been in the south that inter-town marriages there were more frequent.

Until the imposition of currency restrictions, the general pattern had been for the Yoruba to return to Nigeria to marry. In the 1960s, the number of marriages being performed in Ghana increased because it was cheaper, and because marriages were increasingly arranged between families resident there. It appears from Table 6.8 that the Igboho migrants started to perform marriages in Ghana rather earlier than the other two groups – possibly because of

Table 6.6: Origins of friends of Yoruba men living in Northern Ghana, 1969, by occupation.

| Migrants' occupation | Origin of friends | | | | | | Total | |
| | Same Yoruba town | | Other Yoruba town | | Non-Yoruba | | | |
	no.	%	no.	%	no.	%	no.	%
Trading	319	50.6	78	12.4	233	37.0	630	100.0
Other	115	43.1	42	15.7	110	41.2	267	100.0

Plate 6.2: Alhaji Salami, the most senior Yoruba elder in Tamale by the time of the exodus.

Table 6.7: Origins of wives of Yoruba men living in Northern Ghana, 1969, by town.

| | Same town | | Different town | | Non-Yoruba | | | |
	no.	%	no.	%	no.	%	no.	%
Igboho	125	89.9	9	6.5	5	3.6	139	100.0
Ogbomosho	97	91.5	4	3.8	5	4.7	106	100.0
Igbetti	63	91.3	3	4.3	3	4.3	69	100.0
Totals	285	90.8	16	5.1	13	4.1	314	100.0

the very large numbers of Igboho resident in the towns of northern Ghana, compared with the population of the home town.

The low frequency of marriage between Yoruba and Ghanaians has been noted elsewhere in Ghana[26] and marriages between Yoruba women and Ghanaian men in Tamale were particularly rare. There was the rather anomalous case of the Dagomba hotel owner with two Yoruba wives, but his was a lone instance. It was more common for a Yoruba man to have a Ghanaian wife, and these marriages fell into two main groups. First there were established traders who had married local girls as their second or third wives, their first wives being Yoruba. On the other hand, there were the marriages of the younger,

Table 6.8: Places where extant marriages of Yoruba men living in Northern Ghana, 1969, occurred, by year of marriage.

| | Ogbomosho | | Igboho | | Igbetti | | Total | |
	no.	%	no.	%	no.	%	no.	%
Nigeria								
Before 1940	10	9.7	8	5.7	5	7.1	23	7.3
1940–4	10	9.7	9	6.4	5	7.1	24	7.6
1945–9	10	9.7	9	6.4	5	7.1	24	7.6
1950–4	14	13.4	10	7.1	18	25.7	42	13.4
1955–9	12	11.7	20	14.2	6	8.6	38	12.1
1960–4	14	13.6	22	15.6	17	24.3	53	16.9
1965–9	10	9.7	13	9.2	7	10.0	30	9.6
Subtotal	80	77.7	91	64.5	63	90.0	234	74.5
Ghana								
Before 1950	0	0.0	1	0.7	0	0.0	1	0.3
1950–4	0	0.0	4	2.8	0	0.0	4	1.3
1955–9	2	1.9	11	7.8	1	1.4	14	4.5
1960–4	8	7.8	13	9.2	1	1.4	22	7.0
1965–9	13	12.6	21	14.9	5	7.1	39	12.4
Subtotal	23	22.3	50	35.5	7	10.0	80	25.5
Total	103	100.0	141	100.0	70	100.0	314	100.0

educated Yoruba men to educated Ghanaian girls. In the first case, the girls usually came from Dagomba or Gonja families. In the second case, they were more likely to be southerners. There were several examples of the first type of marriage in the northern towns.

Lasisi's half-brother in Ile Olowo had settled in Damongo in the 1950s and established a farm there. He had married a local girl in addition to his two Yoruba wives. His ties with the area were strong, and after the compliance order and a short stay in Igbetti in 1970, he returned to Damongo to continue farming.

Alhaji Oseini, Rafatu's brother from Ogbomosho, had spent a lot of time early in his trading career selling cloth in the rural areas where he had built up an extensive turnover and extensive contacts. In addition to his two Yoruba wives he married the sister of one of his Dagomba friends. She used to help him in his own stall in Tamale while the Yoruba wives had their own businesses. Like Lasisi's half-brother, he felt able to return to Ghana in 1970, where his Ghanaian wife had been managing his market stall for him in his absence.

These two cases have in common the fact that the first wives were Yoruba and both arose out of trading contacts in the rural areas outside Tamale. It is possible that the smaller the Yoruba population in an area, the more the migrant has to rely on the local people for friendship, and the more likely he is to marry a local girl. Both of these men were Muslims in a Muslim area, and both of them had been in Ghana for most of their lives and spoke the local languages perfectly. Interestingly, neither of them had Yoruba tribal marks which would have made them conspicuous in Ghana after the compliance order. Finally both had extensive economic links with the local community in Ghana: Lasisi's brother had used these to obtain farmland, and Oseini in building up his turnover.

Interethnic marriages of the second type were more common in the south of Ghana than in Tamale, though I came across a few examples. In both of the following cases, a temporary affair resulted in pregnancy and then marriage.

Rasidi was the son of an Ogbomosho Mallam, though he no longer 'prayed' himself, or had much to do with his parents. He had fallen out with them over the question of education – he had wanted to go to school with the other boys of his age group, but his father had beaten him when he first suggested it. Eventually he persuaded his mother to send him to school, but his relations with his parents remained strained. While at school, he met a Fanti girl and they became 'friends'. After a series of abortions, she became pregnant in 1969 and this time decided to keep the baby. Rasidi had by this time got a job as a newspaper photographer, and he met the parents of the girl and agreed to pay them NC200 compensation because she had been forced to drop out of school. When I met him he had only managed to pay NC70 of this. His father meanwhile was still suggesting that he should marry a Muslim girl from Ogbomosho, but he had refused.

Bosco was the clerk working for the state distilleries already mentioned in connection with Raliatu, the wife of Alhaji Sani, in Chapter 5. He was born in Koforidua, though his family originally came from Offa. After leaving middle school, he went on to 'commercial' school, where he acquired an Akan girlfriend. She became pregnant by him, and, though at first the parents threatened to take him to court, he eventually made his peace with them. They were married in Koforidua after they had already had two children, and in 1967 she went with him to Tamale where he had been transferred by his firm. In 1968 he married a second time, to an Offa girl whose parents lived in Nsawam. He also had a child by an Ogbomosho girlfriend.

By 1969 there were strains visible in the first marriage. His junior brother who was living with them complained to me about the behaviour of the Ghanaian wife towards him: she was far less respectful, he thought, than she should have been, and far less respectful than the Yoruba wife. The Yoruba girl was a good trader, while the Ghanaian girl was hopeless, and she continually lost money despite the fact that she was literate and should have been able to keep accounts. On one occasion she accused the brother of one of the other women in the compound of stealing money from her, and this caused a lot of ill-feeling between her and the other residents. The Yoruba girl was very reserved, while the Ghanaian girl was constantly gossiping with the other women about her husband and his brother, to which both the brothers objected. The marriage broke up after the compliance order when the elder brother decided to send his two eldest children back to Nigeria with his father's sister and without the knowledge of the wife. In 1970 he resigned from his job, and, together with the brother and the Yoruba wife, returned to Nigeria. The Ghanaian wife stayed in Koforidua with her youngest child, and though the senior brother mentioned the possibility of her eventually joining him in Nigeria, it appeared very unlikely.

Again there are obvious similarities between these two cases, and in the second there is a further clash of values evident. Yoruba women in their relations with their husbands and affines are ideally expected to show deference and respect. Bosco's Ghanaian wife did not, and this, together with her ineptitude in trade, meant that she was constantly being compared unfavourably with Bosco's Yoruba wife, who came much closer to the ideal.

Second, this case brings to the fore the differences in the qualities required of a girlfriend and a wife by the younger Yoruba men. Educated southern girls were in many ways the ideal girlfriends: they were regarded as lively, well-dressed and sexually uninhibited. On the other hand, these were the very qualities which were regarded negatively when it came to discussions of marriage: in these they were described as disrespectful, spendthrift and promiscuous. While many of the younger Yoruba that I talked to in Ghana expressed their preference for local girls as girlfriends, they still intended to marry Yoruba. Yoruba girls on the other hand did not make good girlfriends. For one reason they were 'too money-minded'. One boy complained that 'if you give a Ghanaian girl 20p she will be happy with it, but if you give a Yoruba girl a cedi she will be looking at you, wanting more.' Another complication in the relations between young Yoruba of the opposite sex was that their parents were often actively looking for suitable spouses for them. On his arrival in Tamale, a young Ogbomosho clerk showed a passing interest in an Ogbomosho girl in a neighbouring house. He was in his mid-twenties, good-looking and with a good job. Almost immediately, the girl's mother turned up at his workplace to 'greet' him, and during the conversation she began to drop hints that he might like to consider her elder (and much less attractive) daughter instead. He avoided both girls carefully thereafter.

CRISIS MANAGEMENT:
THE COMPLIANCE ORDER AND ITS AFTERMATH

Despite the intensity of interaction within the Yoruba community, therefore, a significant number of Yoruba migrants had close links with Ghanaians, and this had implications for the political position of the Yoruba both as a group and as individuals. Before Ghanaian independence, the Yoruba in Tamale had tended to support the local regional political party, the Northern People's Party, against the ruling CPP. After the CPP consolidated its power throughout the country, some of the Yoruba leaders in Tamale made a tactical switch and remained members of the CPP until the 1966 coup. This was good for business. The Yoruba with their international links were in a good position to obtain goods in short supply from elsewhere, and it was their links with the party officials which kept them in business as Yoruba trade across the border went on relatively uninterrupted. Many of the Yoruba that I interviewed looked back to the days before 1966 as a golden age compared with the years that followed it. After the coup, links with the authorities had to be rebuilt. The period up to the exodus was marked by arrests of Yoruba traders for smuggling and control price infringements. At the national level events were turning against the migrants, with an ever louder chorus of demands from Ghanaian businessmen to indigenise a wide variety of occupations. The results included the moves against the Lebanese and Indians, the publication of the government's plans for Ghanaian business promotion, and finally the compliance order itself.

Before the 1969 election there had been rumours that the Progress Party, if elected, would take tough measures against the aliens. This was denied by party officials, but the suspicions remained. In Tamale, this suspicion meant that many of the uncommitted aliens who were registered to vote (though technically they were ineligible) did so for the National Alliance of Liberals, which lost the general election but which won the Tamale seat. Officially, of course, the Yoruba were neutral.

In 1969, the election was only one of three main political issues in Tamale. For the Dagomba, the most important of these was the Yendi skin dispute. This exploded into violence immediately after the September election, and many were killed in the disturbances at the Ya Na's palace in Yendi.[27] Overshadowed by both the election and the skin dispute was the long-standing dispute over the Tamale Centre Mosque. One of the leading Mallams in the town, Alhaji Ajura, had broken away to start his own mosque on the Bolgatanga road. Though it was denied by some, it seems that the major lines of cleavage in the town in all three cases tended to converge. Supporters of the Andani faction in the skin dispute were also generally supporters of Alhaji Ajura and NAL, which, it was believed, would decide the skin issue in their favour if it came to power in Accra.

The Yoruba community remained neutral in all these disputes, though individuals became involved because of their local ties. Luke, for instance, supported the Andani faction because of his affinal links, and went to Yendi to join in the celebrations when the Andani candidate was installed. The Yoruba Imam was also involved: he too had a Ghanaian wife and had been giving the Andani gate his spiritual services during the conflict.

The major political issues in Tamale, therefore, mainly concerned the local Dagomba population.[28] Unlike Kumasi, there were no clear-cut divisions in Tamale between the Zongo and the local population. With the exception of the Dagomba villages which it had engulfed, Tamale had an ethnically mixed population in every ward of the town. When the compliance order was announced, therefore, there was considerable sympathy for the position of the immigrants and little of the overt hostility between Ghanaians and migrants that was apparently visible in parts of the south. It was during this period that individual Yoruba were able to mobilise their friendship networks and political contacts either to stay in the country or to salvage their assets and return to Nigeria. It was this crisis which demonstrated the importance of the links which the Yoruba had been able to establish with their hosts.

The order itself was issued with little fanfare, and it took about three days for the Yoruba in the town to realise that it was, in fact, aimed at them. When this became apparent, delegates were sent to the Nigerian High Commission in Accra to find out what the position was. They brought back with them forms which had been hurriedly printed by the High Commission. These were addressed to the Ministry of the Interior, and gave details of the applicant requesting a residence permit. It was in organising the completion of these forms that the Yoruba community in Tamale showed the effectiveness of its communications channels. The news went out in the morning that the forms had to be completed. By three in the afternoon, several hundred passports had been collected and sorted, the forms filled in and the money paid. The secretary of the Nigerian Community flew back to Accra with the forms, passports and money that evening.

However, given the chaos at the Nigerian High Commission and the Ministry of the Interior, it was obvious that it would be long after the deadline of two weeks given by the Government before the forms could be processed, and many of the Yoruba decided to leave in the interim before the position had been clarified. The majority of them left Tamale in the two days immediately preceding the expiry of the compliance order. Many had sold all their goods in the previous two weeks and they lost their money through inflated lorry prices and the low rate of exchange at the border. Others behaved less hastily and fared much better. Nearly all the women and children left for Nigeria, but a few of the men stayed on, and others began to return within a few weeks to clear up their affairs, having seen their families safely home.

It was in the period after this that the ties and contacts which individuals had built up in the town began to take on a special significance. First, they were important in obtaining a residence permit. Ogundiran and Ayoola both headed for Accra where they had contacts in their firms who were able to help them, and they arrived back the following week with residence permits for three months. For the less prominent Yoruba an informal organisation grew up around the immigration office in Tamale itself. The local immigration officer proved willing to help meet the demand for permits at the rate of NC20 for three months. The broker in arranging many of these deals was the new secretary of the Nigerian Community who was able to stay in business himself because of his contacts at the army barracks. In one way or another most of the Yoruba who had either stayed in Tamale or who had returned were able to obtain permits. One way was to claim Ghanaian citizenship. To be able to do this one had to be able to claim at least one Ghanaian parent, but substitutes could be found. Lasisi, to keep his options open, hired an elderly Dagomba lady to swear an affidavit that she was his mother, and soon received a letter from his Progress Party friends in the Ministry of the Interior confirming his claim to Ghanaian citizenship.

Ties with Ghanaians were also important in the disposal of goods and houses. Initially those who did not sell all their goods entrusted the stalls to Dagomba wives or friends who sold off the goods when prices rose again, after the Yoruba exodus. These transactions often demonstrated a considerable degree of trust. In 1971 Lasisi entrusted the sale of his remaining house in Tamale to a Dagomba friend who had been collecting the rent for him in the interim. He later sent one of his daughters over to Ghana to collect the money, buy goods and bring them back to Nigeria.

By the middle of 1970, the black market value of the cedi in Tamale had risen considerably, helped by the easing of border restrictions in both Ghana and Nigeria at the time of the exodus, and by the shortage in some parts of Nigeria, at the end of the civil war, of goods which could be obtained in Ghana and taken across.[29] Many of the Yoruba were able to repatriate most of their assets in one form or another without losing too heavily. In general, it was the migrants with close ties with Ghanaians who came out of the crisis the best. These were the men and women with the largest assets in Ghana, and some of them were to return to Ghana after the 1972 coup which ousted the Busia regime. Lasisi was an exception. Despite his successful claim to Ghanaian citizenship, he stayed in Nigeria where, with the exception of his father Sadiku, he was the most senior member of his descent group. Luke returned to his farm and his grinding mills in Ghana, and the Shaki smugglers also stayed in business. The smuggling trade also apparently attracted new recruits. While checking up on the whereabouts of former migrants to Ghana from Igbetti, I heard that four of them who had found no suitable opportunities to trade in Nigeria, had returned to Ghana to sell smuggled goods in 1970, even though they had not been involved in the trade before.

ETHNICITY AND THE YORUBA IN TAMALE

Let us return to the questions posed at the start of the chapter. Like the Hausa in Ibadan, the Yoruba in Tamale controlled a considerable share of the market in particular kinds of goods, in this case cloth, provisions and *worobo*. Unlike the Hausa, however, they occupied a single level in the market: as middlemen between the importing firms on the one hand and the Ghanaian consumer, or sometimes retailer, on the other. The advantages which the Yoruba possessed in trade came from better access to capital, labour and information than members of other ethnic groups, not because they were able to mobilise to keep others out of these trades. Supplies ultimately came from the large multi-national trading firms, and these the traders could not control. So when the institutions of the Yoruba community became involved in the market, it was usually to sort out problems between the traders and the authorities, rather than try and keep these sectors of the market exclusively Yoruba.

In this process, religion only played a part in so far as it either created or reinforced social links between the Yoruba traders and the 'big men' in the community who could sort out problems with officials if necessary. Unlike the Hausa or the Mossi, the Yoruba were actually divided by religion: Muslims were divided from Christians, and among the Christians church affiliation divided the Igbetti migrants from the others. Whereas Islam brought the Yoruba into greater contact with the rest of the population of Tamale, as was also the case in Kumasi Zongo, Christianity paradoxically did not, given that the Yoruba all belonged to churches where the services were in their own language. What all the Yoruba had in common was language and culture, not

religion: increasingly the Christians and Muslims were becoming closed endogamous and residential groups in Tamale, just as they were in the home towns
in Tamale.[30]

The reasons for these differences can ultimately be traced back to the much
stronger links which the Yoruba retained with their home towns than either
the Hausa or the Mossi. The reasons why this should have been so are complex,
and both ideological and economic factors are often mentioned. For instance,
Schildkrout in her discussion of why the Mossi often failed to retain links with
their home areas, mentions several factors: the poverty of the economy in the
region from which the migrants had come; the acceptance there of permanent
migration as a normal fact of life; the lack of home town ties as the basis
of migrant social organisation; conversion to Islam; the inability of many
migrants to distribute gifts sufficiently lavishly if they did return home; the
accumulation of assets in Ghana in the form of houses and farms which were
not transferable; and shame at not having made regular remittances during the
period of absence. Why the Mossi should be different from their equally poor
neighbours, the Tallensi, who do seem able to return home even after a long
absence, is not entirely clear, though the obstacle of the international boundary
and the costs of crossing it may be significant. But the contrast with the Yoruba
is considerable.[31] The Yoruba came from an area with more land and higher
rainfall, so that returning to farm was a viable option. Their incomes in Ghana
were in general higher than those of the Mossi, and in most cases they were
willing and able to remit substantial sums home, especially for house-building.
Home towns formed the basis of the migrants' social organisation and helped
reinforce links with home, as did the pattern of trade based on the recruitment
of labour through chain migration.

These elements are in turn related to long-term social security. Cohen makes
the point about the Hausa in Ibadan, who, like the Mossi, appeared to retain
few links with home, that begging provided them with an alternative social
security institution.[32] The Yoruba in Ghana saw things very differently. If a
person was really destitute, the advice they usually received was not to beg but
to go home, and friends and relatives would, if necessary, provide the lorry
fare. Long-term security lay ultimately in the home town, and for the Yoruba
to return there was not a myth but a reality.

These on-going links with home affected marriage choices as well. The most
striking feature of Yoruba marriage in Tamale was that not only were there
very few marriages outside the ethnic group, but that there were very few
marriages outside the same town of origin. For a long time, most of the
marriages were actually held in Nigeria, providing the partners as well as their
friends and relatives with a reason to go back home.

But if marriage patterns were exclusive among the Yoruba in Tamale,
residential patterns were not. Many of the Yoruba lived in houses belonging to
themselves, or other kin, but these were not concentrated in a single part of the

town, but were scattered throughout it. In addition, a large proportion of the Yoruba lived in houses belonging to Ghanaians. In Tamale, as in Kumasi, the ethnic mix in a house could be very varied. This may explain why, when it came to friendship networks, so many of the Yoruba had close Ghanaian friends. In many instances, these individual contacts proved to be of crucial importance at the time of the compliance order, as sources of information and official permits, for help with looking after houses and market stalls or storing property, or simply for friendship and support.

It was also through these friendship networks that the individual Yoruba participated in local politics. Luke, Lasisi, Isaac and the others all had good contacts among the local political class, and participated actively in local affairs. On the other hand the Yoruba associations as bodies attempted to stay strictly neutral, particularly in the 1969 general election, even though they made sure that individual members had joined the main political parties so that Yoruba were bound to be on the winning side. In the event, of course, all this had no effect on the politicians that mattered, once the compliance order had been announced. Individuals could use their own networks to gain concessions and residence permits, but the Yoruba associations and the Nigerian Community were powerless to act on behalf of the group as a whole. In fact, the advice of the leaders to the rest of the community was to leave. It is one of the most bitter ironies of the whole affair that the very high level of efficiency and organisation among the Yoruba meant that more of them left the country than might otherwise have been the case, and certainly a higher percentage than among the Mossi and the Hausa.

Ethnic solidarities and stereotypes not only depend on the internal structure of the ethnic community, but also on relations with outsiders. Whatever individual actors feel about the people with whom they come into contact based on their own experience, it is always open to powerful individuals or the state to define the content of ethnic stereotypes, whether through conscious policy, unconscious bungling or default. The history of the compliance order in 1969 is an excellent example of this.[33] On the one side, there was the Ghanaian state. Whether the compliance order was a conscious effort to create employment for the local population, an attempt to bolster the opportunities available for the emerging bourgeoisie, especially those supporting the Progress Party, or simply (as I tend to believe myself) an administrative measure put into effect without proper evaluation of the likely consequences, the government was soon called on to clarify and defend its measure. It did so by seizing on the word 'alien', and making the 'aliens' responsible, in official pronouncements, for all the ills of the country: unemployment, the tottering economy, crime, and even disease. What the individual Ghanaians thought was largely irrelevant: many of them had considerable sympathy for the plight of the aliens, and as individuals went out of their way in many instances to help them, as in the cases of Lasisi, Luke and Isaac. But it was the state rather than the individuals who had access to the media. Other scapegoats have been discovered since to blame for Ghana's economic woes, as the next chapter will show, but 'aliens' remained high on the government hit-list.

I have argued here that it was socio-structural factors which contributed to the hurried departure of the Yoruba from Ghana. In deciding to leave they might have had even more tragic events in the recent past in Nigeria in their minds. There are numerous migrants from the northern Yoruba towns in northern Nigeria, and many of the Yoruba in Ghana either had witnessed at first hand, or had close relatives who had witnessed, the pogroms in the cities of northern Nigeria in 1966, in which thousands of eastern Nigerians had been killed, and the rest forced to flee back home. The Nigerian civil war, it should be remembered, had not yet finished when the compliance order was announced, though it came to an end a few weeks later. With the Ghanaian government's increasingly shrill rhetoric against the 'aliens', and with the Ghanaian media calling on the government, the police and the army to enforce the order with all rigour, a decision to leave first and ask questions afterwards must have seemed to many to be entirely rational. After all, the Yoruba, unlike the Mossi or Hausa, actually had somewhere to go home to, and with the economic difficulties in Ghana, many were reconsidering their position there anyway.

In hindsight, of course, those who sat tight, weathered the storm and waited before disposing of their assets were the ones who were able to salvage most from the situation. The measures actually taken against the aliens who stayed were perfunctory and ineffective. The people who really suffered as a result of the exodus were the poorer traders and their families who lacked the resources to stay. After they had sold their goods at knockdown prices, the low rates of exchange and the high costs of transport home ensured that they finally arrived there penniless. The state, as it turned out, was not yet as willing to use coercion against the traders as it later became. And it is to the aftermath of the exodus and the later policies of the state towards the traders in Ghana that we turn in the next chapter.

7

TRADERS, MIGRANTS AND THE STATE

CHAIN MIGRATION AND TRADE

At the start of this study, I suggested that three levels of analysis were required to do justice to the material: those of the political economy, the networks of social relations, and the level of the individual. To paraphrase Alexander, what we are dealing with is a system of resources, their geographical distribution, production, circulation and control; a structure of formal and informal social institutions through which individuals are linked into complex webs of social relationships; and flows of information through which individuals are able to structure their views of the world and arrive at decisions.[1] What links these three levels together in the case of the Yoruba in Ghana is the process of chain migration.

Chain migration is based on flows of information, and the main channels through which it flows tends to be those of the most significant social relationships in a society. The information is often about economic opportunities and the distribution of resources, and the result can be an extremely rapid movement of people in the direction of those resources. Chain migration has been documented from all over the world: apart from the Yoruba, the best documented example in West Africa seems to be that of the Lebanese.[2] Migration among the Mossi, Hausa and Frafra seems to have been based much less on established chains.[3] The greater degree of poverty and over-population in these areas produced a much more random pattern of migration, with individuals looking for opportunities on their own initiative rather than following in the footsteps of established migrants. Chain migration could have developed in these cases had the initial migrants been as successful as the Yoruba pioneers were, but with more limited capital and without access to resources such as the Yoruba cloth industry, the migration in the Mossi and Frafra cases seems to have remained at the level of random movement. The Hausa case is perhaps more complex: there is no doubt that the Hausa communities studied by Cohen, for instance, were extremely successful in particular niches of the market,[4] but it seems that factors such as the bilateral nature of the Hausa kinship system, and the more limited role of kinship in Hausa society, together with the greater importance of patron–client networks and religion, produced a different pattern of community growth. New migrants appear to have attached themselves to existing networks of patronage, rather than to have been deliberately recruited by senior relatives, as was the case with the Yoruba.

The formal properties of chain migration and its practical implications are extremely interesting however. Historical instances of chain migration are of course products of specific economic and historical situations, but there do seem to be a number of formal similarities which make it possible to compare groups widely separated in time and space.

First, chain migration where it occurs can lead to the extremely rapid and effective mobilisation of manpower, and the rapid colonisation of newly appearing niches in the labour market. This seems to have been the case in Northern Ghana. A number of ethnic groups might have established a trading monopoly in the area in the early part of the twentieth century, but once the early Yoruba pioneers appeared, the combination of kinship-based chain migration and access to supplies of goods in demand, namely Yoruba cloth, meant that the rapid growth of a Yoruba trading community effectively blocked the entry of other groups.

Second, where the migration is based on close kinship links, the mobilis-ation of both information and capital is extremely efficient. This produces a situation in which the chain migrants have a significant competitive advantage over other traders, and this reinforces the tendency for them to dominate particular niches of the market. Information and capital flows can, of course, be managed in other ways, as Cohen's Hausa data demonstrates, but chain migration is an extremely common method of doing it. The result is the rapid reproduction of trading enterprises. It is significant that in other parts of the world, anthropologists have documented the competitive edge which particu-lar groups of migrants have because of their access to capital, and because the migrant communities to which they belong have institutions such as savings or rotating credit associations which can reinforce the maintenance of an adequate supply of capital.[5]

Third, rapid chain migration leads to an oversupply of manpower very rapidly, and the surplus, rather than return home, will begin to look for nearby economic opportunities. In the case of the Yoruba in Ghana, the result was a 'toothpaste tube' effect: an oversupply of traders in the main towns led to a rapid diffusion of traders into the smaller towns and rural areas. The Ogbomosho migrants moved north to Tamale and Wa, and the Igbetti mi-grants moved out from Tamale to Yendi and Damongo, as well as villages such as Sawla, Buipe and Yapei. This diffusion can provide the starting point for new migrant chains, as the history of the large Ogbomosho families in Tamale, or of the Igbetti migrants to Yendi or Damongo, demonstrate.

Fourth, chain migration works extremely well in instances where economic conditions require the mobilisation of large quantities of labour. In the case of the Northern Territories in the early part of the twentieth century, trade had to be labour intensive if it was to succeed at all. The labour of junior relatives was an effective solution to the problem of transport where roads were poor and wheeled transport was at first non-existent. The result was the little caravans of senior traders with their junior relatives and their loads of cloth making their laborious way across the savanna in the direction of Yendi and Tamale in the early part of the century. In later years supplies of labour from the same source was useful in transporting the goods by cycle to the outlying markets, towns and villages, or managing the market stalls and shops in the major towns.

Fifth, rapid chain migration will produce an extremely close-knit community, often with an elaborate internal organisation. Within West Africa the migrants who have well-established, ethnically-based voluntary associations are usually those with high levels of kinship-based chain migration, such as the Yoruba, Igbo and Lebanese. The Hausa and Mossi organise their lives somewhat differently.[6] Trust within the group is the main basis of organisation, and groups in which trust is at a low level, such as the Frafra, may indeed find it difficult to organise at all.[7]

Finally, chain migration tends to continually reinforce the links between migrants and home. The result is very often a group of migrants who see themselves as sojourners rather than as permanent migrants, and the level of assimilation which they achieve with the groups among whom they settle may, as in the Yoruba case, be limited.[8] The Yoruba achieved a degree of residential assimilation and incorporation into the friendship networks of individual Ghanaians, but the links with home remained, and, as we have seen, this had important implications for their behaviour at the end of 1969 when the 'compliance' order was announced. Conversely, their self-definition and presentation as sojourners may lead to others identifying them as the 'enemy within' when looking for scapegoats on which to blame the nation's economic or political woes, an identification which, historically, has been all too common.

THE YORUBA AS MIGRANTS

At the level of the political economy, or in Alexander's terms the system of resources, the Yoruba movement to the Gold Coast in the early twentieth century can be accounted for by the patterns of economic growth within the region, particularly the development of opportunities surrounding the cocoa industry, the availability of wage labour in the army, in the transport industry and the mines, and opportunities for trade to which these gave rise. Parallel developments in the Gold Coast and Western Nigeria meant that there were not only opportunities to be exploited in the Gold Coast, but that there were those in Nigeria with access to the capital necessary to exploit them. The main migration was to the southern Gold Coast, but the north was also colonised by Ogbomosho traders squeezed out of the markets of the south, as well as traders from Shaki, Igboho and the other more marginal towns of the far Yoruba north west.

The scattered and limited demand in the north could only be exploited with access to abundant labour, and this was provided from within the compounds and kin groups of the home towns. If the rate of migration was determined by the patterns of regional economic growth, the incidence was determined by people's position in the social structure, and a few successful early migrants formed the nucleus of the substantial migrant communities that had developed by 1969.

From the point of view of the individual migrant, the expansion of the migration created a new opportunity structure in which to move and work. This remained, however, very much limited by networks of social relations. The migration to the Gold Coast was concentrated in particular towns, and particular compounds within those towns. It did not lead to a generalised 'gold rush'. For many migrants the decision to migrate was taken for them by senior relatives, and for those that did make up their own minds, the experiences of their immediate kin were likely to be the deciding factors. Where the migration did spread between compounds, its diffusion was structured by cognatic kinship links and friendship networks rather than random choice. Individual decisions were very much a function of forces and structures operating at the social and economic levels.

THE YORUBA AS ENTREPRENEURS

The distribution of structural resources in the region also determined the role the Yoruba played when they became established in trade. The growth of wage labour in the southern Gold Coast increased the demand for manufactured goods, in addition to older sales lines such as cloth, kola and natron, and it was the Yoruba who of all the migrant groups were able to move into this niche in the market most readily. Diversification followed as the market expanded: into cocoa brokerage in the Eastern Region, diamond mining and dealing in Akwatia and Akim Oda, and at various times into the long-distance trades in foodstuffs and dried fish throughout the south. Most important of all was the trade in Nigerian cloth, for which demand, particularly in the north, increased in the aftermath of the first World War and remained so until the 1950s, despite an earlier decline in its importance in the south. The Nigerian cloth trade was vertically integrated, with the Yoruba responsible for ordering, purchasing, transporting and distributing it, and it was during the heyday of this trade that the Yoruba 'family firms' in the north developed. With the growth of the trade in imported European manufactures, however, horizontal extension of Yoruba enterprises became a common pattern, the result being the proliferation of small-scale independent enterprises during the 1950s.[9] In the process the Yoruba, like many small-scale entrepreneurs elsewhere, became more and more integrated into a trading system dominated by the large multinational firms. This made them vulnerable in two ways, despite the profitability of the trade. In the first place, they no longer had a monopoly of supply, despite their statistical domination at the retail end of the market, and they could no longer make the kinds of windfall profits that a true monopoly situation would have given them. Second, in the longer term it subjected them to the restrictive trade policies of the large firms, symbolised by the passbooks, and the price control policies of the state. This subordination in the long run reduced the capacity of traders to accumulate capital in the market, and by 1969 the wealthier Yoruba derived much of their income from property. They were also starting to move into farming where, thanks to state loans and subsidies, the returns were higher than they were in the market.

At the level of social organisation, initial penetration of the market was only possible on a large scale with the help of junior relatives and, on occasion, friends. The social structure of the home town provided the labour necessary for the geographical coverage required, particularly in the north where demand was most scattered. With the transition to the sale of manufactured goods, the family groups tended to break up more easily, but the traders were still in the main dependent on senior kin for the capital to start trading themselves. This may explain one of the differences between the organisation of Yoruba trade in Ghana and some parts of Western Nigeria, where individual trade was the norm. Peel's *oṣomaalo* from Ijesha bought goods on credit from wholesalers, including Syrians, in Ibadan and Lagos, and sold on credit in the smaller towns and villages elsewhere in Western Nigeria. The Yoruba in Ghana predominantly bought and sold for cash, and suppliers' credits were not important in getting them established. Help from kin and kinship-based apprenticeships were the norm.[10]

With regard to the system of information flow, social networks had a good deal of influence on the information available to the traders and their decision-making. In day-to-day buying and selling, traders were increasingly constrained by factors such as control prices and market forces. In terms of longer-term investment strategies, the range of options was often limited to those on which information was readily available. That is why the sale of particular commodities was often concentrated in particular groups of related traders or members of the same *egbẹ*, and why information on new investments such as rice farms tended to spread in the same way. The conservatism of Yoruba trade and investment patterns was reinforced by the nature of the available information as much as by constraints on capital, and the room for individual innovation was correspondingly limited.

THE YORUBA AS AN ETHNIC MINORITY

In West Africa, underlying the social significance of ethnic identity in social life are objective differences between groups in the political and economic resources available to them, arising from the pattern of incorporation into the political economy. The fact that capital was more heavily invested in the coastal areas meant that their people were often able to take an early lead in various sectors of the labour market, as well as in administration and politics. Southern Yorubaland was one of the most favoured areas of all in terms of investment and, even though the northern Yoruba towns were more marginal to the regional economy, their people still had easier access to capital and resources than other potential migrants further inland.

Despite Cohen's equation of ethnicity with economic interest, and despite the rather mechanistic discussion of the links between chain migration and competition in trade above, the Yoruba sense of identity and distinctiveness in Ghana came as much from their ongoing links with their home towns as from a need to defend a particular section of the market. In fact, for many years they were successful in defending it, but by the 1960s, Yoruba dominance in the northern Ghana markets was under threat. There were several reasons for this. First, in Tamale, the Dagomba were providing increasingly effective competition in certain sectors of the market as they accumulated capital from farming and the trade in livestock. Second, the high rates of education among the Yoruba meant that resources were diverted from trade and many of their children were moving into other occupations, especially with the slowdown in trade after the coup. Third, the Nigerian economy was starting to pick up as the civil war drew to a close, and some of the traders with difficulties in Ghana were contemplating returning home to trade or farm.

In any case, the situation in the market was hardly one of all-out competition between members of different ethnic groups. Relations between the Yoruba and Ghanaians were, as we have seen, extremely complex and contextual. At the individual level, close friendships existed, the results of factors such as co-residence, Islam, education and interaction in the market. On the other hand, when it came to marriage and voluntary associations, there were more constraints. But here it was specifically town or origin rather than pan-Yoruba identity which was usually significant. Marriages with Yoruba from other towns were nearly as rare as marriages with non-Yoruba, and it was mainly in the Baptist Church and the *Ilu Pejo* that Yoruba, as opposed to Ogbomosho or Igbetti migrants, came together in a more formal way. The ties with people outside the ethnic groups were important as a source of new ideas, access to resources and links with the state, and as a political resource for individuals during crises such as the compliance order.

When it came to information and decisions, therefore, the Yoruba remained in touch with networks of fellow townsmen in Ghana, at home in Nigeria and elsewhere in West Africa. Their links with home were not only a question of personal identity, but also of the resources which could be derived from them: access to land, labour and capital, and security in retirement. Similarly, friendship and clientship relations with Ghanaians were also important, whether in providing access to land, contacts with local officialdom, or simple friendship.

Ethnic identities do not simply emerge in a vacuum. They develop out of a specific political and economic context, and can be articulated and manipulated by other interest groups, including the state. In West Africa in general, if left to themselves, members of different ethnic groups are well able to coexist for long periods with few or no problems. It is often only when national or regional political interest groups make use of ethnic stereotypes for political ends that local issues erupt into violence.[11] There may also be a split between the policies of the state and the local-level attitudes of individuals. In 1969, the state wanted the Nigerians to go. Many of their friends in Ghana did not, and often went to considerable lengths in individual cases to help them. As Brown reminds us, it is common for governments to bolster their legitimacy by looking for scapegoats and 'enemies within'.[12] In the period after 1969, the search for enemies continued to focus on the remaining 'aliens', together with, from time to time, the Ewe, the Togolese, the market mammies and the practitioners of *kalabule* as defined by the state.[13]

The result of their maintenance of links both with Ghana and Nigeria was that the Yoruba approximated much better than either the Mossi or the Hausa to the ideal types of 'middleman minorities' and 'ethnic entrepreneurs'.[14] Like the Asian migrants to the United States or the United Kingdom, their success was based on well-organised associational and credit institutions within the migrant community, which thus provided its members with a measure of protection against the state and support in competition with outsiders. Like the members of many of these migrant groups, the Yoruba in Ghana were 'sojourners',[15] anticipating an eventual return to their home towns in which they continued to invest. Their success also led to heavy investment in education, providing a basis for their children to move out of the market and into more prestigious, lucrative and reliable occupations. Unfortunately, they shared the fate of many other groups of sojourners in other parts of Africa or elsewhere. Faced with chronic economic difficulties for which it could find no lasting solution, the state in Ghana created a series of moral panics about different groups which it blamed for the situation in which it found itself. The 1969 campaign against the 'aliens' was the most dramatic of these in terms of consequences, but it was not the last. After the departure of the most visible aliens, the Yoruba followed by most of the Lebanese and Indians the following year, the state simply turned its attentions elsewhere.

AFTER THE EXODUS

The problems of the Ghanaian economy did not vanish along with the departing Yoruba traders at the end of 1969. Indeed, they were to intensify during the 1970s, so much so that by the early 1980s the country was on the verge of economic collapse.[16] Having consistently portrayed the Yoruba migrant as hero or heroine, and the state as villain, it would be a satisfying ending if I could report that on the departure of the Yoruba, the trading system of the country collapsed rapidly, and that the government thereby learnt the error of its ways. The reality was, of course, rather more complicated.

Whether by design or accident, the Ghana government had chosen a relatively good moment to announce the compliance order so as to minimise the effects on the rest of the economy. The economy was in better shape than it had been since the early 1960s, and probably in better shape than it has been since. As I mentioned earlier, supplies of most essential goods were plentiful and, by 1969, with the slow-down in demand since the coup, there were probably too many market traders relative to the amount of money in circulation. Despite the long empty lines of closed stalls in the market immediately after the exodus, there were few lasting shortages. Gradually new traders arrived to occupy the empty stalls, many of them with the help of political patronage, and the goods which had been bought up from the departing Yoruba were gradually consumed or released back onto the market. Who, then, apart from the Yoruba themselves, did the compliance order harm, or for that matter, benefit?

This is a difficult question, as the results were diffuse, but my own guess is as follows. In the short term, of course, those who reaped enormous benefits included the Togolese currency dealers and transporters who fleeced the departing migrants on the way home. This must have represented a considerable net loss to the Ghanaian economy which I have never seen discussed or quantified. The people who benefited from the compliance order in the longer term within Ghana were the relatively wealthy, and particularly those with links with the new Progress Party government. They were the people with the capital to buy up the goods and the houses which the Yoruba sold off, as well as to occupy their position in the market by renting the empty stalls for themselves, their wives or their relatives. The wealthier members of this group were also to benefit from the departure of the Indians and Lebanese the following year. Indigenisation policies in Africa in general usually reinforce the positions of those with wealth and power already.

But I suspect that the poor must have been net losers from the compliance order in a number of ways. A reduction in the number of traders, particularly in the more remote rural markets, almost certainly meant less selection and higher prices, as well as the end of established credit relationships. The polarisation of the rich and the poor, and the increasing control of the economy, whether openly or behind the scenes, by those in power, became one of the main factors in the increasing unpopularity of successive administrations in the late 1970s and early 1980s, helping to pave the way for the two Rawlings coups.

The point I want to make here, however, is not that the compliance order completely wrecked the Ghanaian economy. It clearly did not, even though it may have weakened it: perhaps the short term loss of migrant cocoa labourers was more serious than the loss of the migrant traders.[17] What it did do, however, was reveal a certain set of assumptions held by the state – assumptions about migrants, about market traders as an occupational group, about the roots of the economic crisis and how to deal with it politically, and about relations with the neighbouring countries in West Africa. I would argue that these assumptions, and the policies which arose out of them, did the economy a great deal of damage in the years that followed. Thus, just as so often the activities of the Yoruba traders had shown up the contradictions and absurdities in economic policy before 1969, so the compliance order made explicit a number of issues which were to assume importance in its aftermath.

The status of the aliens was only one of a number of contentious issues in the relations between the traders and the state throughout this period: others included regulation of imports and exports, control of foreign currency dealings, control of prices, and control of the channels for the distribution of essential goods. These had been areas of conflict for many years, indeed since well before independence. Colonial officials had, as we have seen, had occasion to comment on the prevalence of smuggling, the 'parasitic' middlemen who pushed up the prices of goods, and the 'alien traders' who drained capital and resources out of the country. Since independence, successive regimes in Ghana have used much the same imagery and rhetoric, and yet the policies with which they have attempted to solve the problems of the economy have generally been counterproductive. It is really only since 1983 that there has been a substantial re-evaluation of policy towards the small-scale entrepreneurs in the economy, and the removal of some of the more serious constraints on their activities.

Many of these problems, it might be supposed, could have been avoided had the Ghanaian government listened to some of the more vocal critics of colonial and post-colonial economic policies. In the 1950s, Bauer had been saying that less rather than more government intervention in trade was required if the economy was to be allowed to grow, and he continued to argue that outsiders (such as the Lebanese) had an important role to play in providing new ideas and competition for the established multinational firms. He also contested the view that a multiplicity of middlemen in the market was inefficient and led to higher prices. If people could save money by dealing directly with each other and eliminating middlemen, then they would act accordingly. The compulsory elimination of classes of intermediaries would only lead to a rise in the cost of marketing services, not its reduction. Marketing arrangements in Africa might be technically primitive, but they suited African conditions. Attempts to reform the system led to waste of capital and skilled manpower, and raised the real cost of marketing.[18]

Berg argued along similar lines.[19] The post-colonial states of Africa, like their colonial predecessors, were *dirigiste* in nature, profoundly suspicious of the disorderly and wastefully competitive market, which in any case was often dominated by outsiders. On the other hand, attempts to establish state organisation to bypass the market traders were usually unsuccessful or, as in the cases of Guinea and Tanzania, simply disastrous. Much of the argument had direct relevance to Ghana. Administrative ineptitude had resulted in shortages, the growth of a black market, and massive smuggling over the international boundaries in response to price differentials. Like Bauer, Berg argued that state intervention in trade is wasteful, as it involves employing skilled manpower to do what the market does anyway. State firms need bigger inventories, better storage facilities and more elaborate accounting procedures than the private traders. Opportunities for corruption on the part of state officials are multiplied, and given the low levels of their wages and salaries, they find them difficult to resist. It is impossible to separate politics from economics, and where the state controls the market, decisions are likely to be made on political rather than economic grounds. Given that Africa has the highest ratio of frontiers to area of any continent, international boundaries are impossible to police effectively, so uneven subsidies and pricing policies between countries will lead to massive smuggling, often with the collusion of customs officials. Smuggling is also difficult to control because the same ethnic group often lives on both sides of the boundary, and because everybody, except the government, seems to benefit from it: producers, consumers, and traders alike:

> The smuggler casts a long shadow in Africa. He imposes restraints . . . on independent economic policies. All of the instruments of direct economic control, as well as price policies generally, will – unless they are in harmony with those prevailing in surrounding countries – threaten to activate or enlarge the current of contraband trade – Unless common policies are laid down by geographically-related groups in African states, each of them is at the mercy of policies followed by their neighbors . . . Socialism in one country is not possible in Africa.[20]

The interesting question is why this kind of advice, which in hindsight seems so obvious, was ignored for so long. Bates provides one possible answer.[21] Often, he argues, the economists and international organisations, such as the World Bank, have assumed economic rationality. African politicians are indeed involved in purposeful behaviour, but they are motivated by political rather than economic logic. Time and again particular policies are preferred because they are more useful politically to particular interest groups, even though they are less economically efficient. It is important to appease these interests if they want to stay in power. The experience of Ghana in the early 1970s is a case in point. Regulation of the market, by price controls, restrictions on imports and so forth, might have been economically counterproductive, but they provided lucrative opportunities for the bureaucracies which had the task of enforcing them, including the army and the police. Second, the overvalued cedi tended to decrease local agricultural and industrial production in the face of cheap imports, but it also meant cheap food in the urban markets, and cheaper imported consumer goods. The devaluation of the cedi at the end of 1971 very quickly resulted in higher prices, urban discontent and a military coup.[22] After this, successive Ghanaian leaders were very unwilling to devalue the cedi, even when its black market value had dropped to only a tiny fraction of its official value.

As Ghana's leaders were finding, continued appeasement of powerful interests is expensive, and the costs may well undermine the economy to such an extent that political instability is inevitable anyway. The government might attempt to buy time by printing money, but expansion of the money supply only undermined the currency still further. Ghana's problems were symptomatic of a general crisis in the political economy of the region, according to Hart the result of overdeveloped states resting on backward small-scale agricultural economies.[23] To resolve the crisis, he argued, either agricultural productivity had to rise, or the political economy had to sink to a level compatible with that of its pre-industrial base. Expanding agricultural productivity could only be achieved by reversing policies aimed at providing cheap food for the urban sector, by increasing incentives to producers and lowering the exchange rate. He thought that a more likely outcome was a form of political economy relying on predatory force to sustain an urban elite at the expense of a permanently impoverished rural majority. In the case of Ghana, however, the government did eventually decide to restructure the economy, but only after more than a decade of increasing political and economic trauma.

THE COLLAPSING GHANAIAN ECONOMY

In the 1950s, the Ghanaian economy had been the most prosperous in Africa, supported by high commodity prices and with a government in power committed to economic expansion and the creation of an industrial base and a welfare state. In the early 1960s, growth came to a halt as the price of cocoa fell, and as the reserves were exhausted by the ambitious development programme, much of it ill-conceived and expensive. The resulting crisis led to the downfall of Nkrumah and the first period of military rule in 1966. Large numbers of workers were laid off as projects were cut back or abandoned, but increased cocoa revenues combined with cautious NLC economic policies helped stabilise the situation. The cedi was devalued from $1.40 to $0.98, and some progress was made with the rate of inflation. Having achieved modest success, the soldiers, perhaps wisely, retired to their barracks before the next crisis could materialise.

It was not long in coming. Some elements of the Progress Party programme, such as the expenditure on agriculture and infrastructure, were welcomed, but the rise in cocoa producer incomes helped fuel a consumer boom, and imports rapidly increased. The proceeds from high cocoa prices were soon spent, and continuing demand for consumer goods fuelled inflation. Bank lending also expanded rapidly.[24]

The imports boom helped mask the potentially disruptive effects on distribution of the departure of the Yoruba at the end of 1969, followed by most of the Lebanese and Indians in 1970, but the government's political popularity suffered from other heavy-handed measures, such as the sacking of civil servants who had supported the opposition in the 1969 election campaign. By late 1971, the economic crisis which resulted from the government's expansionary economic policies led to a further devaluation, and the military took over once more early in 1972, with the formation of Acheampong's National Redemption Council.

National redemption became increasingly necessary as the 1970s dragged on. After two years of relatively successful political and economic management (in part because it was able to reap the benefits of the PP investment programme),[25] the NRC faced increasing problems from 1975. Cocoa prices were falling, the rest of the agricultural sector was suffering from the effects of the drought, and the price of oil rose as a result of the Arab-Israeli war. The long-term effects of inadequate capital investment, inflation, poor infrastructure, an under-trained labour force and over-centralised government were all becoming apparent. The increasing corruption and ineptness of the regime, now relabelled the Supreme Military Council, destroyed its credibility, and Acheampong was replaced as leader by Akuffo in 1978. By this time inflation stood at over 100 per cent, the GDP was declining, government expenditure was increasing, financed by the printing of more money, and foreign debts and the trade deficit were rising rapidly. The price of food more than doubled during 1977, and there were increasing reports of hardship and malnutrition in the rural areas. The black market value of the cedi dropped, and now stood at between a tenth and an eighth of its official value.[26]

The Akuffo regime which followed fared little better. The cedi was devalued from $0.86 (not much less than the parity which had existed a decade earlier, during my fieldwork) to $0.36, but it was still over-valued. Attempts were made to control government spending, and the currency was replaced at a discount of 30 per cent to mop up excess liquidity.[27] There was flagrant corruption among both senior officers and bank officials as the exercise proceeded, fuelling discontent among those worst hit, the low income workers and farmers. Shortages of goods and queues in the markets continued to grow. A young Air Force officer, Flt Lt Jerry Rawlings, staged an unsuccessful coup in May, but feeling in the ranks of the armed forces was such that he was released from prison by his supporters to lead a successful coup on 4 June. The Armed Forces Revolutionary Council, as the new regime was called, saw its main purpose as conducting a short but brutal 'housecleaning' operation, executing either senior members of former regimes, including three former heads of state.[28] Meanwhile it allowed the return to civilian rule, which was already under way, to continue, and in October of the same year it handed over power to the newly elected government of Dr Hilla Limann.

The effects of these upheavals on trade and distribution were disastrous. As the economic crisis had grown worse during the 1970s, the government had looked for scapegoats, and had once more begun to blame the petty traders, and particularly the 'market mammies' for the shortage of goods and the high level of prices. A new word, *kalabule*, entered the language to denote all forms of corruption and campaigns were initiated to eradicate it.[29] These efforts intensified under the AFRC, resulting not only in the executions, but also a concerted campaign against the market traders, to enforce the control prices and to crack down on hoarding and smuggling. Market women were assaulted, publicly whipped and even killed.[30] Traders that refused to come to market had their goods seized and distributed by the troops, police and vigilante groups. Hoarded goods were seized, and some of the stores blown up. The large firms sold off their stocks, and the goods were snapped up at the low control prices by anyone with the capital to buy them. Finally, the largest market in Accra, Makola No. 1, the alleged centre of all that was wrong with the economy, was razed to the ground. Similar demolitions took place in some of the other main towns.[31] None of the measures helped the situation. Indeed the price control enforcement was described by a *Financial Times* correspondent as 'economic suicide' because it increased consumption when supplies were tight.[32] After the brief bonanza, many goods simply vanished from the market.

Having come to power under the shadow of the AFRC, the Limann regime was faced with the constant possibility of another military takeover. The twenty-seven months that it was in power were marked by political inertia and continued economic deterioration. Limann could do little but condone the activities of the vigilante groups who continued to terrorise the traders in the name of 'enforcement' of the regulations, while vainly promising to 'flood the markets' with imported goods.[33] The newspapers were full of reports of 'profiteers' being given exemplary sentences, like the woman at Elmina jailed for six months for selling a plastic comb for 80p instead of 55p, or the eighteen-year-old Winneba schoolboy who was given three years with hard labour for selling a box of matches for c8 instead of c1.32.[34] In 1981, in a desperate attempt to increase the inflow of goods, the government decreed that anyone with their own sources of foreign exchange could import the goods under open general licence, with no questions asked.[35] A list of fifteen essential commodities was drawn up, and distribution of them channelled through government organisations.[36] After the publication of a budget at the end of 1981 which manifestly failed to acknowledge the seriousness of the situation, the armed forces acted again, and Rawlings staged yet another coup on 31 December.

THE PNDC: RAWLINGS'S SECOND COMING

Initially, the policies of the People's National Defence Committee (PNDC) looked very much like those of the Armed Forces Revolutionary Council (AFRC), though Limann and his ministers escaped the fate of Acheampong and Akuffo. (Less fortunate were the organisers of the various coup attempts which shook the PNDC at regular intervals during its first few years in office.) Outwardly, the rhetoric was much the same as in 1979. There was to be a war against *kalabule*, and attacks started again against the foreign exchange dealers of Cow Lane in Accra, and the market women in Accra, Takoradi and Kumasi. Traders were warned that 'revolutionary measures' would be necessary if prices did not fall, but were told that illegal profits could be retained if they identified the managers and middlemen selling at above the controlled prices.[37] Market stalls were destroyed in Kumasi and Takoradi as a warning to those who withheld goods rather than reduce their prices. The government announced that 'people's shops' were to be set up, to provide goods at fair prices and to bypass the market traders.[38] New lists of control prices were issued, and, in a move reminiscent of the Akuffo era, c50 notes were withdrawn from circulation in a further attempt to reduce liquidity and eliminate hoards of illegally acquired cash.[39] The result, yet again, was an attack on the savings of the poor whose money was only returned, if at all, after more than a year of galloping inflation. Citizens' Vetting Committees were set up to investigate the assets and activities of former party members and politicians.[40]

However, there was an increasing realisation in some quarters that the measures were misdirected. As one commentator put it:

Although it was to be conceded that they [i.e. the market mammies] have been taking full advantage of the scarcities in the system, and sometimes creating the scarcities, they no longer occupy a dominant position in the economy, having [been replaced] by well-educated and sophisticated women, sometimes wives of senior civil servants, army officers, highly-placed politicians and their hangers on, and the managerial class. This class of women through a system of carefully worked out alliances with the managerial class have so far managed to beat every distribution system devised. The level at which they operate does not bring them into direct contact with the consumer so they are less well known.[41]

Another writer, complaining about lawlessness among the military, noted that rural producers were finding it easier and cheaper to let food rot in the ground rather than bother to harvest and market it:

There is always the fear that it might be snatched from them before it can even reach the market, or that they might be beaten for even possessing it, or that one of the PDCs [People's Defence Committee] will force them to sell it at a controlled price well below production costs. Even if none of these things happen, there is nothing to buy with the money that they make from it.[42]

There were reports that in some parts of the country, the PDCs were themselves involved in illegal grain dealing. Meanwhile, the numbers of Ghanaians fleeing to 'Agege' (Nigeria) was increasing by the day.[43] Those who stayed were involved in a process of 'disengagement' from the official economic and administrative structures, establishing informal and illegal, but at least functioning, alternatives.[44]

The crisis continued into 1983. From 21 January it became an offence for traders to display and sell goods without clearly marked prices, and market women in Accra and Tema were required to obtain identity cards. The government might complain of 'sudden and unjustified' price increases[45] but the fact was that shortages were increasingly acute. They were made more so both by another drought and by the arrival early in the year of hundreds of thousands of Ghanaians repatriated from Nigeria.[46]

It was these events which finally forced the government into the arms of the IMF, which had been advocating a massive devaluation, a 300 per cent rise in producer prices, a curb on state expenditure, and an end to subsidies and price controls. The deal with the IMF precipitated a political crisis within the regime, and more coup attempts were uncovered.[47] By the end of the year the results of the economic U-turn, managed by Kwesi Botchwey, the PNDC's finance secretary, were becoming apparent. Price controls on locally produced foodstuffs were lifted. Early in 1984 the Chairman of the Public Tribunals admitted that the price controls prosecutions had failed to get at the big profiteers.[48] The cedi was further devalued in August 1984, to $1 = c38.50. In October, the governor of the Bank of Ghana, J.S. Addo, expressed the view that rigid price controls should be scrapped if the recovery programme was to succeed. Deregulation of prices, he thought, would encourage producers to work and improve on the supply situation.[49]

Other policies fell into line. Gradually foreign exchange controls were liberalised, and the cedi was allowed to find its own level on the market. It sank like a stone, and by the late 1980s stood at £1 = c450. There was no longer any necessity to prevent open currency dealing. Foreign exchange bureaux were set up and began to compete successfully with the dealers of Cow Lane.[50] The People's Shops, set up originally to bypass the market traders, were themselves allowed to wither on the vine.

The other result of a relaxation of controls was that the need for smuggling lessened. The collapse of the black market and the rising prices of cocoa and consumer goods meant that the profits to be made from selling them over the border for CFA francs were reduced. However, border restrictions continued to be enforced for political reasons. Relations with Togo were strained, and there were allegations by both countries that dissidents were being harboured and coups plotted on the other side of the border.[51]

Daily life in Ghana returned to a degree of political and economic stability, and the markets were better stocked than at any time since 1970. However, all this was at a severe cost: the political bloodletting of 1979 and 1982–4, the harassment of thousands of market traders and other civilians, and a massive exodus of the best-educated and skilled Ghanaians both to other West African countries and elsewhere. Some who went to Nigeria were repatriated in 1983 and 1985, or returned as the Nigerian economy itself went into recession, but others have settled abroad permanently, and there will have to be massive improvements in Ghana's situation before they can be enticed back. With 70 per cent of foreign exchange earnings going to service loans from the IMF and elsewhere, and with the economy still largely dependent on an ageing cocoa industry, the long-term outlook still remains uncertain, despite the relaxation of control by the state over some areas of the economy.

YORUBA MIGRANTS AND PUBLIC POLICY

Two sets of factors were at work in the sad decline of the Ghanaian economy. The first was related to the world system, and particularly the structure of the international commodity market over which Ghana had relatively little control. However, within this wider context there were also problems peculiar to Ghana. Undoubtedly, many of the country's problems were self-inflicted, and as the economic crisis deepened, many of the policies used to deal with it – particularly the attempts to control smuggling, prices, the distribution system and the exchange rate – were counterproductive. This takes us back to the issues raised by Bauer, Bates and Berg and discussed earlier in the chapter.

As we have seen from the Yoruba case material, it is virtually impossible to prevent smuggling in the West African context for three reasons. First, the long undefined land boundaries are either impossible to police effectively or policing more heavily brings diminishing returns. Second, border guards whose incomes have been eroded over the years as badly as everyone else's are always susceptible to bribery. The experience of Ghana is that the problem only gets worse as the economic crisis bites and incomes of producers and border guards alike are further eroded. Vigilante tactics breed violence, hostility and more corruption, and do not solve the problem; neither do vague appeals to patriotism by regimes which lack stability and legitimacy. Third, public opinion is usually on the side of the smuggler. Smuggling reduces prices, increases the variety and quality of goods available, and helps people defend themselves against the effects of the government's more damaging economic policies. The only long-term way of dealing with smuggling, therefore, is to abandon the more contradictory policies and to harmonise economic policy across the region in such a way as to make the kind of smuggling of essential goods in which the Yoruba were involved unprofitable. A smuggling trade in illicit or luxury goods would no doubt continue, but at least the massive cross-border movements of cheap cotton cloth, milk, sardines, cigarettes and soap powder – to say nothing of cocoa and staple foodstuffs – would be significantly reduced.

As we have also seen from the Yoruba material, price controls do not work either, and, where such a large number of traders are at work, it is impossible to enforce them. The Ghanaian experience suggests that, if anything, they drive up prices and cause goods to vanish from the market, either because consumption is increased and/or a black market develops. The system of small-scale trade is competitive enough to drive down prices as far as is economically possible. The Yoruba material suggests that when distribution is in the hands of small-scale traders, hoarding is also relatively uncommon; few, apart from the wealthiest traders, have the capital to speculate against an eventual price rise sufficient to offset the loss of turnover in the meantime. Storage in itself involves cost. Many of the 'hoards' identified in the campaigns of 1979 and 1982 were probably simply traders' normal stocks. The dividing line between regular inventory maintenance and 'hoarding' is an extremely fine one. Hoarding by wealthy members of a political class and their relatives, however, is another matter: they have the capital to speculate on a large scale, and are also likely to be untroubled by government anti-hoarding campaigns. As I have argued above, exercises such as the compliance order only served to accelerate the concentration of economic power in their hands.

The various attempts by the Ghanaian state to develop alternative ways of distributing goods channels have usually failed either to improve supplies or reduce prices. Given West African conditions in retail trade, it is virtually impossible for large organisations with heavy overheads of labour, rent and transport, to undercut the small-scale trader, as the commercial trading companies long since discovered. Ghana's experience with state trading over the years has not been a particularly happy one. After the nationalisation of AG Leventis to form the Ghana National Trading Corporation in 1962, the firm quickly established a reputation for inefficiency and corruption, culminating in the scandal surrounding the purchase of 700,000 watch straps at a cost of c29m in the early 1980s.[52] The diversion of supplies of fifteen types of essential goods in the 1980s away from the market simply gave rise to more opportunities for corruption and embezzlement. The performance of the other innovation of the early Rawlings period, the People's Shops, was also disappointing. As the Yoruba experience with the storekeepers showed, employees entrusted with distribution are in control of a scarce resource, and, in the absence of sanctions, they can make a good deal of money out of this. They reap the benefits of shortages of goods, but do not have to risk their own capital. The market traders, by contrast, make money out of rapid turnover. They have few alternative sources of income, and gain little from hoarding in anticipation of a future price rise as it ties up capital, cuts down turnover, and is inherently risky. The inference is that the elimination of small-scale traders from the market by government usually results in higher costs to the consumer, a less flexible and efficient system, and a more regressive distribution of income because those with power use it to make more money.

Finally, maintaining an overvalued currency, however functional for the political élite in the short term, is unlikely to succeed in the long term because a black market, impossible to control effectively, will always develop to subvert it. Government pronouncements on exchange-rate policy in Ghana up to the early 1980s always had an air of unreality about them. The rhetoric implied a self-sufficient economy with water-tight boundaries and an all-powerful state ready to discipline anybody breaking the regulations. The reality was, of course, very different, as the Yoruba material illustrates: an efficient and pervasive regional currency market, which responded rapidly to changing price levels and other market forces, and which was largely beyond the control of the state, simply because the agents of the state were themselves frequently involved in it. The Ghanaian government finally gave up the attempt to control the currency market, allowing the cedi to find its own level, and authorising the opening of foreign exchange bureaux. These quickly did more damage to the profits of the unofficial currency dealers of Cow Lane in Accra than had the previous 20 years of police raids.

From the point of view of economic constraints, therefore, it would seem that the structure of trade, based on international networks and enormous numbers of small operators, makes it virtually impossible for governments in the region to pursue import, pricing and foreign exchange policies which differ widely from those in surrounding countries. The solutions to the 'problems' of smuggling, price-control evasion and illegal currency dealing would seem to lie in harmonising fiscal policies across the region in such a way that the problems simply go away. Given the geography of the region, international trade and therefore migration are bound to continue, as most countries are simply not self-sufficient in basic resources. To take these arguments to their logical conclusion, and to argue for maximum liberalisation of the cross-border movement of people and goods throughout the region, is only to restate the official aims of ECOWAS, the Economic Organisation of West African States. So far the implementation of the ECOWAS programme, including the liberalisation of trade, a common currency, and the right of free movement and residence, has been slow. There are frequent setbacks, whether in the form of border disputes and closures, or the expulsion of foreign residents from one country or another, and the question is frequently raised as to whether the political will actually exists among the member states to achieve these objectives.[53]

The problems of both Ghana and ECOWAS seem to point to the existence of conflicting agendas which operate both in the relations between states as well as in the internal policies of individual states. First there is an agenda which arises from the geographical and economic realities of the region, which I have already outlined: the lack of self-sufficiency of individual countries, the long arbitrary frontiers, impossible to police, and the inequalities in the distribution of capital and of natural and human resources. The inference is that the region needs a much greater degree of economic and political co-operation than it has achieved to date. Apart from Nigeria, the other West African countries are too small to achieve balanced and diversified economic growth in isolation. This is an agenda to which the migrant traders would subscribe. There are tremendous obstacles to international trade, of course. The process of balkanisation and the proliferation of different currency systems which followed independence have not helped, while frequent disputes and border closures between neighbouring countries have meant that little has been done to improve the communications network across frontiers. The road and rail maps remain much as they were in 1960, with the majority of routes directed towards the capital on the coast, the link between the colonial and metropolitan economies. Borders can be crossed easily on foot or by bicycle, so that the role of the small-scale trader in international trade remains vital. Nevertheless, the flow of lorry traffic is hampered by cumbersome bureaucracy, poor roads, hostile and corrupt border guards, and frequent closure. The progress towards regional economic co-operation remains very slow indeed, despite the fact that all the governments in the region pay lip-service to it.

This fact may be partly accounted for by a second agenda in which the economy, and particularly trade, are subordinated to national interests. We have seen that in the colonial period the European powers attempted, largely unsuccessfully, to control trans-frontier trade for their own purposes, rather as the major kingdoms of the region had done before them. This strategy was pursued more rigorously after independence, as neighbouring states pursued increasingly divergent economic policies. It has resulted in barriers, restrictions and, of course, bottlenecks in supply. These have made things difficult for the international trader, though for those with either the capital or the political contacts to exploit the situation it has meant a range of new income opportunities. The same cannot be said for the consumer for whom this agenda has generally meant shortages, queues, black markets and, of course, higher prices.

A third agenda, which is really an extension or subtext of the second, and which – for obvious reasons – does not receive the publicity of the other two despite its importance, is one in which the economy becomes a resource which members of particular classes or interest groups can exploit for their own ends. This kind of agenda often underlies policies which are formulated using the rhetoric of 'the national interest', but where benefits are clearly unequally distributed. The various classes and factions which make up the contemporary African state have their own particular interests and agendas. Barriers, bottlenecks and bureaucratic restrictions continue to exist, not as some Weberian survival from the past, but because they suit the purposes of particular officials and administrators at the present. Erecting barriers to trade does not mean that trade stops – it has to go on simply because people need to eat, drink and clothe themselves – but that gatekeepers, whether in the public or the private sector, can exact a toll as people and goods pass through the gates that they control. The most literal manifestations of this are the men in blue, black and khaki who man the numerous roadblocks throughout the region, collecting the tribute from passing drivers – although they have their counterparts in all other areas of public life. In trade, the costs are greater uncertainty and higher overheads for the trader, which result in higher prices for the consumer. The rewards for the gatekeepers, however, are of course considerable.

These different agendas seem to underlie the conflicts which exist at a number of different levels within the political system: at the grass-roots level, in the relationships between people and the agents of the state; at the national level, in the struggles over the formulation of policy; and at the international level, in the relations between states. At the local level, the contradictions between them are reflected in the interference of state officials in the market, of which this study has presented many instances. At the national level they are reflected in the tendency of governments to cling to policies which appear to be economically disastrous, in part because they continue to benefit particular interest groups. And at the level of regional relations, the conflict underlies the reluctance of states to abandon their short-term interests, even while paying lip-service to rosy visions of economic integration in the future.

This notion of conflicting agendas may shed some light on some of the more seemingly bizarre policies of the Ghanaian state over the years. Despite their diversity and the undoubted complexity of the historical circumstances in which they were conceived, there is a lowest common denominator to do with questions of power and accumulation. The expulsion of the Nigerians gave the party faithful access to stalls in the market, as well as providing immigration officials with a lucrative source of income as the migrants tried to rearrange their lives. The exodus of the Lebanese and Asians similarly provided the Ghanaian middle classes with a wider base for business activities. Price control and import restrictions provided sources of income for the police, the price control officials, the border guards and the storekeepers. The overvalued cedi provided a rich source of economic opportunities for those with access to foreign exchange at the official rate. The diversion of supplies of essential goods from the market provided opportunities for a new breed of middle-class traders with direct links with officials and the military. The currency exchange exercises benefited those with bank accounts rather than cash, as well as those with contacts with bank officials to get their money changed. The list goes on endlessly. What it all adds up to is the gradual economic consolidation of the political and administrative class, and the progressive subordination, marginalisation or elimination of groups that stand in the way, whether they be migrants or market mammies.

Without resorting to explanations in terms of historical teleology or conspiracy theory, it is perhaps not difficult to see why Ghana's decision-makers have taken decisions on so many occasions which, directly or indirectly, have benefited themselves or their immediate circles of friends and relatives.

The history of the Yoruba in Ghana illustrates this clash of agendas well, first because they were strangers, and, second, because they were traders. As strangers, they were the heirs of the Hausa and Mande of the pre-colonial period, organised into an international diaspora which flowed through and around the boundaries of the colonial and post-colonial states. They drew on resources from across the region in conducting local trade, and thus showed up many of the contradictions between the realities of regional economic interdependence and the pretensions of national economic independence. As traders, they worked within a regional economy in which manpower was more readily available than capital, and this resulted in an endless search for new niches in the market and new ways of speeding up turnover. And as the prosperity and numbers of the traders grew, so the ability of the state to control their activities according to its own agenda declined. It was perhaps inevitable, given the new emphasis placed on national independence and bureaucratic control by the emerging political and administrative class, that at some point there should have been a crisis involving a confrontation between the migrant traders and the Ghanaian state: it was also ironic that when this happened the social institutions which had served the Yoruba traders so well as a buffer against the power of the state should have led to such a complete and rapid exodus.

But the eventual costs of national rulers pursuing their own interests, even when it is advertised as the national will or as being in the national interest, may be high, not only for the greater mass of the population, but even for the rulers themselves in terms of loss of support or legitimacy, leaving it open to rival factions and groups to claim that their own agendas reflect the national will rather better. In general, as this study will have shown, I tend towards the populist view that the masses are generally better at developing strategies which benefit them than are their rulers. Trade is a case in point. As the examples of the Yoruba and countless other migrants in West Africa show, the peoples of the region are extremely quick to perceive and respond to economic opportunities, even in the most unlikely settings. The economic isolation, sparse population, lack of infrastructure or markets, and limited development of a cash economy did not make the Northern Territories at the start of the colonial period look a particularly inviting area in which to trade. The Yoruba traders showed that there were opportunities to be exploited there, and their trade flourished over a period of sixty years, just as it did in Niger and Upper Volta in what seemed to be the most impoverished areas of the Sudan and Sahel. They created a trading network on foot, before cheap motorised transport was available, and they did it with their own resources and without subsidies from either the foreign firms or the state. In contrast, by the early 1980s the Ghanaian state appeared to have succeeded in letting much of the country's trading network wither: the most dynamic groups of immigrant merchants had departed, the Ghanaian market traders were being regularly assaulted by the military on the pretext of eliminating *kalabule*, and the result was a withdrawal from trade and a crisis as food was left rotting on the farms. Even the key institution in the Ghanaian economy, the Cocoa Marketing Board, lacked the resources to collect and transport the cocoa harvest, and it eventually required the mobilisation of university students and the drafting in of extra labour from unconventional sources – such as police stations and supermarket queues – in order to shift it.[54] Given the unprecedented magnitude of the crisis, it is understandable that for once the country's rulers, certainly with one eye on the international financial community and perhaps with the other on their own chances of survival, backtracked and adopted a less regulatory agenda, even at the expense of dissent within their ranks. Given that the interests of rulers and officials in the short term are best served by regulation rather than its opposite, it will be interesting to see whether, and in what ways, the pendulum will begin to swing back in the other direction. In general it seems possible that over the next few years, with a continuing economic crisis in the region, the economic policies of many of its constituent states may well oscillate between those which fit the geography and the dictates of the international financial institutions, and those which suit the interests of their political élites.

It would be nice to think that over time, an agenda geared to the economic integration and development of the whole region will prevail, and that the frontiers in West Africa will once more become as porous as they were during the early colonial period, allowing labour to migrate to where it is required in the regional economy and allowing the migrants some degree of protection by the state. But this is perhaps naive, and the omens are not good. Members of the political and administrative classes and their dependents are now entrenched in trade and commerce and seeking to consolidate their positions. These are the groups which have most to gain when policies of 'indigenisation' are implemented in the 'national interest', replacing the increasingly vulnerable 'aliens' who created and developed many sectors of the market. Even within national boundaries, the position of migrants from other regions is not necessarily secure, as Nigeria's history since 1966 has shown. With the development of the class structure the importance of the long-distance small-scale migrant traders in West Africa may well be on the wane, and an important turning point in their fortunes was the events in Ghana in December 1969. Those of them who, like the Yoruba in Ghana, are using their earnings abroad to build houses in their home towns as a form of long-term security are probably still wise to do so.

APPENDIX: A NOTE ON METHODS

The exodus of one's informants halfway through fieldwork is a relatively unusual event in anthropology, so an account of the effects it had on the research may be helpful. I had originally planned to spend about eighteen months in the field, divided between Tamale and Bawku in Ghana, and to end with a brief visit to Nigeria, visa permitting. Before going to Ghana, I spent six months learning Yoruba through weekly visits to SOAS in London. As I came to realise, Hausa, which all the Yoruba in Ghana spoke as a *lingua franca*, would have undoubtedly been easier to learn as it is less tonal, and it would have allowed me to communicate more freely with members of other ethnic groups as well. As things turned out, however, my Yoruba eventually proved useful, as I spent more time in Nigeria than originally intended. It eventually became fluent enough in Nigeria to cope with conversations about matters relating to trade and migration, though it was less adequate on other occasions, where I still often required help. Having so many people about who could speak either West African or standard English was always extremely useful, even though it created a less than ideal environment for learning Yoruba. Conversations in Nigeria with some of my most valuable older informants took place in a cheerful jumble of languages which often changed in mid-sentence.

I arrived in Ghana in April 1969, and arrived in Tamale at the end of the month. Thanks to the help and advice of friends, I found little difficulty settling into a house in Tamale and making contact with the local Yoruba community. Niara Sudarkasa, who was just finishing her own research in Kumasi, had suggested that I contact the Nigerian High Commission, and a letter of introduction from them opened many doors. She also put me in touch with Ganiyu Gbademasi who had been working with her and who proved an invaluable helper and source of information until he left the country in December. The organisation of the Yoruba in Tamale described in chapter 6 made it very easy to track down association secretaries and the Christian and Muslim leaders, but despite this, the initial progress of research was slow as I soon developed the usual range of tropical diseases and ended up in hospital. By the time I had recovered, the Ghanaian general election campaign was in full swing, and the Yoruba decided to suspend association meetings until September when it was all over. Immediately after, my wife Carla arrived in Ghana to take up a teaching job in Bawku, which fitted in with my plan to start work there after finishing in Tamale. This was not to be, however, as the Ghanaian government issued its compliance order in December, and most of the Yoruba left the country in the following weeks. By then I had a reasonably good idea of the structure of the Yoruba community and their life in Tamale, but little systematic quantitative data either on individual migration or trade.

In the first half of 1970 I continued collecting various types of data, including court records, archival material and life histories. I was helped with the latter mainly by Lasisi Lawal, who had remained in Ghana and who was a neighbour in Sakasaka. Most of the relatively few Yoruba who had stayed on in Tamale were simply waiting to sell their houses and were no longer working, and so had much more time to sit and talk to me than they had done the previous year. By the middle of the year thanks to Ibrahim Tahir – then a fellow-graduate student at Cambridge – I was able to obtain a Nigerian visa, and so my wife and I set off for the towns from which the migrants had come. As most of them were from a relatively small number of compounds it proved very easy to make contact once more, and for the next eleven months we divided our time between Igbetti and Ogbomosho with about a month in Igboho, interviewing as many people as we could find who had been in Tamale or other parts of Northern Ghana. We also spent some time collecting material on the returnees from Ghana from the Ministries in Ibadan. Our main helpers in Nigeria were Yekini Yusuf from Ogbomosho and Felicia Sangotowo from Igbetti, who had been a student at Carla's secondary school in Ghana. With her help, Carla was able to interview many of the women while I concentrated on the men. In the end, in addition to more general information we obtained systematic information on 382 adults (195 men and 187 women) who had been in Northern Ghana, relating to migration, work, marriage and family, education, religion and, in the case of the men, friends. Many of the tables in this book are based on sub-sets of this material, in most cases collected from former traders who had lived in Tamale. The statistics are descriptive rather than analytical. The people interviewed were simply those who were available rather than a proper probability-based sample, and I have therefore not presented a more elaborate statistical analysis. Figures on turnover have to be treated with particular caution as they were based on reminiscences, but many people seemed more willing to talk freely about trade in Ghana once it was in the past, and in most cases the figures were more or less in line with what I had seen in the market stalls in Tamale. The most they can do is give a general impression of the level of trade among the Yoruba on the eve of the exodus.

NOTES

CHAPTER 1

1. The Yoruba population of Ghana according to the 1960 census was 100,560 (*Population Census of Ghana, 1960*, Report 'E', Table S1, pp. c3–c9). Assuming a growth rate of 5 per cent per annum to include both natural increase and net immigration, the Yoruba population would have risen to 153,000 in 1969. Sudarkasa's estimate (1974: Appendix C) is that the population of Nigerian origin in Ghana in 1969 was 300,000, including 150,000 Yoruba, 92,400 Hausa and 21,000 Igbo. She estimates that 145,000 of the Yoruba left as a result of the compliance order. In terms of order of magnitude, these figures are broadly consistent with those of the Ministry of Economic Planning and Rehabilitation in Ibadan which registered 88,104 returnees between December 1969 and April 1971, assuming a registration rate of 50–60 per cent.
2. See Nypan (1960: 16) and Sudarkasa (1985: 51). In 1968 1,732 of the traders in Kumasi Central Market were Yoruba, i.e. 23 per cent. They were legal tenants of 17 per cent of the stalls, occupying others through subletting.
3. On the exodus, see Peil (1971), Eades (1987b), and Sudarkasa (1979). On the position of aliens in Ghana and elsewhere in West Africa, see also Skinner (1963), Peil (1974, 1979).
4. Hopkins (1987: 136).
5. References to corruption in the literature on Ghana are legion: perhaps surprisingly the only full-length study of the subject is LeVine (1975).
6. Hill (1970a) and Sudarkasa (1974, 1975) provide analysis of the 1960 figures on the Yoruba. The main source on the 1969–70 repatriation figures is Hundsalz (1972), though we consulted the same ministry later than he did when more material had been collected. Our material modifies his findings in detail but not in overall substance. The other main ethnographic sources besides this book are Stapleton (1958, 1959), Oyedipe (1967), Sudarkasa (1974, 1975, 1979, 1985), and Eades (1975, 1977, 1979, 1987b).
7. Eades (1980).
8. Amin (1974). The argument in this section is developed at greater length in Eades (1987a). Much of the earlier conventional wisdom on migration research is summarised in the papers in Jackson (1969).
9. On international migration within West Africa, see Zachariah and Condé (1981). On migration from Upper Volta see Skinner (1960), and Coulibaly *et al.* (1980). On migration to Ghana, see Rouch (1956) and Schildkrout (1978). The classic account of the Ghanaian cocoa industry is Hill (1963). On the effects of the 1969 exodus on the industry, see Addo (1970, 1972).
10. The main accounts of the Nigerian cocoa industry are by Galletti *et al.* (1956), Berry (1975), Beer (1976), Beer and Williams (1976), Peel (1983: Chapter 7) and Berry (1985: Chapters 3–5).
11. The distinction between the rate and incidence of migration comes from Mitchell (1970). Mitchell's most recent formulation (1985) which distinguishes between the 'setting' and 'situation' of migration has elements in common with the approach adopted here.

12. For discussions of chain migration, see Price (1969: 210–12) and Eades (1987b). On the distribution of the Yoruba from different Yoruba towns in Ghana, see also Hundsalz (1972).

13. Hart (1973), one of a series of papers (the others are Hart 1970, 1975, 1986) in which his views on the informal sector evolved.

14. The best brief discussion of this debate is Moser (1978). For its relevance to Ghanaian markets, see also Robertson (1984: 3–7).

15. Eades (1987a:). Alexander (1987) makes a similar distinction between 'trade', 'traders', and 'trading', corresponding to the economic and administrative context, the structure of social relations, and the process of decision-making itself.

16. See, for example, Bascom (1942), Lloyd (1955, 1962, 1966), Bender (1970, 1972), Eades (1980: Chapter 3), Peel (1983: Chapter 3), Berry (1985).

17. A preliminary move in this direction is my attempt to write a computer simulation of Yoruba trading activity, as part of the Kent Social Anthropology and Computing Teaching Initiative.

18. On the Ghanaian economy during the Nkrumah period, see Birmingham et al. (1966), Genoud (1969), Berg (1971), Jones (1976), Killick (1978) and Hutchful (1987). Of these, Jones and Berg are the most hostile and Hutchful the most sympathetic. On the NLC period see also Pinkney (1972: 29–33) and Esseks (1975). For the years from 1968–9 onwards, an annual survey is available in *Africa Contemporary Record*.

19. The fullest account is Cohen (1969). See also Cohen (1965, 1966, 1971a) on trade, and Cohen (1967, 1971b, 1974b) on ethnicity, religion and politics.

20. The fullest account is Schildkrout (1978). On generational differences see also Schildkrout (1974a), and on Kumasi religion and politics see Schildkrout (1970a, 1970b, 1974b, 1978: Part III).

21. Schildkrout (1978: 43–5), Cohen (1969: 41–2).

22. It is clear from the accounts both of Schildkrout (1978) and Winchester (1976) that the Mossi and Hausa communities continued to function, despite the compliance order.

23. For accounts of the Ghanaian economy during this period see Killick (1978), Esseks (1975) and Huq (1989). For a critical account of the role of foreign capital and the IMF, see also Hutchful (1987).

24. Eight leaders were executed by the AFRC, including three former heads of state, Generals Afrifa, Acheampong and Akuffo, along with General Uteka, the head of the border guards.

25. A fuller account is given in Chapter 7 below. On the Rawling's period and Ghana's economic collapse, see Chazan (1983) and Pellow and Chazan (1986). Ray (1986) analyses the Rawling's period as a Marxist revolution, an analysis that is much less convincing now, perhaps, than when he wrote it. For the assault by the regime on market traders during this period see also Chapter 7 below together with Robertson (1984: 243–5), Brown (1983), and Clark (1988).

CHAPTER 2

1. Eades (1980: Chapter 1).
2. Berry (1975), Gusten (1968).
3. Eades (1980: 18); Smith (1969: Chapter 2).
4. The main study of Oyo is Law (1977), particularly Chapter 10 on the economy.
5. On West African trade in the pre-colonial period in general, see Hopkins (1973:

Chapter 2). On the trade from Ashanti to Hausaland, see Lovejoy (1980), Adamu (1978).

6. On the collapse of Oyo, see Law (1977: Part III). On the successor states see O'Hear (1983) (Ilorin), Awe (1967) (Ibadan), Smith (1962) (Ijaye), and Biobaku (1957) (Abeokuta).

7. For nineteenth-century estimates of the size of these towns, see Mabogunje (1968: 93).

8. On the changes in the settlement pattern in the Oke Ogun see Babayemi (1971). The general problems of these towns are discussed by Mabogunje and Oyawoye (1961).

9. On Yoruba settlement patterns and rural-urban links, see Lloyd (1962), Krapf-Askari (1969), Peel (1983: Chapters 3–4), and Bender (1972).

10. The most famous example is that of continuing conflict between the residents of Modakeke in Ife who are descended from nineteenth century Oyo refugees, and the rest of the town (Oyediran, 1974).

11. On town improvement associations, see Mabogunje (1972: 83–7) and Peel (1983: Chapter 9).

12. On Hausa trade, see Cohen (1965, 1966), and on the Lebanese see Winder (1962).

13. On Ijesha trade, see Peel (1983: Chapter 8), and on the Ijebu see Mabogunje (1967), Aronson (1971, 1978).

14. Hundsalz (1972) is based on the ministry registration forms. These were completed by returning migrants in offices set up in the main towns affected. The forms were later sent to Ibadan for processing and storage, and we had access to them in April 1971, after Hundsalz. Between his visit and ours, more forms had been processed. Some of the data had been classified by the Ministry for its own use. Data on the town of residence in Ghana had to be extracted from the forms themselves. We worked through all the forms for Oyo North, but due to constraints of time we decided to take a 25 per cent sample of the forms from Egba and Oshun North West and a 10 per cent sample of those from other divisions. In the tables drawn up on the basis of this data, 'ministry figures' refers to figures compiled by ministry officials, and 'registration forms' refers to data we extracted ourselves.

15. Sudarkasa (1974: 95–8; 1975: 98). There is a problem with the 1948 census figures because of its inadequate classification of ethnic groups. Listed in the tables are four groups of Nigerian origin, 'Hausa', 'Southern Nigerians', 'Northern Nigerians', and 'Nigerians'. Given that the Yoruba in Ghana were universally known as 'Lagosians' or 'Nigerians' it is probable that the 'Nigerians' were Yoruba. Probably the bulk of the 'Southern Nigerians' were as well, as the age distribution of the Igbo in 1960 suggests that they were recent arrivals. This leaves the problem of the Northern Nigerians. Some of them may have been Hausa, but the category could also have included Yoruba from the then Northern Region of Nigeria, mainly from Ilorin and Offa. The classification also seems to have been applied differently in different parts of the country. In many parts of the country all the Nigerians were classified as 'Northern' or 'Southern', whereas in Krachi they were simply categorised as 'Nigerians'. Tables 2.1 and 2.3 give figures (a) assuming that the Yoruba were the 'Southern Nigerians' and (b) including the 'Nigerians' and 'Northern Nigerians' as well. Sudarkasa (1975: 98, n.1) suggests that for Kumasi in 1921, at least a third of the 3,135 'Northern Nigerians' enumerated were Yoruba from the Northern Region.

16. This has been done on the basis of the maps in the 1960 census volumes showing the two sets of boundaries. The major change in boundaries was the transfer of Kadjebi and Ho to Buem-Krachi Division in 1960. Given this, and the problems of the 1948

Krachi ethnic classification, it is difficult to calculate the intercensile shift in the ratios for these two areas.

17. Hill (1970a: 54).
18. Sudarkasa (1975).
19. Hill (1970a: 11).
20. Hill (1970a: 33).
21. Hundsalz (1972).
22. Aronson (1971, 1978), Mabogunje (1967).
23. Sudarkasa (1975: 112).
24. Hundsalz (1972).
25. On the economy of Bolgatanga, see Hart (1974, 1978). On the geography of the north of Ghana, see Dickson (1969). The Northern Territories of the Gold Coast on independence became the Northern Region of Ghana, and in 1961 it was divided into the Northern and Upper Regions. In 1980, the Upper Region was subdivided into the Upper East and Upper West Regions.
26. Shepherd (1978, 1981).
27. Ladouceur (1979: 34–5), Wilks (1975: 308).
28. Johnson (1966), Wilks (1971, 1975: Chapter 7), Lovejoy (1982).
29. Adamu (1978: 63).
30. Lovejoy (1980).
31. O'Hear (1983).
32. Law (1977: 204–5), O'Hear (1980), Bray (1968, 1969a, 1969b).
33. Sudarkasa (1975: 95–6).
34. Johnson (1966: 1/1).
35. See SAL/22/2, SAL/3/1 (David Asante), SAL/16/34 (Lonsdale, SAL/63/1 (Rowe), SAL/18/3 (von Francois), SAL/12/2 (Wolf) and SAL/19/4, SAL/19/11 (Binger) in Johnson (1966). Binger, who visited the town in 1896, estimated that 40 per cent of the inhabitants were Gonja, 20 per cent each Hausa and Dyula, with the remaining 20 per cent made up of a mixture of other groups, including 'Nago and Yoroba of the coast' (SAL/19/4). He estimated the fixed population of the town at around 3,000. The Anago are one of the southern Yoruba-speaking subgroups, while 'Yoroba' probably refers to Oyo Yoruba from Ilorin and other towns further north.
36. Braimah and Goody (1967).
37. Quartey-Papafio (1911: 438–9), Sudarkasa (1975: 96).
38. Skinner (1974: 26).
39. Wilks (1968).
40. *Annual Report, North East Province of the Northern Territories*, 1908.
41. Bening (1973b).
42. Staniland (1975: 72).
43. Bening (1974).
44. Szereszewski (1965).
45. Kirk-Greene (1980), Killingray (1982).
46. Quartey-Papafio (1911: 438–9); Sudarkasa (1975: 96). Many of these troops seem to have come from Ibadan and towns under its control after the end of the Kiriji war in 1893 (Akintoye, 1971). They may have included recruits from Ogbomosho: Chief Akintola's father took refuge with Ogbomosho soldiers in Ibadan during political disturbances in 1916 (Osuntokun 1984: 4–6).
47. On the Nigerian railway industry, see Oyemakinde (1974). According to Jeffries (1973: 12), unskilled Nigerian labour remained important for the Gold Coast railways throughout the colonial period. On road labourers, see Sudarkasa (1975: 96).

48. Crisp (1984: 35), Sudarkasa (1975: 97).
49. Mabogunje (1972: 125–7).
50. Beckman (1976: 47).
51. Sudarkasa (1985: 46).
52. Agiri (1972).
53. The major sources on the administration and development of the Northern Terri-tories during the colonial period include Staniland (1975: Chapters 3–6), Ladou-ceur (1979), Shepherd (1978, 1981), Konings (1986) and the series of papers by Bening (1971, 1973a, 1973b, 1974, 1975a, 1975b, 1975c, 1977, 1983), Thomas (1973, 1974, 1975), and Sutton (1983, 1989). On the political economy of the Gold Coast in general see Kay (1972) and Howard, 1978).
54. Cited in Bening (1975c: 72).
55. Bening (1975c: 79).
56. *Annual Report for the Northern Territories*, 1910: 16. Cf. *Annual Report for the Northern Territories*, 1914: 7 and 1917: paragraph 72.
57. Northcott (1899: 47), *Annual Report for the Northern Territories*, 1908: 7.
58. Watherstone (1908: 368–9).
59. *Annual Report for the Northern Territories*, 1912: 9.
60. By the 1960s the rise of the Volta Lake made the ferry service lengthy and infrequent, and the only alternative was the road through Kintampo which remained untarred until the 1970s.
61. Arhin (1979: 84).
62. Patterson (1983) estimates that 10 per cent of the population died in the epidemic.
63. Thomas (1973).
64. Thomas (1975), Killingray (1982).
65. *Annual Report for the Northern Territories*, 1926–7: para 324.
66. *Annual Report for the Northern Territories*, 1929–30.
67. *Annual Report for the Northern Territories*, 1930–1: 1.
68. *Annual Report for the Northern Territories*, 1923–4: 7.
69. *Annual Report for the Northern Territories*, 1928–9.
70. *Tamale District Census Reports*, 1931.
71. *Lawra Tumu District Census Report*, 1931.
72. *Kusasi District Handing-Over Notes*, 1931.
73. *Dagomba District Annual Report*, 1937–8: para 46.
74. *Annual Report for the Northern Territories*, 1938–9: 18.
75. *Kusasi District Handing-Over Notes*, 1939.
76. Bray (1968).
77. Barbour and Simmonds (1971).
78. Sudarkasa (1974: 70).
79. Cf. Sudarkasa (1975: 95).
80. Sudarkasa (1975: 99–100). Alhaji Karimu, who died in 1970, was the last Yoruba chief in Tamale. By 1969 he had retired semi-permanently to Ogbomosho.
81. *Dagomba District Annual Report*, 1935–65.
82. *Annual Report for the Northern Territories*, 1936–7.
83. Peel (1983: Chapter 8).
84. The Ilorin remained one of the largest groups of Yoruba in Accra and one of the largest in Kumasi. However, although Ilorin remained a major centre of cloth production, much of the trade in the town and the surrounding rural areas has been taken over by Yoruba from Ogbomosho, Offa and elsewhere. O'Hear (1983) discusses the reasons for this.
85. Sudarkasa (1974: 69–70).
86. Wilks (1968).

CHAPTER 3

1. Lloyd (1962: 53) pointed out that if the populations of the more sparsely and more densely populated areas are averaged out, the overall density approximates that for the rest of the country.
2. Clarke (1972: 74–6).
3. The Lander brothers in 1830 reported that they 'entered a town of prodigious extent called Bohoo. Its immense triple wall is little short of twenty miles in circuit ... By the hasty view we obtained of it, the town is not much unlike Kano. Bohoo was formerly the metropolis of Yoruba. It is still considered a place of great importance, the second town in the kingdom' (1832: 144–6). For a period in the sixteenth century it had been the capital of the whole kingdom (Smith 1965). By the time Clarke visited it in 1854, much of it lay in ruins (1972: 68).
4. Shaki was also protected by fortifications, as well as by the hills surrounding it. Clarke described it as having one of the finest markets in the country with 'the commercial spirit ever observable' (Clarke, 1972: 57, 61). On its problems in the twentieth century, see Mabogunje and Oyawoye (1961).
5. On Yoruba migrants in French-speaking West Africa see Sudarkasa (1985: 58–60). Mabogunje (1972) gives the following figures for Shaki migrants in West Africa in 1967: Ghana 2500, Dahomey (Benin) 1,800, Togo 1,500, Upper Volta (Burkina Faso) 1,900, Niger 1,420, Ivory Coast 500, Mali 1,870, Sierra Leone 400, Guinea 790, Senegal 200, making a total of 12,880.
6. E.R Hislop in the *Annual Report for Oyo Province*, 1949. Ironically, *irẹpọ* in Yoruba means 'unity'.
7. Cited in O'Hear (1983: 17–18).
8. On the commercial importance of Igbetti, see Sudarkasa (1973), Gusten (1968) and Anthonio (1967). Its market handled a quarter of the yam trade between Oyo Province and Ibadan.
9. Political problems have bedevilled Nigeria's attempts to hold a census since independence (Aluko 1965). The 1962 and 1974 figures were scrapped, and the 1963 figures were probably inflated for some parts of the country, including Northern Oyo and Oshun North West Divisions. In the late 1960s Milone and Green were working on estimates of the populations of the northern Yoruba towns based on aerial photography and sample surveys of occupancy rates (Milone and Olaore, 1971; Green 1974). The available figures for the four towns are as follows:
   Igbetti: 1952 – 10,955; 1963 – 28,000; 1970 (est.) – 10–15,000
   Igboho: 1952 – 8,476; 1963 – 45,000; 1970 (est.) – 10–15,000
   Ogbomosho: 1952 – 139,535; 1963 – 313,000; 1970 (est.) 80–100,000
   Shaki: 1952 – 22,983; 1963 – 75,000; 1970 (est.) – 28,000
   The very high figure for Ogbomosho in 1963 is not perhaps surprising, given that Chief Akintola was regional Premier at the time.
10. Osuntokun (1984: 3–4).
11. O'Hear (1983: 294), Killingray (1982), Kirk-Greene (1980).
12. On Ogbomosho migration to Jos, see Plotnicov (1967: 85–110). The Ogbomosho *parapọ* in Jos paid for the legal training in the UK of the young S.L. Akintola (Osuntokun, 1984: 16).
13. In 1914 the ruler of Ogbomosho was deposed by the Alafin of Oyo, and Ogbomosho remained under Oyo administration until the creation of Ibadan Division in 1934 (Atanda, 1973: 136–8).
14. *Annual Report, Oyo Province*, 1948.

15. *Annual Report, Oyo Province, 1949*. The main force for progress in the town, the British view, was Chief Nathaniel Oyerinde, Ogbomosho's first graduate and author of an important history of the town (Agiri, 1979).
16. The history of the Baptist Mission in Ogbomosho dates back to Bowen's arrival in 1855. He settled there having been refused permission to reside in Ilorin (1857: 203–4). In addition to the educational institutions, Ogbomosho also has a large Baptist hospital.
17. For a brief summary of Yoruba politics in the 1960s, see Eades (1980: 109–115).
18. On the importance of progressive unions in Yoruba towns, see Berry (1985: Chapter 7), and Peel (1983: Chapter 9). Mabogunje's figures (1972: 137) show that in addition to private remittances, Shaki migrants in the late 1960s were contributing over £8,000 a year to development projects at home through their associations.
19. For fuller accounts of Yoruba towns and settlement patterns, cf. Lloyd (1962: Chapter 3), Krapf-Askari (1969), and Eades (1980: Chapter 3).
20. The strength of the cognatic element varies between different areas of Yorubaland. For a fuller discussion see Eades (1980: 49–61) together with Lloyd (1966) and Bender (1972).
21. Bascom (1942).
22. Fadipe (1970: 105–13).
23. Berry (1985: 64).
24. Cf. Peel (1983: 146–59).
25. Schiltz (1982). For a full-length account of women traders in or near Oyo, see Sudarkasa (1973).
26. Ile Olowo and Ile Isale are both pseudonyms, as are the names of the individuals within them. The Ile Olowo material was previously presented in Eades (1975). For a description of the compound in 1970, see Eades (1980: 46–8).
27. Sadiku was brought up by his parents as a Muslim on the advice of the Ifa oracle.
28. Although the demand for Yoruba cloth declined in the southern Gold Coast in the 1930s (Sudarkasa, 1975: 99), it held up well in the north of the country. Yoruba *aṣọ ofi* is similar to Dagomba cloth, though of finer quality and with a wider range of designs.
29. An earlier version of this case study is presented in Eades (1979).
30. On the restrictions on the export of Yoruba cloth and their effects on the Ilorin weaving industry, see O'Hear (1983: 152–3). In the Gold Coast, the 1930s were a disastrous period for the rural community including the agricultural migrants, as cocoa production levelled off and disputes over marketing developed. See Van Hear (1982: 121). On the other hand, demand for foodstuffs for the troops stimulated production for the market, as food prices climbed to two or three times their pre-war level by 1943/4 (Van Hear, 1982: 121).
31. On the post-war economy, see the essays in Birmingham *et al.* (1966), and for the period after 1960 see Killick (1978). For political development see Austin (1964), Pinkney (1972), Jones (1976). On developments in northern Ghana see Ladouceur (1979), Staniland (1975), Shepherd (1978) and Van Hear (1982).
32. Robertson (1984: 39). The results of the official investigation into the riots were issued in the Watson Report. See especially paragraphs 164–79, reprinted in Kay (1972).
33. The producer price varied from 78 per cent of the world price in 1956/7 to 38 per cent of the world price in 1953/4 and 1954/5 (Beckman, 1976: 292).
34. Robertson (1984: 39).
35. Van Hear (1982: 255).
36. Van Hear (1982: 255). On the cattle trade, cf. Hill (1970b: Chapter 5).

37. Garlick (1971: 7). As a means of building up a regular clientele, the firms instituted a system whereby regular customers could deposit sums of money with them, usually not less than £50, and obtain goods up to the value of this deposit. Transactions were recorded in a passbook. When they had sold the goods and made up the deposit again, more goods could be obtained. In addition to preference in the supplies of the goods available, the traders also received a small commission on goods bought from the firm, and they would either receive this as cash at regular intervals or have it added to their deposits. A trader well-known to a branch manager might in time be allowed goods of greater value than the deposit, for which he would pay at the end of the month. Technically it is only these customers who were credit customers: most passbook customers were in fact lending money to the firms. According to informants, credit was more readily available in the 1950s when goods were in plentiful supply. With the increasing shortages of goods after 1961 the firms increasingly restricted credit sales, and the passbook system took on a new lease of life. Even passbooks became more difficult to obtain as the demand for them increased. If a trader had a larger sum of money to deposit, usually upwards of £500, he could become a licensed agent for a particular firm. A number of Yoruba in northern Ghana had become agents in this way, particularly in the smaller towns where the large firms could not afford to operate directly. On abuses of the system, cf. Jones (1976: 256–9).
38. Berg (1971), Killick (1978: 43–54), Genoud (1969). For a recent more sympathetic evaluation of CPP policy, cf. Hutchful (1987).
39. Killick (1978: Chapters 7–8).
40. The fear of unemployment was a factor lying behind the creation of the Worker's Brigade and the state farms (Killick, 1978: 217).
41. Genoud (1969: 147–8).
42. Pinkney (1972: 140). Killick (1978: 73–9) notes that the 1970 Census failed to reveal as large a rise in unemployment as had been expected, and suggests that the drop in male employment was offset by an increase in female participation in the labour force.
43. Kay (1972).
44. Garlick (1971: 118).
45. Garlick (1971: 71), Jones (1976: 187–90).
46. Garlick (1971: 71), cf. Kumar (1973).
47. Pinkney (1972: 29–32).
48. Skinner (1963), Austin (1964: 110), Schildkrout (1970a: 263).
49. The main items were: The Ghana Nationality and Citizenship Act, 1957; the Deportation Act, 1957; the Immigration Act, 1957; the Deportation (Amendment) Acts of 1958 and 1959; the Ghana Nationality Act of 1961 (amended 1967, 1969 and 1972); the Aliens Act of 1963 (amended 1968); the Ghana Enterprise Decree (1968); and the Ghana Business (Promotion) Act of 1970.
50. Ofosu-Amaah (1971: 92).
51. Birmingham et al. (1966: 266ff), Stapleton (1959), Mabogunje (1972: 134–5).
52. NLC Decree 259, July 1968 (Pinkney, 1972: 32). Cf. Mabogunje (1972: 125–7).
53. Bauer (1954: Chapter 12).
54. Peil (1971: 211–2).
55. Peil (1971: 206).
56. Ewusi (1976).
57. Cf. Hart (1974).
58. Cf. Gaveh (1961).
59. Pinkney (1972: 32).

60. Lisk (1976).
61. For a description of the daily contribution savings system, see Chapter 5 below. Similar systems are described by Lewis (1976: 141–2) and Yusuf (1975).
62. Cf. Sudarkasa (1985: 55).
63. Cf. Sudarkasa (1975: 54–5).
64. This was the start of the rice boom in the Tamale area, which involved a number of the wealthier Yoruba and which continued after their departure (Shepherd, 1978). For the situation elsewhere in the north, see Goody (1980), Shepherd (1981), Konings (1986).
65. Traditionally Yoruba roofs were thatched, but with the introduction of corrugated iron sheeting 'pan' roofs quickly became popular. Although they made the interior of the house hotter, they were more durable and made the collection of clean water much easier during the rains. By the late 1960s there were very few thatched roofs left in the towns, but they were still the norm in the farm villages of northern Yorubaland.
66. Unlike Ogbomosho, Igboho and Shaki, where the main group of Christians were the Baptists, most of the Igbetti Christians belonged to the United Missionary Church of Africa, founded by the United Missionary Society, a small American mission with other congregations at Share and Jebba in Kwara State to the north. The doctrines, ritual and organisation of individual churches in the two missions are extremely similar.
67. Eades (1980: 61–3).
68. Similar processes are described in Ilesha, Iganna and Ife by Peel (1983), Schiltz (1982), and Berry (1985).
69. Property ownership in Lagos and Ibadan, where there is considerably more pressure on housing, can be extremely lucrative. See the discussion in Barnes (1986: Chapter 3).

CHAPTER 4

1. The individuals whose cases are discussed here were all members of what might loosely be called my 'network' in Tamale, and thus, although I lack the kinds of systematically collected data presented by Plotnicov (1967) and Aronson (1978), I do have enough material scattered throughout my fieldnotes to build up a reasonably full picture of their economic and social lives in the late 1960s. A brief description of this network is in order as it serves to illustrate the multiplex nature of the ties binding the Yoruba community together. The first of the traders I came to know was Limata who was the mother of one of my research assistants. She rented a shop in a house belonging to the sons of Mustafa Iyanda, an Ogbomosho trader who had died two years before my arrival. Rahimi lived in the same house and his aunt lived next door. She and Ogundiran's wife were good friends. Mustafa Iyanda had been a close friend both of Alhaji Lasisi and Raliatu's husband, Alhaji Raji. There were other links. One of Raliatu's 'boyfriends', Bosco, lived in a house owned by Lasisi, while Limata had been brought to Tamale initially by a friend of Lasisi's father, Sadiku. Raliatu, her husband, Ogundiran and Iyanda were all from the same ward of Ogbomosho. Caleb was the odd man out in all this. He lived in a different area of the town, came from Igboho and had a network of friends based on his church rather than on the market.
2. For a comparison with Kumasi, see Sudarkasa (1974: 86).
3. In Kumasi, co-wives living in separate buildings were apparently the norm (Sudarkasa, 1974: 86).

4. On the division of household expenditure between husband and wife in Yoruba society, see Sudarkasa (1973).

5. This was significant. Lasisi had been one of the strongest supporters of the exiled ruler of Igbetti, the Onigbetti who had been an Akintola supporter and the local parliamentary representative until 1966. The majority of people in Igbetti had supported the rival Action Group and after the Nigerian coup of January 1966, in which Akintola was killed, the Onigbetti was forced into exile. After he left the town, his house and car were burnt by an angry crowd, and the ruins, including the wreck of the car in the garage, had remained untouched.

6. The theme of the mystical dangers of interethnic marriage is a familiar one in West Africa. See for instance Cohen (1969: 53–4).

7. In the 1969 election Tamale was one of the few 'marginal' seats and the outcome was in doubt right up until the poll. It was won by the General Secretary of the National Alliance of Liberals. See Staniland (1975) for the political background to the Tamale campaign.

8. On market periodicities in Ghana as a whole see Fagerlund and Smith (1970). The fullest account of marketing in the Northern Region of Ghana, including Tamale and the markets around, is Mann (1977). The fullest source in English is Van Apeldoorn (1971). On the Tamale/Yendi area cf. McKim (1978).

9. Ẹko is described by Bascom (1951: 128) as a warm, thin corn starch gruel usually eaten like soup with a spoon. In Tamale the Yoruba normally sweetened it with sugar and ate it with beancakes sold every morning by Dagomba women in the neighbourhood.

10. These were the largest beer bars in the town and were much frequented by the salaried workers, especially after pay-day. The music was either provided by the resident band of the cafe, by local army bands, or by the usual assortment of popular 'high life' and 'soul' records, especially those of James Brown.

11. The Yoruba Imam, Alhaji Bello, and his assistants presided over most of the muslim rites of passage within the Yoruba community in Tamale. See Chapter 6 below.

12. On Ile Oke, see Chapter 3 above. On the organisation of the First Baptist Church see Chapter 6 below, and Eades (1977).

13. Presumably this was to evade the Nigerian export restrictions (O'Hear, 1983: 152–3).

14. The Ogboni cult is common throughout Yorubaland, where it formerly wielded considerable political power (see the references in Eades, 1980: 98–9). A number of the senior Yoruba in Tamale were thought to be members, despite the disapproval of the Baptist church. The Oddfellows had only two Yoruba members, Ogundiran and his friend Ayoola, the secretary of the Nigeria Community. Their activities for the most part seemed to consist of expensive feasting, but it was widely believed by others in the Yoruba community that Ogundiran derived spiritual powers from his membership, no doubt on the analogy of the Ogboni. Masonry and similar associations are popular among the elite in West Africa (cf. Cohen 1971b): in recent years in Ghana they have been under attack as hotbeds of anti-government dissent.

15. The word is derived from la oju, to open one's eyes. English-speaking Yoruba usually translate the word as 'civilisation' but perhaps a better translation would be 'sophistication'. Cf. Peel (1978).

16. Ogundiran's monogamy was all the more remarkable in that he had no sons, only two teenage daughters.

17. On the circumstances surrounding the formation of the Second Baptist Church see Chapter 6 below and Eades (1977).

18. Even allowing a profit margin of 10 per cent on the cost price of goods and a turnover of NC800 a month, Raliatu would at most have had an income in the region of NC1000 a year, which would have been barely sufficient to finance her house. Probably her turnover was rather higher than the figure she gave us. It was still the highest figure given to us by a Yoruba woman who had been in Tamale. Sudarkasa's estimate of profit margins in Kumasi is very low indeed (1974: 76). It is possible that they were higher in Tamale where there was less competition.

19. Star Beer was the leading local brand of lager beer in both Nigeria and Ghana, and the Star Beer bottle was a convenient and universally recognised liquid measure, holding just over a pint.

20. The house had a tap in the central courtyard, but water was very scarce in Tamale in 1969. Often the supply was only turned on for a couple of hours at night. Rainwater was therefore an important alternative to the municipal water carts that used to tour the streets intermittently when the shortage was particularly acute.

CHAPTER 5

1. Cf. Sudarkasa (1974: 78–9), who implies that in Kumasi traders retiring to Nigeria simply sold up their businesses and repatriated the capital.

2. Cf. Aronson (1970: 26–7) and Bascom (1969: 58) on the pattern of self-reliance training in Yoruba society.

3. See for instance Peel (1983: 152–9). The *oṣomaalo* traders from Ilesha seem to have based their whole operations on credit sales from the European and Levantine firms in the large towns. As they did not rely on their kin for capital, this might explain the difference between the one-man Ilesha enterprises and the larger kin-based groups involved in the trade to Ghana.

4. Cf. Bascom (1952). Ardener (1964) brings together a multitude of different examples from other parts of the world. See also Light (1972).

5. Katzin (1964: 191–2) describes a similar system operating in Onitsha. The first daily contribution collectors in Tamale were Yoruba, but they had Dagomba as well as Yoruba clients.

6. *Tiro* is used as eye shadow by both men and women. Natron (*kaun* in Yoruba and *kanwa* in Hausa) has a wide range of uses in medicine, cooking, feeding livestock, soap production, dyeing, tanning and preparing chewing tobacco (see Lovejoy, 1980:123–4).

7. On market cycles, see Van Apeldoorn (1971), Fagerlund and Smith (1970) and Smith (1971).

8. Cf. Hart (1969: 221–4) on the vital role of credit in the lives of lower-paid urban workers.

9. The main discussion of price control for this period is Killick (1973). Despite these and similar criticisms, successive governments persisted in enforcing controls with increasing brutality and with disastrous results until 1983.

10. Some examples are sugar 8 per cent, sardines 10 per cent, matches 12 per cent, batteries 13 per cent, tomato paste 15 per cent and toilet soap 17 per cent. The difference between the retail and wholesale price on all textiles was NC1.00 which translated into a margin of 9.5 per cent on cheap local prints, and of less than 5 per cent on the better quality imported prints which cost twice as much. I would agree with Garlick in questioning Nypan's figure of 25–30 per cent margins on goods sold in the market, though admittedly this is based on little data. So is Sudarkasa's much lower estimate (1974).

11. The most famous market for foreign exchange was in Cow Lane in Accra, which from the late 1970s became a major target in the war against corruption or *kalabule*

(see below, Chapter 7). In recent years the traders have had to put up with severe competition from the official foreign exchange bureaux.

12. On Yoruba education, see Abernethy (1969).
13. See Abernethy (1969) together with Foster (1965) on the development of education in Ghana. In the Northern Territories educational development had been seriously hampered by the unwillingness of the administration to let the missions operate freely on the grounds that it would alienate local Islamic sentiment. The result was an imbalance in education between the north and south of the country which has persisted until the present. See Thomas (1974), and Ladouceur (1979).
14. Cf. Hart (1970: 111–2), Garlick (1971: 55).
15. See above, Chapter 3 note 64.
16. Even in 1937, Bascom noted that traditional marriage payments in cash were only a fraction of the total wedding expenditure, and that a wedding even then in Ife could cost upwards of £50 (1969: 60). NC400 may be a low estimate: one of the migrants spent N£400 on his wedding in Nigeria after his return, and Oyedipe (1967: 47) describes a naming ceremony as costing NC400 in Accra.
17. Peel (1983), Peace (1979).

CHAPTER 6

1. Cohen (1965, 1966, 1967, 1969, 1971a), Schildkrout (1974b, 1978).
2. Cohen (1969: 201–11).
3. Cohen (1974a, 1974b).
4. Cf. Schildkrout (1978: 8–17).
5. Sudarkasa (1979: 147–65).
6. On West Africa, see Little (1957, 1965), Barnes and Peil (1977). On Latin America see the summary in Butterworth and Chance (1981).
7. Modeke is the oldest centre of Islam in Igboho, and the Modeke people argued that the central mosque should be sited there. The other sections of the town agreed on an alternative site, resulting in two mosques in Igboho and a split in the ranks of the migrants abroad. Also underlying the split was a long-standing dispute about the relative status of the ruler of Igboho and the chief of Modeke.
8. The other figures were: Igbetti 135, Igboho (Okegboho and Obago quarters) 90, Ogbomosho Muslims 95 (all married men), Ogbomosho Christians 90 (including unmarried men). I was unable to trace figures for the Igboho migrants from Modeke quarter.
9. The fullest description of patron–client politics and informal leadership in a Yoruba community is Barnes (1986). See especially Chapter 4.
10. Cf. Mabogunje (1972: 136–7), Peel (1983: Chapter 9).
11. The conflict dated back to 1958 when Ajura, a CPP supporter, signed a petition demanding the deposition of the Ya Na, Abudulai III (Staniland, 1975: 156).
12. An earlier version of this section is contained in Eades (1977).
13. In general the protestant missions had a 'gentlemen's agreement' not to duplicate mission work in each other's areas, but there was a good deal of informal collaboration between them. The Baptists were based at Ogbomosho, with large churches in Igboho and Shaki. The UMS were based in Ilorin, with outstations at Igbetti, Share and Jebba, on the Niger. In addition to the work in Ghana, which arose out of the Yoruba migration, there are also large Baptist congregations in the major towns of Northern Nigeria, again with a large northern Yoruba component.
14. This is a pattern which goes back to the early part of the century in Accra (Quartey-Papafio 1911, Oyedipe 1967: 3, Acquah 1958: 101) and Kumasi (Sudarkasa, 1979: 147–52, Schildkrout 1970a, 1970b, 1978: 194–206).

15. This is the Tamale equivalent of the Kumasi Yoruba Community, described by Sudarkasa (1979: 157–60), which operated from 1959–69.
16. While in Tamale I was given access to local court records covering 146 of the 336 months between 1941 and 1969. There were only nineteen examples of cases between two Yoruba, an average of one case every 7.5 months. This is remarkably small considering that the majority of cases involving Yoruba were to do with trade and the market, and given the complexities of credit within the Yoruba community.
17. Cf. Sudarkasa (1979: 158).
18. E.g. Schildkrout (1978).
19. Oyedipe (1967).
20. On education rates among the Yoruba, see above, Chapter 5, Tables 5:11, 5:15.
21. This has generated a large literature, much of it summarised in Goody (1982). On Yoruba fostering, see Sudarkasa (1973: 132–44, 1974: 79–80).
22. Oyedipe (1967: 66).
23. The idea was suggested by Roger Sanjek who was working in Adabraka at the time (Sanjek, 1972). Cf. Peil (1975, 1981).
24. The figures are 58.2 per cent for Ogbomosho, 60.9 per cent for Igbetti and 62.3 per cent for Igboho. Compare the figures of 79 per cent and 76 per cent recorded by Peil in Ajegunle and Kukuri (Peil, 1975: 116).
25. Cf. Sanjek (1972) who argued that in Adebraka, a middle-class suburb of Accra, class rather than ethnic identity was becoming the main determinant of social interaction.
26. The Yoruba had a reputation for exclusivity when it came to marriage. Cf. Goody (1970), Skinner (1974: 122), Peil (1975: 110), Sudarkasa (1979: 156–7). As a comparison, Schildkrout found that 28 per cent of the marriages of Mossi male first-generation migrants, and 37 per cent of those in the second generation were outside the ethnic group. Out-marriage by Mossi women was much less common, the figures being 2 and 10 per cent for the two generations (1978: 178).
27. The violence was triggered by the release of the Mate-Kole commission of Enquiry into the affair, which declared that the enskinment of Na Andani in 1968 was null and void, Andani himself having died in March. The ruling was important as it virtually eliminated the Andani ruling family from future access to the chiefship. For a full account, see Ferguson and Wilks (1970), Ladouceur (1972), Staniland (1975). Since Staniland's book was published, the affair has continued to rumble on, with another set of rulings being handed down by the Ghana courts in 1986, and with more trouble in Yendi reported in 1987. This left the Andani claimant occupying the skin, with the Abudulai faction still contesting the decision. See the articles in *West Africa*, 1981, p. 1001; 1986, p. 2379; and 1987, pp. 393 and 1131.
28. Schildkrout (1970a, 1970b, 1974b, 1978: Chapter 8).
29. The Nigerian civil war finished on 15 January, 1970.
30. Cf. Schildkrout (1978: 90). On the distribution of the world religions among the Yoruba, see Eades (1980: Chapter 6), and Peel (1967).
31. Schildkrout (1978: 43–7). Cf. Hart (1975).
32. Cohen (1969: 41–6).
33. Eades (1987b).

CHAPTER 7

1. Alexander (1987: 2).
2. The account with most similarities to the pattern of migration among the Yoruba is that of Khuri (1965).

3. This would appear to be clear from Cohen (1969), Schildkrout (1978), and a number of Hart's papers (e.g. 1971).
4. Cohen (1965, 1966).
5. This is one of the main points made by Ivan Light in his survey of why some American migrant groups succeed in business and others do not. (Light, 1972).
6. That is to say on the basis of Islam, ethnic chiefship and patron–client ties (Cohen 1969, Schildkrout 1978). Perhaps the most elaborate degree of ethnic organisation based on migrant kinship is that of the Chinese (Watson, 1977), but a large number of other examples could be cited, including the Pakistanis in the United Kingdom (Ballard 1987, Werbner 1987), the Sikhs (Ballard and Ballard 1977), the Italians in the United States (Ianni 1972) and many of the examples cited in the surveys by Bonacich (1973) and Light (1972).
7. On this point, see Hart (1988).
8. The underlying model is that of Bonacich (1973).
9. On the horizontal and vertical dimensions of trade organisation, cf. Werbner (1987: 220–2).
10. Peel (1983: 154, n.9).
11. For comparable case studies from Nigeria, see Melson and Wolpe (1971).
12. Brown (1982, 1983).
13. On the position of the Ewe in Ghanaian politics, see Price (1974), Brown (1983), Chazan (1983: 224), Pellow and Chazan (1986: 48, 85–6), Horowitz (1985: 513). On women traders, see Frake and Harrell-Bond (1979), Robertson (1984: 243–7) and Clark (1988). On *kalabule* see Jeffries (1982), Pellow and Chazan (1986: 168–70), Sandbrook (1985: 142–4).
14. Cf. Light (1972), Bonacich (1973), Bonacich and Modell (1980), Ward and Jenkins (1984), Werbner (1987).
15. Bonacich (1973).
16. The best discussions of this period are those of Chazan (1983) and Pellow and Chazan (1986).
17. According to Schildkrout (1978: 43), the effects on the cocoa industry were probably short term as the compliance order had little effect on the size of the Mossi population in Ghana, unlike that of the Yoruba. Most of the Mossi who actually left Ghana in 1969–70 soon returned.
18. Bauer (1954, 1968: 57–9).
19. Berg (1968).
20. Berg (1968: 44–5).
21. Bates (1981: 4–6).
22. Bates (1981: 30).
23. Hart (1982, 1986).
24. Killick (1978: Chapter 11).
25. Chazan (1983: 168).
26. Chazan (1983: 173).
27. Hanson and Collins (1980).
28. That is, Generals Afrifa (who had just been elected to Parliament), Acheampong, and Akuffo. Significantly, given the AFRC's tough line on corruption, the executed also included General Uteka, formerly head of the border guards.
29. One derivation of the word is from the Hausa *kere kabure* meaning 'keep it quiet' (Jeffries, 1982: 307).
30. See the examples in Frake and Harrell-Bond (1979), and the account in Clark (1988).
31. *West Africa*, 1979: 1539–40, 1589. There was a further raid on the market early in 1982 (*West Africa*, 1982: 333) after Rawlings's return to power.

32. *West Africa*, 1979: 1185.
33. *West Africa*, 1979: 2009, 2062, 2210, 1980: 848, 2329.
34. *West Africa*, 1979: 2079; 1980: 1259.
35. *West Africa*, 1981: 194.
36. *West Africa*, 1981: 773.
37. *West Africa*, 1982: 285.
38. Ray (1986: 79–80).
39. Pellow and Chazan (1986: 82), *West Africa*, 1982: 433, 536.
40. *West Africa*, 1982: 482.
41. E. Hanson in *West Africa*, 1982: 1125–9.
42. *West Africa*, 1982: 1855.
43. Originally a road junction, this has now developed into a major commercial town (Peace, 1979). Because of its proximity to the border, it also became an area of Ghanaian settlement until the expulsions of 1983 and 1985. Cf.*West Africa*, 1983: 213.
44. On the strategies available to Ghanaians during this period, see Chazan (1983: 191–7).
45. *West Africa*, 1983: 235.
46. For reports on the 1983 expulsions, see *West Africa*, 1983: 243–6, 303–9, 382–6. It is also discussed in Gravil (1985), Aluko (1985), and Brydon (1985). There was a further round of expulsions in May, 1985 (*West Africa*, 1985: 867, 988–9, 1032–3, 1103).
47. Ray (1986: 103–11).
48. *West Africa*, 1984: 433–4.
49. *West Africa*, 1984: 2075.
50. *West Africa*, 1988: 680.
51. For a survey of Ghana–Togo relations, see *West Africa*, 1988: 1435. Other issues included smuggling, and the refugees who fled into Togo from Northern Ghana during inter-tribal fighting in 1985.
52. *West Africa*, 1981: 1196; 1982: 1029.
53. *West Africa*, publishes regular features on ECOWAS, usually at the time of the annual conference in May or June. See for instance *West Africa*, 1985: 1047–63; 1986: 1363–7; 1987: 1286–1300; 1988: 1196.
54. *West Africa*, 1982: 482, 960, 536.

BIBLIOGRAPHY

Abernethy, D. (1969) *The Political Dilemma of Popular Education* Stanford: (Stanford University Press)

Acquah, I. (1958) *Accra Survey* (London: University of London Press).

Adamu, M. (1978) *The Hausa Factor in West African History* (London: Longmans).

Addo, N. (1970) 'Immigration into Ghana: some social and economic implications of the Aliens Compliance Order of 1st November, 1969', *Ghana Journal of Sociology*, 6, 20–42.

Addo, N. (1972) 'Employment and labour supply on Ghana's cocoa farms in the pre- and post-Aliens Compliance Order era', *Economic Bulletin of Ghana*, 2, 34–50.

Agiri, B.A. (1972) 'Kola in Western Nigeria 1850–1950' (PhD thesis, Madison: University of Wisconsin).

Agiri, B.A. (1979) 'Chief N.D. Oyerinde and the political, social and economic development of Ogbomosho, 1916–1951', *Journal of the Historical Society of Nigeria*, 10, 86–112.

Akintoye, S.A. (1971) *Revolution and power politics in Yorubaland 1840–1893: Ibadan expansion and the rise of Ekitiparapo* (London: Longmans).

Alexander, J. (1987) *Trade, traders and trading in rural Java, Singapore* (Singapore: Oxford University Press).

Aluko, O. (1985) 'The expulsion of illegal aliens from Nigeria: a study in Nigeria's decision-making', *African Affairs*, 84(337), 539–60.

Aluko, S.A. (1965) 'How many Nigerians? An analysis of Nigeria's census problems', *Journal of Modern African Studies*, 3(3), 371–92.

Amin, S. (1974) 'Introduction', in S. Amin (ed.) *Modern Migrations in West Africa* (London: Oxford University Press for the International African Institute).

Anthonio, Q.B.O. (1967) 'The supply and distribution of yams in Ibadan markets', *Nigerian Journal of Economic and Social Studies*, 9, 33–49.

Ardener, S. (1964) 'The comparative study of rotating credit associations', *Journal of the Royal Anthropological Institute*, 94, 201–29.

Arhin, K. (1979) *West African Traders in Ghana in the Nineteenth and Twentieth Centuries* (London: Longmans).

Aronson, D.R. (1970) 'Cultural stability and social change among the modern Ijebu Yoruba', (PhD thesis, Chicago: University of Chicago).

Aronson, D.R. (1971) 'Ijebu Yoruba urban-rural relationships and class formation', *Canadian Journal of African Studies*, 5, 263–80.

Aronson, D.R. (1978) *The City is our Farm* (Boston: G.K. Hall).

Atanda, J.A. (1973) *The New Oyo Empire* (London: Longmans).

Austin, D. (1964) *Politics in Ghana, 1946–1960* (London: Oxford University Press).

Awe, B. (1967) 'Ibadan, its early beginnings', in P. Lloyd, A. Mabogunje and B. Awe (eds.) *The City of Ibadan* (Cambridge: Cambridge University Press).

Babayemi, S.O. (1971) 'Upper Ogun: an historical sketch', *African Notes*, 6, 72–84.

Ballard, R. (1987) 'The political economy of migration: Pakistan, Britain, and the Middle East', in J.S. Eades (ed.) *Migrants, Workers and the Social Order* (London: Tavistock).

Ballard, R. and Ballard, C. (1977) 'The Sikhs: the development of South Asian settlements in Britain', in J.L. Watson (ed.) *Between Two Cultures* (Oxford: Blackwell).

Barber, K. (1991) *I Could Speak Until Tomorrow: Oriki, Women and the Past in a Yoruba Town* (Edinburgh: Edinburgh University Press for the International African Institute).

Barbour, J. and Simmonds, D. (1971) *Adire Cloth in Nigeria* (Ibadan: Institute of African Studies, University of Ibadan).

Barnes, S.T. (1986) *Patrons and Power: creating a political community in metropolitan Lagos* (Manchester: Manchester University Press for the International African Institute).

Barnes, S.T. and Peil, M. (1977) 'Voluntary association membership in five West African cities', *Urban Anthropology*, 6(1), 83–106.

Bascom, W.R. (1942) 'The principle of seniority in the social structure of the Yoruba', *American Anthropologist*, 44, 37–46.

Bascom, W.R. (1951) 'Yoruba cooking', *Africa*, 21, 125–37.

Bascom, W.R. (1952) 'The esusu: a credit institution of the Yoruba', *Journal of the Royal Anthropological Institute*, 82, 63–9.

Bascom, W.R. (1969) *The Yoruba of Southwestern Nigeria* (New York: Holt, Rinehart and Winston).

Bates, R.H. (1981) *Markets and States in Tropical Africa*, (Berkeley and Los Angeles: University of California Press).

Bauer, P.T. (1954) *West African Trade* (Cambridge: Cambridge University Press).

Bauer, P.T. (1968) 'Some aspects and problems of trade in Africa', in R. Moyer and S.C. Hollander (eds.) *Markets and Marketing in Developing Economies'* (Homewood, Ill.: Irwin).

Beckman, B. (1976) *Organizing the Farmers: cocoa, politics and national development in Ghana* (Uppsala: Scandanavian Institute of African Studies).

Beer, C. (1976) *The Politics of Peasant Groups in Western Nigeria* (Ibadan: Ibadan University Press).

Beer, C. and Williams, G. (1976) 'The politics of the Ibadan peasantry', in G. Williams (ed.) *Nigeria: Economy and Society* (London: Rex Collings).

Bender, D.R. (1970) 'Agnatic or cognatic? a re-evaluation of Ondo descent', *Man*, 5, 71–87.

Bender, D.R. (1972) 'De facto families, and de jure households in Ondo', *American Anthropologist*, 73, 223–41.

Bening, R.B. (1971) 'The development of education in Northern Ghana 1908–1957', *Ghana Social Science Journal*, 1, 23–25.

Bening, R.B. (1973a) 'Indigenous concepts of boundaries and significance of administrative stations and boundaries in Northern Ghana', *Bulletin of the Ghana Geographical Association*, 15, 1–21.

Bening, R.B. (1973b) 'The definition of the international boundaries of Northern Ghana, 1888–1904', *Transactions of the Historical Society of Ghana*, 14, 229–61.

Bening, R.B. (1974) 'Location of regional and provincial capitals in Northern Ghana 1897–1960', *Bulletin of the Ghana Geographical Association*, 16, 54–66.

Bening, R.B. (1975a) 'Location of district administrative capitals in the Northern Territories of the Gold Coast (1897–1951)', *Bulletin de l'IFAN*, Series B 37(3), 646–66.

Bening, R.B. (1975b) 'Foundations of the modern native states of Northern Ghana', *Universitas*, 5, 116–38.

Bening, R.B. (1975c) 'Colonial development policy in Northern Ghana, 1898–1950', *Bulletin of the Ghana Geographical Association*, 17, 65–79.

Bening, R.B. (1977) 'Administration and development in Northern Ghana, 1898–1931', *Ghana Social Science Journal*, 4(2), 58–76.

Bening, R.B. (1983) 'The administrative areas of Northern Ghana, 1898–1951', *Bulletin de l'IFAN*, Series B 45, 325–56.

Berg, E.J. (1968) 'Socialist ideology and marketing policy in Africa', in R. Moyer and S.C. Hollander (eds.) *Markets and Marketing in Developing Countries* (Homewood Ill.: Irwin).

Berg, E.J. (1971) 'Structural transformations versus gradualism: recent economic development in Ghana and the Ivory Coast', in P. Foster and A. Zolberg (eds.) *Ghana and the Ivory Coast* (Chicago: University of Chicago Press).

Berry, S.S. (1975) *Cocoa, Custom and Socio-Economic Change in Rural Western Nigeria* (Oxford: Clarendon Press).

Berry, S.S. (1985) *Fathers Work for Their Sons: accumulation, mobility and class formation in an extended Yoruba community* (Berkeley: University of California Press).

Biobaku, S.O. (1957) *The Egba and their Neighbours 1842–1872* (Oxford: Clarendon Press).

Birmingham, W., Neustadt, E. and Omaboe, E. (eds.) (1966) *A Study of Contemporary Ghana, Vol. 1: The Economy of Ghana* (London: George Allen & Unwin).

Bonacich, E. (1973) 'A theory of middleman minorities,' *American Sociological Review*, 38, 583–94.

Bonacich, E. and Modell, J. (1980) *The Economic Basis of Ethnic Solidarity: small business in the Japanese American community*, (Berkeley: University of California Press).

Bowen, T.J. (1857) *Adventures and Missionary Labours in Several Countries in the Interior of Africa from 1849 to 1856* (London: Frank Cass) [1968 reprint].

Braimah, J.A. and Goody, J.R. (1967) *Salaga: the struggle for power*, (London: Longmans).

Bray, J.M. (1968) 'The organization of traditional weaving in Iseyin, Nigeria', *Africa*, 38, 270–80.

Bray, J.M. (1969a) 'The craft structure of a traditional Yoruba town', *Transactions of the Institute of British Geographers*, 46, 179–93.

Bray, J.M. (1969b) 'The economics of traditional cloth production in Iseyin, Nigeria', *Economic Development and Cultural Change*, 17, 540–51.

Brown, D. (1982) 'Who are the tribalists? Social pluralism and political ideology in Ghana', *African Affairs*, 81(322), 37–69.

Brown, D. (1983) 'Sieges and scapegoats: the politics of pluralism in Ghana and Togo,' *Journal of Modern African Studies*, 21, 431–60

Brydon, L. (1985) 'Ghanaian responses to the Nigerian expulsions of 1983', *African Affairs*, 84 (337), 561–85.

Butterworth, D. and Chance, D.K. (1981) *Latin American Urbanization* (Cambridge: Cambridge University Press).

Charbonneau, J. and Charbonneau, R. (1961) *Marchés et marchands d'Afrique noire* (Paris: La Colombe).

Chazan, N. (1983) *An anatomy of Ghanaian politics: managing political recession, 1969–1982* (Boulder, Colorado: Westview).

Clark, G. (1988) 'Price control of local foodstuffs in Kumasi, Ghana 1979 in G. Clark (ed.) *Traders versus the State: anthropological approaches to unofficial economies* (Boulder: Westview).

Clarke, W.H. (1972) *Travels and Explorations in Yorubaland (1854–1858)* (Ibadan: Ibadan University Press).

Cohen, A. (1965) 'The social organization of credit in a West African cattle market', *Africa*, 35, 8–20.

Cohen, A. (1966) 'Politics of the kola trade', *Africa*, 36, 18–36.

Cohen, A. (1967) 'The Hausa', in P. Lloyd, A.L. Mabogunje and B. Awe (eds.) *The City of Ibadan* (Cambridge: Cambridge University Press).

Cohen, A. (1969) *Custom and Politics in Urban Africa* (London: Routledge and Kegan Paul).

Cohen, A. (1971a) 'Cultural strategies in the organization of trading diasporas', in C. Meillassoux (ed.) *The Development of Indigenous Trade and Markets in West Africa* (London: Oxford University Press for the International African Institute).

Cohen, A. (1971b) 'The politics of ritual secrecy', *Man*, 6, 427–8.

Cohen, A. (1974a) 'Introduction: the lesson of ethnicity', in A. Cohen (ed.) *Urban Ethnicity* (London: Tavistock).

Cohen, A. (1974b) *Two-dimensional man: an essay on the anthropology of power and symbolism in complex society* (London: Routledge).

Coulibaly, S., Gregory, J. and Piche, V. (1980) *Les migrations voltaïques I: Importance et ambivalence de la migration voltaïque* (Ottawa: Centre de recherches pour le développement international).

Crisp, J. (1984) 'The labour question in the Gold Coast, 1870–1906', in B. Munslow and H. Finch (eds.) *Proletarianization in the Third World* (London: Croom Helm).

Dickson, K.B. (1969) *A Historical Geography of Ghana* (Cambridge: Cambridge University Press).

Eades, J.S. (1975) 'The growth of a migrant community: the Yoruba in northern Ghana', in Jack R. Goody (ed.) *Changing social structure in Ghana: essays in the comparative sociology of a new state and an old tradition* (London: International African Institute).

Eades, J.S. (1977) 'Church fission in a migrant community: Yoruba Baptists in northern Ghana', *Savanna*, 6(2), 167–78.

Eades, J.S. (1979) 'Kinship and entrepreneurship among Yoruba in northern Ghana', in William A. Shack and E.P. Skinner (eds.) *Strangers in African Societies* (Berkeley: University of California Press).

Eades, J.S. (1980) *The Yoruba Today* (Cambridge: Cambridge University Press).

Eades, J.S. (1987a) Anthropologists and migrants: changing models and realities, in J.S. Eades (ed.) *Migrants, Workers and the Social Order* (London: Tavistock).

Eades, J.S. (1987b) 'Prelude to an exodus: chain migration, trade, and the Yoruba in Ghana', in J.S. Eades (ed.) *Migrants, Workers and the Social Order* (London: Tavistock).

Esseks, J.D. (1975) 'Economic policies', in Dennis Austin and Robin Luckham (eds) *Politicians and Soldiers in Ghana* (London: Frank Cass).

Ewusi, K. (1974) 'The growth rate of urban centres in Ghana, and its implications for rural-urban migration', *Nigerian Journal of Economic and Social Studies*, 16, 479–91.

Ewusi, K. (1976) 'Disparities in levels of regional development in Ghana', *Social Indicators Research*, 3.

Fadipe, N.A. (1970) *The Sociology of the Yoruba* (Ibadan: Ibadan University Press).

Fagerlund, V.G. and Smith, R.H.T. (1970) 'A preliminary map of market periodicities in Ghana', *Journal of Developing Areas*, 4(3), 333–48.

Ferguson, P. and Wilks, I. (1970) 'Chiefs, constitutions and the British in Northern Ghana', in M. Crowder and O. Ikime (eds.) *West African Chiefs: their changing status under colonial rule and independence* (Ile-Ife: University of Ife Press).

Foster, P.J. (1965) *Education and Social Change in Ghana* (London: Routledge).

Frake, A. and Harrell-Bond, B. (1979) 'Feminine influence', *West Africa*, 3254, 2182–6.

Galletti, R., Baldwin, K.D.S., and Dina, I.O. (1956) *Nigerian Cocoa Farmers* (London: Oxford University Press).

Garbett, K. and Kapferer, B. (1971) 'Theoretical orientations in the study of labor migration', *New Atlantis*, 1(2), 179–97.

Garlick, P.C. (1971) *African Traders and Economic Development in Ghana* (Oxford: Clarendon Press).

Gaveh, G. (1961) 'Tamale: a geographical study', *Bulletin of the Ghana Geographical Association*, 3, 12–29.

Genoud, R. (1969) *Nationalism and Economic Development in Ghana* (New York: Praeger).

Goody, E.N. (1982) *Parenthood and Social Reproduction: fostering and occupational roles in West Africa* (Cambridge: Cambridge University Press).

Goody, J.R. (1970) 'Marriage policy and incorporation in Northern Ghana,' in R. Cohen and J. Middleton (eds.), *From Tribe to Nation in Africa: studies in incorporation processes* (Scranton, Pa.: Chandler).

Goody, J.R. (1980) 'Rice burning and the Green Revolution in Northern Ghana', *Journal of Development Studies*, 16, 136–55.

Gravil, R. (1985) 'The Nigeria Aliens Expulsion Order of 1983', *African Affairs*, 84(337), 523–37.

Green, L. (1974) 'Migration, urbanization and national development in Nigeria', in Samir Amin (ed.) *Modern Migrations in West Africa* (London: Oxford University Press for the International African Institute).

Gusten, R. (1968) *Studies in the Staple Food Economy of Western Nigeria* (Munich: Weltforumverlag).

Hanson, E. and Collins, P. (1980) 'The army, the state, and the "Rawlings revolution" in Ghana', *African Affairs*, 79, 3–23.

Hart, J.K. (1969) 'Entrepreneurs and migrants: a study of modernization among the Frafas of Ghana', (PhD thesis, Cambridge: University of Cambridge).

Hart, J.K. (1970) 'Small-scale entrepreneurs in Ghana and development planning', *Journal of Development Studies*, 6, 104–20.

Hart, J.K. (1971) 'Migration and tribal identity among the Frafras of Ghana', *Journal of Asian and African Studies*, 7, 21–35.

Hart, J.K. (1973) 'Informal income opportunities and urban employment in Ghana', *Journal of Modern African Studies*, 11, 61–89.

Hart, J.K. (1974)) 'Migration and the opportunity structure: a Ghanaian case study', in Samir Amin (ed.) *Modern Migrations in West Africa* (London: Oxford University Press for the International African Institute).

Hart, J.K. (1975) 'Swindler or public benefactor? The entrepreneur in his community', in Jack Goody (ed.) *Changing Social Structure in Ghana* (London: International African Institute).

Hart, J.K. (1976) 'The politics of unemployment in Ghana', *African Affairs*, 75, 488–97.

Hart, J.K. (1978) 'The economic basis of Tallensi social history in the early twentieth century', in G. Dalton (ed.) *Research in Economic Anthropology*, 1, 185–216, (Greenwich, Conn.: JAI Press).

Hart, J.K. (1982) *The Political Economy of West African Agriculture* (Cambridge: Cambridge University Press).

Hart, J.K. (1986) 'Some contradictions in postcolonial state formation: the case of West Africa', *Cambridge Anthropology*, 10 (3).

Hart, J.K. (1987) 'Rural-urban migration in West Africa', in J.S. Eades (ed.) *Migrants, Workers and the Social Order* (London: Tavistock).

Hart, J.K. (1988) 'The Frafra' in D. Gambetta (ed.) *Trust* (Cambridge: Cambridge University Press).

Hill, P. (1963) *Migrant Cocoa Farmers of Southern Ghana* (Cambridge: Cambridge University Press).

Hill, P. (1970a) *The Occupations of Migrants in Ghana* (Ann Arbor: University of Michigan Museum of Anthropology).

Hill, P. (1970b) *Studies in Rural Capitalism in West Africa* (Cambridge: Cambridge University Press).

Hopkins, A.G. (1973) *An Economic History of West Africa*, (London: Longmans).

Hopkins, A.G. (1987) 'Big business in African studies', *Journal of African Studies*, 28, 119–40.

Horowitz, D.L. (1985) *Ethnic Groups in Conflict* (Berkeley: University of California Press).

Howard, R. (1978) *Colonialism and Underdevelopment in Ghana*, (London: Croom Helm).

Hundsalz, M. (1972) 'Die Wanderung der Yoruba nach Ghana und ihre Rückkehr nach Nigeria', *Erdkunde*, 26, 218–30.

Hutchful, E. (ed.) (1987) *The IMF and Ghana: the confidential record* (London: Zed Books).

Huq, M.M. (1989) *The Economy of Ghana* (London: Macmillan Press).

Ianni, F. (1972) *A Family Business* (London: Routledge and Kegan Paul).

Jackson, J.A. (ed.) (1969) *Migration* (Cambridge: Cambridge University Press).

Jeffries, R. (1973) *Class, Power and Ideology in Ghana* (Cambridge: Cambridge University Press).

Jeffries, R. (1982) 'Rawlings and the political economy of underdevelopment in Ghana', *African Affairs*, 81(324), 307–17.

Johnson, M. (ed.) (1966) *Salaga Papers* (Legon: Institute of African Studies, University of Ghana).

Jones, T. (1976) *Ghana's First Republic 1960–1966: the pursuit of the political kingdom* (London: Methuen).

Katzin, M. (1964) 'The role of the small entrepreneur', in M.J. Herskovits and M. Harwitz (eds.) *Economic Transition in Africa* (Evanston, Ill.: Northwestern University Press).

Kay, G.B. (ed.) (1972) *The Political Economy of Colonialism in Ghana*, (Cambridge: Cambridge University Press).

Khuri, F.I. (1965) 'Kinship, emigration and trade partnership among the Lebanese of West Africa', *Africa*, 35, 385–95.

Killick, A. (1973) 'Price controls in Africa: the Ghanaian experience', *Journal of Modern African Studies*, 11.

Killick, A. (1978) *Development Economics in Action: a study of economic policies in Ghana* (London: Heinemann).

Killingray, D. (1982) 'Military and labour recruitment in the Gold Coast during the Second World War', *Journal of African History*, 23(1), 83–95.

Kirk-Greene, A.H.M. (1980) '"Damnosa hereditas": ethnic ranking and the martial races imperative in Africa', *Ethnic and Racial Studies*, 3(4), 393–414.

Konings, P. (1986) *The State and Rural Class Formation in Ghana: a comparative analysis* (London: Kegan Paul International).

Krapf-Askari, E. (1969) *Yoruba Towns and Cities* (Oxford: Clarendon Press).

Kumar, A. (1973) 'Smuggling in Ghana: its magnitude and economic effects' *Universitas (Legon)*, 2, 119–40.

Ladouceur, P. (1972) 'The Yendi chieftaincy dispute and Ghanaian politics', *Canadian Journal of African Studies*, 6, 97–116.

Ladouceur, P. (1979) *Chiefs and Politicians: the politics of regionalism in Northern Ghana* (London: Longmans).

Lander, R. and Lander, J. (1832) *Journal of an Expedition to Explore the Course and Termination of the Niger* (London: John Murray), 3 vols.

Law, R. (1977) *The Oyo Empire c.1600–c.1836: a West African imperialism in the era of the slave trade* (Oxford: Clarendon Press).

Leighton, N.O. (1979) 'The political economy of a stranger population: the Lebanese of Sierra Leone', in W.A. Shack and E.P. Skinner (eds) *Strangers in African Societies* (Berkeley: University of California Press).

LeVine, V.T. (1975) *Political Corruption: the Ghana case* (Stanford, Cal.: Hoover Institute Press).

Lewis, B.C. (1976) 'The limitations of group action among entrepreneurs: the market women of Abidjan, Ivory Coast', in Nancy Hafkin and Edna Bey (eds.) *Women in Africa* (Stanford: Stanford University Press).

Light, I. (1972) *Ethnic Enterprise in America: business and welfare among Chinese, Japanese and Blacks* (Berkeley and Los Angeles: University of California Press).

Lisk, F. (1976) 'Inflation in Ghana, 1964–75: its effects on employment, incomes and industrial relations', *International Labour Review*, 113, 359–75.

Little, K. (1957) 'The role of voluntary associations in West African urbanisation', *American Anthropologist*, 59, 579–96.

Little, K. (1965) *West African Urbanisation* (Cambridge: Cambridge University Press).

Lloyd, P.C. (1955) 'The Yoruba lineage', *Africa*, 25(3), 235–51.

Lloyd, P.C. (1962) *Yoruba Land Law* (London: Oxford University Press).

Lloyd, P.C. (1966) 'Agnatic and cognatic descent among the Yoruba', *Man (NS)*, 1(4), 484–500.

Lovejoy, P.E. (1980) *Caravans of Kola: the Hausa kola trade 1700–1900* (Zaria: Ahmadu Bello University Press).

Lovejoy, P.E. (1982) 'Polanyi's "ports of trade": Salaga and Kano in the nineteenth century', *Canadian Journal of African Studies*, 16(2), 245–77.

Mabogunje, A.L. (1967) 'The Ijebu', in P.C. Lloyd, A.L. Mabogunje and B. Awe (eds.) *The City of Ibadan* (Cambridge: Cambridge University Press).

Mabogunje, A.L. (1968) *Urbanization in Nigeria* (London: University of London Press).

Mabogunje, A.L. (1972) *Regional Mobility and Resource Development in West Africa* (Montreal: McGill-Queen's University Press).

Mabogunje, A.L. and Oyawoye, M.O. (1961) 'The problems of northern Yoruba towns: the example of Shaki', *Nigerian Geographical Journal*, 4(1), 3–10.

Mann, C. (1977) *Periodische Märkte und Zentrale Orte-Raumstrukturen und Verflechtungsbereiche in Nord-Ghana* (Heidelberg: Geographical Institute, University of Heidelberg).

McKim, M. (1978) 'The periodic market system in northeastern Ghana', *Economic Geography*, 333–44.

Melson, R. and Wolpe, H. (eds.) (1971) *Nigeria: Modernization and the Politics of Communalism* (East Lansing: Michigan State University Press).

Milone, V. and Olaore, G.O. (1971) 'Tentative population projections for Western Nigeria from air photographs and house occupancy measurements', *Nigerian Opinion*, 7(4–6), 71–5.

Mitchell, J.C. (1970) 'The causes of labour migration' in John Middleton (ed.) *Black Africa: its peoples and their cultures today* (London: Collier-Macmillan).

Mitchell, J.C. (1985) 'Towards a situational sociology of wage-labour circulation', in R.M. Prothero and M. Chapman (eds.) *Circulation in Third World Countries*, (London: Routledge).

Moser, C. (1978) 'Informal sector or petty commodity production?', *World Development*, 6, 1041–64.

Northcott, H.P. (1899) *Report on the Northern Territories of the Gold Coast* (London: HMSO).

Nypan, A. (1960) *Market Trade: a study of market traders in Accra* (Achimota: Economic Research Division, University College of Ghana.

Ofosu-Amaah, G. (1971) 'Review of the position of aliens in Ghana', *Review of Ghana Law*, 3, 88–106.

O'Hear, A. (1980) 'Ilorin: the history of the weaving industry and the trade in woven cloth', seminar paper, (Ilorin: Social Science Faculty, University of Ilorin).

O'Hear, A. (1983) 'The Economic History of Ilorin in the Nineteenth and Twentieth Centuries: the rise and decline of a middleman society', (PhD thesis, University of Birmingham).

Osuntokun, A. (1984) *Chief S. Ladoke Akintola: his life and times*, (London: Frank Cass).

Oyedipe, F.O. (1967) 'Some Sociological Aspects of the Yoruba Family in Accra', (MA thesis, Legon: University of Ghana).

Oyediran, O. (1974) 'Modakeke in Ife: historical background to an aspect of contemporary Ife politics', *Odu (NS)*, 10, 63–78.

Oyemakinde, W. (1974) 'Railway construction and operations in Nigeria, 1895–1911. Labour problems and socio-economic impact', *Journal of the Historical Society of Nigeria*, 7(2), 303–24.

Patterson, K.D. (1983) 'The influenza epidemic of 1918–19 in the Gold Coast', *Journal of African History*, 24(4), 485–502.

Peace, A. (1979) 'Prestige, power and legitimacy in a modern Nigerian town', *Canadian Journal of African Studies*. 13(1), 25–51.

Peel, J.D.Y. (1967) 'Religious change in Yorubaland', *Africa*, 37, 292–306.

Peel, J.D.Y. (1978) 'Olaju: a Yoruba concept of development', *Journal of Development Studies*, 14, 135–65.

Peel, J.D.Y. (1983) *Ijeshas and Nigerians: the incorporation of a Yoruba kingdom, 1890s–1970s* (Cambridge: Cambridge University Press).

Peil, M. (1971) 'The expulsion of West African aliens', *Journal of Modern African Studies*, 9, 205–29.

Peil, M. (1974) 'Ghana's aliens', *International Migration Review*, 8, 367–81.

Peil, M. (1975) 'Interethnic contacts in Nigerian cities', *Africa* 45, 107–21.

Peil, M. (1979) 'Host reactions: aliens in Ghana', in W.A. Shack and E.P. Skinner (eds.) *Strangers in African Societies* (Berkeley: University of California Press).

Peil, M. (1981) *Cities and Suburbs: urban life in West Africa* (New York and London: Africana).

Peil, M. (1984) *African Urban Society*, (Chichester: Wiley).

Pellow, D. and Chazan, N. (1986) *Ghana: coping with uncertainty*, (Aldershot: Gower).

Pinkney, R. (1972) *Ghana under Military Rule, 1966–69* (London: Methuen).

Plotnicov, L. (1967) *Strangers to the City* (Pittsburg: University of Pittsburg Press).

Price, C. (1969) 'The study of assimilation', in J.A. Jackson (ed.) *Migration* (Cambridge: Cambridge University Press).

Price, R.M. (1974) 'The pattern of ethnicity in Ghana: a research note', *Journal of Modern African Studies*, 11, 470–5.

Quartey-Papafio, A.B. (1911) 'Native Tribunals of the Akras (Part III)', *Journal of the African Society*, 10, 434–46.

Ray, D.I. (1986) *Ghana: politics, economics and society* (London: Frances Pinter).

Robertson, C.S. (1984) *Sharing the Same Bowl: a socioeconomic history of women and class in Accra* (Ghana, Bloomington, Indiana: Indiana University Press).

Rouch, J. (1956) 'Migrations au Ghana (Gold Coast): enquête 1953–55', *Journal de la Société des Africanistes*, 36, 33–193.

Sandbrook. R. (1985) *The Politics of Africa's Economic Stagnation* (Cambridge: Cambridge University Press).

Sanjek, R. (1972) 'Ghanaian Networks: an analysis of interethnic relations in urban situations', (PhD thesis, New York: Faculty of Political Science, Columbia University).

Sanjek, R. (1977) 'Cognitive maps of the ethnic domain in urban Ghana: reflections on variability and change', *American Ethnologist*, 4, 603–22.

Schildkrout, E. (1970a) 'Strangers and local government in Kumasi', *Journal of Modern African Studies*, 8, 251–69.

Schildkrout, E. (1970b) 'Government and chiefs in Kumasi Zongo', in M. Crowder and O. Ikime (eds) *West African Chiefs: their changing status under colonial rule and independence* (Ile-Ife: University of Ife Press).

Schildkrout, E. (1974a) 'Ethnicity and generation differences among urban immigrants in Ghana', in Abner Cohen (ed.) *Urban Ethnicity* (London: Tavistock).

Schildkrout, E. (1974b) 'Islam and politics in Kumasi: an analysis of disputes over the Kumasi Central Mosque', *Anthropological Papers of the American Museum of Natural History*, 52(2).

Schildkrout, E. (1978) *People of the Zongo* (Cambridge: Cambridge University Press).

Schiltz, M. (1982) 'Habitus and peasantization in Nigeria: a Yoruba case study', *Man*, 17, 728–46.

Shepherd, A. (1978) 'The Development of Capitalist Rice Farming in Northern Ghana', (PhD thesis, Cambridge: University of Cambridge).

Shepherd, A. (1981) 'Agrarian change in Northern Ghana: public investment, capitalist farming and famine', in J. Heyer, P. Roberts, and G. Williams (eds) *Rural Development in Tropical Africa*, (New York: St Martins Press).

Skinner, E.P. (1960) 'Labour migration and its relationship to socio-cultural change in Mossi society', *Africa*, 30, 375–401.

Skinner, E.P. (1963) 'Strangers in West African Societies', *Africa*, 33, 307–20.

Skinner, E.P. (1974) *African Urban Life: the transformation of Ouagadougou* (Princeton, NJ: Princeton University Press).

Smith, R.H.T. (1971) 'West African market places: temporal periodicity and locational spacing', in C. Meillassoux (ed.) *The Development of Indigenous Trade and Markets in West Africa* (London: Oxford University Press for the International African Institute).

Smith, R.S. (1962) 'Ijaiye, the western Palatinate of the Yoruba', *Journal of the Historical Society of Nigeria*, 2(3), 329–49.

Smith, R.S. (1965) 'The Alafin in exile: a study of the Igboho period in Oyo history', *Journal of African History*, 6(1), 57–77.

Smith, R.S. (1969) *Kingdoms of the Yoruba* (London: Methuen).

Staniland, M. (1975) *The Lions of Dagbon: political change in Northern Ghana* (Cambridge: Cambridge University Press).

Stapleton, G.B. (1958) 'Nigerians in Ghana with special reference to the Yoruba', Ibadan: *NISER Conference Proceedings*, 159–63.

Stapleton, G.B. (1959) 'Nigerians in Ghana', *West Africa*, no. 2814, 175.

Sudarkasa, N. (1973) *Where Women Work* (Ann Arbor: University of Michigan, Museum of Anthropology).

Sudarkasa, N. (1974) 'Commercial migration in West Africa with special reference to the Yoruba in Ghana', *African Urban Notes*, Series B 1, 61–103.

Sudarkasa, N. (1975) 'The economic status of the Yoruba in Ghana before 1970', *Nigerian Journal of Economic and Social Studies*, 17, 93–125.

Sudarkasa, N. (1979) 'From stranger to alien: the socio-political history of the Nigerian Yoruba in Ghana, 1900–1970', in W.A. Shack and E.P. Skinner (eds) *Strangers in African Societies*, (Berkeley: University of California Press).

Sudarkasa, N. (1985) 'The role of Yoruba commercial migration in West African development', in Beverly Lindsay (ed.) *African Migration and National Development* (University Park and London: Pennsylvania State University Press).

Sutton, I.B. (1983) 'Labour in commercial agriculture in Ghana in the late 19th and early 20th centuries', *Journal of African History*, 24(4), 461–83.

Sutton, I.B. (1989) 'Colonial agricultural policy: the non-development of the Northern Territories of the Gold Coast', *International Journal of Historical Studies*, 22(4), pp. 637–69.

Szereszewski, R. (1965) *Structural Change in the Economy of Ghana, 1891–1911* (London: Weidenfeld and Nicolson).

Thomas, R. (1973) 'Forced labour in British West Africa', *Journal of African History*, 14, 79–103.

Thomas, R. (1974) 'Education in Northern Ghana, 1906–1940: a study in colonial paradox', *International Journal of African Historical Studies*, 7, 427–67.

Thomas, R. (1975) 'Military recruitment in the Gold Coast during the First World War', *Cahiers d'études africaines*, 15(1).

Todaro, M.P. (1971) 'Income expectations, rural–urban migration and employment in Africa', *International Migration Review*, 104, 387–413.

Van Apeldoorn, G.J. (1971) 'Markets in Ghana: a census and some comments. Volume I: Northern and Upper Regions', Technical Publication Series no. 17, Institute of Statistical, Social and Economic Research, Legon: University of Ghana.

Van Hear, N. (1982) 'Northern Labour and the Development of Capitalist Agriculture in Ghana', (PhD thesis, Birmingham: Centre for West African Studies).

Ward, R. and Jenkins, R. (eds) (1984) *Ethnic Communities in Business*, (Cambridge: Cambridge University Press).

Watherstone, A.M.C. (1908) 'The Northern Territories of the Gold Coast', *Journal of the African Society*, 7, 344–73.

Watson, J.L. (1977) 'The Chinese: Hong Kong villagers in the British catering trade', in J.L. Watson (ed.) *Between Two Cultures* (Oxford: Blackwell).

Werbner, P. (1987) 'Enclave economies and family firms: Pakistani traders in a British city', in J.S. Eades (ed.) *Migrants, Workers and the Social Order* (London: Tavistock).

Wilks, I. (1968) 'Interdisciplinary Seminar in Field Methods, Summer 1968.' Legon and Evanston: University of Ghana and Program of African Studies, Northwestern University (Mimeographed).

Wilks, I. (1971) 'Asante policy towards the Hausa trade in the nineteenth century', in C. Meillassoux (ed.) *The Development of Indigenous Trade and Markets in West Africa* (London: Oxford University Press).

Wilks, I. (1975) *Asante in the Nineteenth Century* (Cambridge: Cambridge University Press).

Winchester, N.B. (1976) 'Strangers and Politics in Urban Africa: a study of the Hausa in Kumasi, Ghana', (PhD thesis, Bloomington: University of Indiana).

Winder, R.B. (1962) 'The Lebanese in West Africa', *Comparative Studies in Society and History*, 4, 296–333.

Yusuf, A.B. (1975) 'Capital formation and management among the Muslim Hausa traders of Kano, Nigeria', *Africa*, 45(2), 167–82.

Zachariah, K.C. and Condé, J. (1981) *Migration in West Africa: demographic aspects* (London: Oxford University Press for the World Bank).

OFFICIAL SOURCES

Annual General Reports for the Northern Territories of the Gold Coast, Northern and Southern Provinces 1927–32 (Tamale: National Archives of Ghana).

Annual Report, North-East Province of the Northern Territories of the Gold Coast, 1908 (Tamale: National Archives of Ghana).

Annual Reports for the Northern Territories of the Gold Coast, 1902– (London: Colonial Office).

Annual Reports, Oyo Province, 1948–9 (Ibadan: Nigerian National Archives).

Census of Population 1948, Report and Tables, 1950 (London: Gold Coast Census Office).

Dagomba District Annual Reports, 1935–8 (Tamale: National Archives of Ghana).

District Census Reports, 1931 (Tamale: National Archives of Ghana).

Kusasi District Handing-over Notes, 1931 (Syme to Oliver), 1939 (Syme to Parkinson) (Tamale: National Archives of Ghana).

Population Census of Ghana, 1960. Special Report 'E': Tribes in Ghana, 1966 (Accra: Government Printer), 1966.

Population Census of Nigeria, 1963.

Population Census of the Western Region of Nigeria 1952, 1953, 1954 (Lagos: Government Statistician.

INDEX

'n.' signifies a note on that page. An italic entry signifies a table or illustration.

EU Authorised Representative: Easy Access System Europe Mustamäe tee 5
0, 10621 Tallinn, Estonia gpsr.requests@easproject.com

Printed and bound by CPI Group (UK) Ltd, Croydon, CR0 4YY

16/04/2025

01846986-0001